Mary Meade's ◎ ◎ ◎
MODERN
HOMEMAKER
COOKBOOK

■ ■ ■ ■ ■
◎

Mary Meade's
■ MODERN ■
■ HOMEMAKER ■
■ COOKBOOK ■

By Ruth Ellen Church

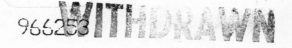

RAND McNALLY & COMPANY
CHICAGO · NEW YORK · SAN FRANCISCO

The color photographs in this book were made by
Earl Gustie, Chicago Tribune staff photographer

FOR HOLLY KAPPLE FIELD
Young Modern Homemaker

▼ FOREWORD ▼

Much of modern cooking is the inspiration of the moment; little of it has roots in the past. Grandma's hand-me-down recipes aren't merely out of date; some of them actually won't work. For not only has our way of living changed drastically in the past several decades, not only have food preferences changed, but food itself has changed.

Even such basic ingredients as flour, sugar, and butter have appeared in new forms. The packaged cake mix has its own canned frosting; the frozen vegetable, even the canned one, has its sauce already applied; one buys coleslaw dressing, hollandaise sauce, potato salad mixings, or the potato salad itself in a jar. Sauces and gravies come in packets; so do salad dressings. There are various flavors even for everyday catsup.

A hundred kinds of biscuits, rolls, and breads may be baked fresh from the package. Orange juice, dairy dips, and eggnog are delivered routinely by the milkman. There are barbecued chicken, crisp fried fish, ready-cooked corned beef at the supermarket to make meal-getting easy.

Our modern homemaker has ninety-six more "things to do" than her Mom had. Even if she does not go to work every day, she is family shopper, launderer, errand runner, housekeeper, and chauffeur. She needs all the meal-getting helps available. Only on weekends or for special occasions has she time to *really* cook.

Today's family doesn't always have its meals around the dining table. There are too many meetings, there is too much tempting television, and too much getting home late. In the pace of today's living we must all be careful that mealtime doesn't degenerate into something resembling a stop at a filling station to gas up the car!

We ought to keep some of the niceties, some of the old-time ritual of dining. When meal preparation itself is so simple, a little thought might be given to the setting. Sometimes the table is the only family meeting place for members who at other times fly off in different directions. If we make it an inviting conference table, no member will ever want to miss a meeting!

How shall we do this? How provide a calm, happy rest-stop and gracious family dining in a kind of existence that whirls and swirls about us?

By something as simple as setting a pretty table, complete with fruit, if not flowers and candles for centerpiece, polished glasses and silver (or stainless steel flatware, which needs so little care). Attractively patterned paper and plastic place mats, tablecloths which need no ironing are available to help.

Women with large families sometimes find it easier on week nights to feed youngsters early, get them off to bed or homework, then set the table again for a cozy twosome, just husband and wife, who can eat then with more leisure and have time to talk over the problems of the day, with perhaps a glass of wine or two to help them relax.

Speaking of wine, I have suggested one to accompany every main course among the recipes in this book. All are domestic wines from California mainly, but also from New York and Ohio, our other great wine-growing regions. Americans at last have realized that not all of the best wines are imports. Our State Department recommends the serving of American wines at all diplomatic functions. Royalty and distinguished guests from other countries have enjoyed our best American wines. Some of them are now being sold in Paris and London as well as in other parts of the world. It is time we knew them better ourselves!

PLEASE ALL FIVE SENSES WITH DINNER

Good food pleases all five senses. Appetites are stimulated by the smell of something cooking. A simmering barbecue sauce, spice cookies coming from the oven, a steak being grilled, the pungency of garlic smashed against the sides of a salad bowl or vinegar on its way to a dressing— all these fragrances prickle our taste buds and make us eager to eat.

The bustling sounds of a busy kitchen help, too: the plopping of coffee in the percolator, the ring of a lid lifted to test a vegetable, the sizzle of chops, the clink of ice in a glass, the swish of plates being taken from a stack and placed on the table, and the rattle of silverware—even, the happy humming of a good cook!

Nose and ear having been pleased, we look at the food. Does it please the eye? Not if it isn't colorful! Imagine a dinner plate bearing a portion of poached white-fleshed fish, a scoop of mashed potatoes, a serving of creamed cauliflower! What a disappointment for eye and nose! Take away the potato and cauliflower. Replace them with a branch of broccoli and a baked tomato. Before you've even sauced the vegetable with hollandaise (from a jar!), bringing yellow into the color picture, your appetite has revived! Color matters.

Arrangement on the plate matters, also, and contrasts in size and shape of the food. If we have sliced potatoes, we don't need sliced carrots—whole ones will look ever so much more appealing. If the meat is chopped, let the potatoes be whole.

Food needn't be garnished to the teeth, but it should make a pretty picture on the plate. The occasional sprig of parsley or watercress helps.

Part of a pretty picture is space to set off the food. Like a mat around a painting, the rim of the plate frames its contents. A crowded plate depresses the appetite. Let portions be small and neat. One may always ask for more.

When we are ready to taste, there should be contrasts—some foods hot, some cold, something soft or jellied, something else firm and crisp or crunchy. Variety in textures pleases our sense of touch.

The last sense we please or do not please—taste—is affected by how well or poorly we have pleased all the others, and by our care in seasoning the food we've chosen for quality, compatability with its platemates, and contrasts in flavor.

Never have cooks had so many handy helpers to make foods taste good. Herbs and spices, herb and spice blends, the flavor-boosts offered by chicken and beef concentrates and broths, canned soups, packaged soup mixes and salad dressing mixes, and wines are only the beginnings of a list. Good butter is one of the best of seasoners, and no cook should be without the benefits of lemon, onions, and garlic in some form.

But we must remember that all good cooking begins with choice food, carefully chosen and carefully handled.

SERVE HOT FOODS HOT, COLD FOODS COLD

The novice, in struggling to get all the various parts of a meal onto the table at the same time, may overlook one of the basic principles of good cooking: Hot foods should be served really hot; cold foods should be cold, though not necessarily icy.

It takes only a few minutes to warm the plates, but warm plates make a difference. If you serve hot meat on a cold platter, or ladle the soup into chilly bowls, you've instantly reduced the heat in your food.

Chilling salad plates and sherbet glasses in the refrigerator before putting food in them is a thoughtful practice. I do think that chilling sometimes is overdone, however. Water glasses are overloaded with ice cubes and sometimes ice even comes in fruit juice, tomato juice, or milk, beverages which should not be diluted.

Fruits have more flavor if they are not served too cold. The same is true of wine. The bouquet of a white wine is inhibited by cold; likewise, a peach or cantaloupe loses fragrance with overchilling. An hour and a half in the refrigerator usually is sufficient for wine or fruit. Red wines, it should be noted, are better appreciated served cool, not cold.

Ice is a modern handy helper in the kitchen. Radishes, celery, carrot sticks, and other raw vegetables will be crisper and crunchier if they are chilled in a bowl with ice cubes for half an hour or more before dinner. When a cold soup is served on a hot summer day, it is a welcome sight nestled in a container of crushed ice. If you are giving a party, why not plan ahead well enough so that you can spoil your guests with such flattery as cold soup or a seafood cocktail bedded in ice?

With such principles as the foregoing in mind, hundreds of successful meals can be prepared with the recipes in this book, I think. In choosing them I have kept the needs of today's busy young homemaker in mind. Many recipes begin with a prepared or semi-prepared ingredient, or several. They are dishes which have been popular lately with the thousands of modern homemakers who read the food pages of *The Chicago Tribune.* Some of them came from friends among the home economists whose work is simplifying cooking procedures for the home. Several are even from men who have found short-cuts to good food.

Many of my own favorites are included. My hope is that this is a book whose pages will become somewhat spattered and grease-stained because it is used every day. I couldn't wish for more!

R. E. C.

CONTENTS

◎ ◎ ◎

Mary Meade's ◎ ◎ ◎
MODERN HOMEMAKER COOKBOOK

■ ■ ■ ■ ■

◎

◎ ◎ ◎ ◎ ◎

APPETIZERS

AN APPETIZER is supposed to arouse appetite, not satisfy it. That is why most appetizers are small bites of something piquantly seasoned. If you are having a dinner party, it is a mistake to allow the cocktail "hour" to extend beyond an hour's time, for hungry guests will overdo on both the goodies offered and the drinks. They may not be able to enjoy the dinner.

The cocktail hour has definite advantages. It allows guests to mix informally and become better acquainted, and it gives the hostess needed time for last minute fixings in the kitchen. After greeting everybody, she can excuse herself for these tasks—providing her husband or someone else keeps glasses filled, and assuming that she has set out a dip with some potato or corn or coconut chips and crisp raw veg-etables for munching.

It's possible to give a cocktail party without making a lot of fancy appetizers, although more food is expected if dinner is not to follow. The gourmet food sections of most supermarkets offer all kinds of packaged and jarred and sacked tidbits, including so many kinds of crackers, chips, nuts, toasted seeds, ready-made spreads and the like as to make one dizzy. Here are baby sardines and smoked oysters, herring in sour cream, antipasto, cocktail sausages. There are

onion dips and blue cheese dips, ready mixed in the refrigerated cases. Olives, and fancy pickles, and cheese. . . .

Ah, and cheese! One or two good kinds of cheese on a
tray, crackers and a knife, and you can be all set. Choose
Camembert and a very old Cheddar. Or a sharp Swiss and
Port du Salut. Or a smoky cheese and a creamy dip. Edam
from Holland, Samsoe from Denmark, Fontina from Italy,
Caerphilly from Britain, Roquefort from France—offer an
international selection if you wish. Do have some firm-tex-
tured cheeses and some softer ones, some mild, some sharp.
Cheese is a particularly good idea if you are serving wine;
red wine such as Burgundy or Bordeaux, California Pinot
Noir or Cabernet Sauvignon goes well with many kinds of
cheese.

EVERYBODY LOVES SHRIMPS!

If you can afford them, do serve shrimps at your cocktail
party. I have found that if I serve shrimps two ways, plain
chilled, with a cocktail sauce, and curried or pickled or marinated in a savory sauce, the plain shrimps disappear first.
There's something about spearing a shrimp on a pick, dip-
ping it into cocktail sauce (there are such good bottled sauces
that it isn't necessary to make one), and popping it in the
mouth that appeals to munchers of every age.

DIETERS LIKE TO CRUNCH!

Crisp raw vegetables are appreciated by many at cocktail
parties. And they look very pretty on a tray. Radishes with
a bit of stem (sometimes it is hard to find them with leaves
any more), green onions, crisp, crunchy cauliflower, cucumber sticks, celery with fringed ends (ice water makes them
curl), carrot sticks, even thin slices of fresh turnip offer
munching pleasure whether a dip is provided for them or
not. Baby tomatoes small enough to pop in the mouth in a
single bite are perfect appetizers, too. So are bite-size pieces
of melon, mandarin orange sections, pineapple chunks, sliced
apples, and even whole fresh strawberries.

APPETIZERS

TRY FRESH MUSHROOMS

There's hardly a more toothsome appetizer than fresh raw mushrooms with or without salt. Just try them and see!

HOW ABOUT CAVIAR?

Imported caviar is expensive, and if you can't afford it, settle for cheaper fish eggs. Inexpensive black and red caviars from less rare fish than sturgeon are available. Mix them with fluffy cream cheese or serve them on quartered deviled eggs. Usually it is a good idea to squeeze a little onion juice and lemon juice over caviar you use for canapés.

The almost priceless Beluga is served in its own jar which is bedded in crushed ice, and it usually is accompanied with sour cream, chopped onion, lemon juice, and melba toast. Nothing more. Oh, well, *champagne,* of course!

POPCORN, ANYONE?

Freshly popped, warm corn, well seasoned and dressed with a little butter is always popular. Season the butter with garlic salt, if you wish, or sprinkle the freshly popped corn with Parmesan cheese along with the butter.

OH, AND SAUSAGE!

Many kinds of sausage are appealing with cocktails, particularly the highly seasoned cervelats and salamis, and pepperoni, which is really hot. An assortment of sausages can be as appealing as an assortment of cheese. And there's no work for the cook!

Read on for more ideas.

ANCHOVY CHEESE DIP
FOR FRESH VEGETABLES

Six SERVINGS

Crisp celery, cauliflowerets, cucumber and carrot sticks, turnip slices and radishes are the kind of thing you dip into this mix.

1 package (8 ozs.) cream cheese
2 tablespoons sour cream
1 tube anchovy paste
1 tablespoon minced onion
1 sliver garlic, minced
1 teaspoon lemon juice
   Dash Tabasco sauce

Combine ingredients very well and chill. Serve surrounded by groupings of the crisp vegetables, cut munchable.

BABY FOOD DIP

One CUP

Use the old imagination and you can make any number of peppery dips from Baby's lamb, chicken, liver, or other meaty food. Keep Baby out of it, though!

1 jar (3½ ozs.) junior or strained beef
3 ounces cream cheese
1 teaspoon horseradish
¼ cup chopped chutney
   Dash of salt

Mix, chill, and serve with crackers or cocktail rye bread.

CHOPPED CHICKEN LIVERS · *Eight* SERVINGS

Serve as a first course, on lettuce, or place in a bowl on the hors d'oeuvre tray.

```
  2  medium onions, sliced
 ¼  cup (1 stick) butter
  1  pound chicken livers
  2  hard-cooked egg yolks
1½  teaspoons salt
 ¼  teaspoon freshly ground coarse black pepper
```

Sauté the onions until yellow in the butter, remove from the pan and brown the chicken livers. Cook about 10 minutes, no more. Chop or grind onions, livers, and egg yolks, mix with seasonings and chill.

CHEESED OLIVES · *Four* DOZEN

These hot little morsels will be gone in a twinkling. Make them early; bake them when the crowd has gathered and everybody has a glass in hand.

```
  2  cups grated sharp Cheddar cheese
 ½  cup soft butter
  1  cup flour
 ½  teaspoon salt
  1  teaspoon paprika
  4  dozen stuffed olives (the little ones)
```

Mix cheese and butter. Work in flour, salt, and paprika. Mold a teaspoon of the mixture around each olive, concealing it. Bake at 400° F. for 12 to 15 minutes.

Olives may be omitted and mixture shaped and baked in small balls.

CHEESE LOG

One ROLL

That handy onion soup mix gives a lot of zip to this spread.

1 package (8 ozs.) cream cheese, softened
1 jar (5 ozs.) blue cheese spread
1 can or packet dry onion soup mix
3 tablespoons piccalilli
½ cup finely chopped pecans

Blend cheeses, add soup mix and pickle. Shape into a roll (10x2½ inches), wrap in waxed paper, and chill several hours. Remove paper and roll the log in nuts.

DELICIOUS CHEESE WAFERS

Eight to Ten DOZEN

With salads and cocktails you'll love them!

1 pound American cheese, grated
½ cup butter, melted
1½ teaspoons salt
½ teaspoon cayenne pepper
2 cups sifted flour

Add butter to cheese. Add salt and cayenne to flour and resift to blend. Add to cheese and work with fingers as in making pastry. When well blended, press with hands into two long rolls. The mixture will be crumbly but will hold together with pressure. Wrap tightly in waxed paper and chill in refrigerator overnight. Cut in very thin slices no thicker than the blade of a knife. Bake on cooky sheet at 450° F. for 5 to 7 minutes, or until crisp and lightly puffed. Remove from sheet immediately. The dough will keep in your refrigerator for about a month.

CHEESEY PUFFS　　　　　*About Three* DOZEN

The sharper the cheese, the better these morsels will taste.
Serve them with salads as well as with drinks.

¼ cup (½ stick) butter
2 cups grated sharp Cheddar cheese
1 cup flour
½ teaspoon salt
½ teaspoon dry mustard
½ teaspoon paprika
　　Dash onion and garlic powders (optional)
　　Dash cayenne pepper

Blend butter and cheese. Mix in combination of dry ingredients, kneading with your hands and shaping a ball. Break off bits of the cheese mixture, about a teaspoon at a time, and shape into balls, rolling on a board or between your palms. Bake on cooky sheets at 350° F. for about 12 to 15 minutes. Serve warm or cold. Warm ones are better!

△

COTTAGE CHEESE DIP　　*Two and a half* CUPS

Tomato tints and flavors this savory mixture of three kinds
of cheese.

1½ cups dry cottage cheese
1 package (3 ozs.) cream cheese
1 jar (3 ozs.) or link of onion
　　cheese spread
⅓ cup tomato paste
¼ cup catsup

¼ cup mayonnaise
¼ teaspoon garlic salt
½ teaspoon salt
　Pepper
　Dash of sugar, if you like

Sieve cottage cheese if you haven't a blender to mix the whole deal in. Mix well and refrigerate several hours ahead of time to allow mixture to thicken and meld flavors. Good with chips, crackers, or vegetables.
　　The rest of the can of tomato paste can go into hamburgers or soup.

21

CURRIED CHICKEN TIDBITS   *Four* DOZEN

*These spicy morsels helped an American team win honors in
the "Culinary Olympics." Freeze them ahead if you can.*

  1 cup cooked chicken, ground fine
  1 teaspoon curry powder
  3 tablespoons chutney sirup
    Salt, pepper as needed
½ cup minced parsley

Mix all but parsley, form small balls and coat with parsley. Chill and
serve with picks. A melon ball scoop will be helpful in shaping.

⚠

DOTTIE HOLLAND'S   For *Four* or *Five*
HOT CRABMEAT APPETIZER

*This is one of my favorites, perfectly delicious with crisp
cold cauliflower.*

  1 package (8 ozs.) cream cheese
  1 can (6½ ozs.) crabmeat, flaked
  2 tablespoons finely chopped onion
  1 tablespoon milk
½ teaspoon creamy horseradish
¼ teaspoon salt
    Dash pepper
⅓ cup sliced almonds, toasted

Combine all ingredients except almonds, mixing until well blended.
Spoon mixture into an 8-inch pie plate or a good-looking ovenware dish.
Sprinkle with almonds. Bake 15 minutes at 375° F. and serve hot with
cold crisp pieces of raw vegetables.

COCONUT CRABMEAT DIP   *Three* CUPS

This is one of the most delicious of all dips, I think. You can make it with shredded coconut if you'll give it a whirl in your electric blender.

2 cups sour cream
4 green onions with tops, cut fine
2 teaspoons curry powder
  Pepper
½ teaspoon salt
1 cup flake coconut or fresh grated coconut
1 can or 6 to 8 ounces crabmeat, shredded

Mix ingredients and chill several hours for flavors to blend. Serve with crackers, melba toast, or potato chips.

GUACAMOLE   *One and a half* CUPS

This is an authentic Mexican mixture, hot but tantalizing.

1 ripe tomato, seeds removed
3 soft-ripe avocados
2 tablespoons lemon juice
2 green onions with tops
1 teaspoon salt (about—keep tasting!)
2 canned green chili peppers, drained
  Pinch of coriander, optional

Chop ingredients rather than mixing them smooth, combine and serve with corn chips, raw vegetables, or quartered tortillas fried in deep fat.

MUSHROOM CHEESE PUFFS   *Three* DOZEN

The canned broiled mushrooms work fine for these delicious morsels.

36 mushrooms caps, browned in butter
36 bread rounds, slightly larger than mushroom caps
 6 ounces cream cheese
 1 egg yolk, beaten
 ⅛ teaspoon scraped onion

Mix cream cheese, egg yolk, and onion. Toast rounds on one side, place dab of cheese mixture on untoasted side of each round. Top with mushroom caps, round side down, and cover mushroom cap with cream cheese mixture. Broil until puffy and slightly brown. Serve hot.

X

CHRISTMAS STRAWBERRIES   *Four* DOZEN

Beautiful morsels like these might be served at any season, but they're especially inviting during the holidays.

 1 pound liver sausage
 ½ cup (3 ozs.) blue cheese
 1 package (3 ozs.) cream cheese
 2 teaspoons minced onion
   Mayonnaise
   Fine, red-colored bread crumbs
   Parsley bits, green picks

Mix liver sausage, cheeses, and onion with enough mayonnaise to blend and shape by tablespoonfuls into strawberries. Roll in the red crumbs (color by mixing food color with a little water and shaking crumbs in a jar with the solution, then drying out in the oven). Make leaves from bits of parsley and stems from half-picks. Chill and serve on a bed of holly leaves or watercress.

24

SNOWBALL PATÉ
Serves *Twelve*

This is all you need with the exception of melba toast to spread it on, and glasses of whatever you're drinking.

- 1 pound liver sausage
- 1 tablespoon minced onion
- ¼ cup lemon juice
- ¼ cup mayonnaise
- 1 package (8 ozs.) cream cheese
- ¼ cup cream or sour cream

Mix liver sausage, onion, lemon juice, and mayonnaise with electric mixer until smooth and pack into a round mold or a deep, round-bottomed bowl. Cover and chill overnight. Loosen gently with spatula and turn out on a serving plate. Spread with mixture of cheese and cream, whipped until fluffy. Ring the mold with watercress, if you wish.

On occasion you might like to coat the cheese with toasted slivered almonds or chopped parsley or cress. But then you'd have to call this appetizer by another name.

PEANUT AND CHEESE NIBBLERS
One QUART

Something different! Here's good television snacking or party fare.

- ⅓ cup butter, melted
- 4 teaspoons Worcestershire sauce
- 2 teaspoons seasoned salt
- 7 slices white bread, cubed
- 1 jar (9 ozs.) dry roasted Spanish peanuts
- ⅓ cup cubed Cheddar cheese
- 5 strips cooked bacon, crumbled

Combine melted butter, Worcestershire, and seasoned salt and toss with bread cubes in a roasting pan. Bake at 350° F. for about 30 minutes or until toasty-brown, stirring occasionally. Cool. Combine with cheese, peanuts, and bacon.

MRS. MAC'S SPREAD

*Use this mixture as a sandwich spread or a dip; it's versatile.
This recipe makes enough for several parties.*

2 large cans deviled ham
½ pound cream cheese
½ pound liver sausage
1 medium sweet onion, ground
1 large dill pickle, ground

Combine ingredients thoroughly and store mixture in covered jar in refrigerator to use as needed.

COCKTAIL MEAT BALLS   About *Fifty*

*The only work involved is shaping the meat. Keep the good
morsels hot over a candle warmer.*

1½ pounds ground beef
1 can onion dry soup mix
1¼ cups water
½ cup catsup
1 tablespoon sweet pickle relish
1 teaspoon prepared mustard

Combine beef and 2 tablespoons soup mix. Shape into 50 small balls.
Brown in a skillet (with a tablespoon of butter, if you wish). Pour off
fat, add other ingredients, cover, and cook over low heat 20 minutes.
Stir now and then. Uncover the last 5 minutes to thicken the sauce.
Serve on toothpicks.

Use a dry red wine for part of the water, if you wish. The flavor
might be even better!

BETH'S DEVILED MEAT BALLS

Two and a half DOZEN

Meat balls should be mixed gently, not squeezed, if they are to be tender and tempting.

¼ pound Roquefort cheese
¼ cup mayonnaise
2 tablespoons Worcestershire
    sauce
1 teaspoon prepared mustard
2 cups corn flakes, slightly
    crushed

⅓ cup milk
1 egg, slightly beaten
1 pound ground beef
1½ teaspoons salt
⅛ teaspoon pepper

Crumble cheese with a fork. Blend in mayonnaise, Worcestershire and mustard. Combine with rest of ingredients, mix lightly, and shape into 1-inch balls. Broil or pan-fry in butter just until well browned.

RUMAKI

Four DOZEN

Sometimes these are done without the soy sauce and brown sugar, but they're more exotic soaked and coated. Everybody adores them!

1 dozen chicken livers, quartered
2 dozen slices bacon, precooked until limp, cut in half
1 dozen water chestnuts, sliced
    Soy sauce, brown sugar

Soak livers in soy sauce for several hours, drain, and wrap in bacon half-slices along with sliced water chestnuts, securing each little packet with a pick. Dip in brown sugar, place on a rack in a shallow roasting pan, and bake at 400° F. for 15 minutes or until bacon is crisp.

And of course you know that if you just wrap half a chicken liver in half a strip of bacon and broil it or bake it, you have an even simpler, almost as tempting a delicacy.

ANGELS ON HORSEBACK   *Six* SERVINGS

In England these savories are served on toast at the end of the meal.

2 dozen large oysters
12 slices bacon, cut in half
½ teaspoon salt
⅛ teaspoon pepper
2 tablespoons chopped parsley
Lemon juice

Drain oysters and pick over for bits of shell. Lay each on a half slice of bacon, sprinkle with seasonings, parsley, and lemon juice. Roll bacon around oysters and secure each with a pick. Bake at 450° F. for 6 to 8 minutes or until bacon is crisp.

TERIYAKI (A JAPANESE APPETIZER)   *Six* to *Eight* SERVINGS

Cooking is usually done over charcoal, but broiling works well, too.

1 pound tender beefsteak (sirloin is O.K.)
¼ cup soy sauce
1 tablespoon sugar
1 clove garlic, minced
1 teaspoon ginger (fresh), chopped fine

Slice meat in thin strips across the grain. Place on bamboo sticks (100 for 25 cents, in Chinatown). Mix soy sauce, sugar, garlic, and ginger. Soak meat in sauce 30 minutes or more, turning to marinate evenly. Broil on a cooky sheet 5 minutes on each side before serving hot.

LIVER SAUSAGE DIP   *Two* CUPS

This simple mixture is very good with beer or a red wine.

½ pound liver sausage
1 cup sour cream
1 envelope onion soup mix
1 teaspoon Worcestershire sauce
Dash Tabasco sauce

28

Mix ingredients in mixer or blender until smooth and chill before serving with crackers, chips, or crisp vegetables.

SHRIMP INDIENNE DIP
Two CUPS

Tangy and unique, this dip really prickles those taste buds!

- 1 can frozen shrimp soup
- 1 package (8 ozs.) cream cheese
- ¼ teaspoon curry powder
- ½ cup chopped stuffed olives
- 2 teaspoons lemon juice
- 1 clove garlic, crushed
- Salt, pepper

Remove soup from can and nearly thaw in a bowl. Add rest of ingredients and beat until well blended. Cover and chill for several hours. Transfer to a small bowl and serve on a tray with big potato chips.

BUFFET SHRIMPS
Eight to ten SERVINGS

Keep them a week in the refrigerator, if you wish; they're great for a party.

- 2 pounds fresh or frozen shelled, deveined shrimps
- 2 onions, sliced thin
- 8 bay leaves
- 1¼ cups salad oil
- ¾ cup white or rosé wine vinegar
- 1½ teaspoons salt
- 2½ teaspoons celery seed
- 2½ tablespoons capers and juice
- Dash tabasco sauce

Mix oil and remaining ingredients and pour over combination of shrimps, onions, and bay leaves in a shallow dish. Chill at least 24 hours.

TUNA PATÉ FOR A PARTY *Three and a half* CUPS

Whip it together in your mixer or blender. Serve it with crackers or as filling for appetizer puffs or cocktail biscuits.

  1 package (8 ozs.) cream cheese
  2 tablespoons chili sauce
  2 tablespoons minced parsley
 ¼ cup minced green onion
  1 tablespoon Worcestershire sauce
 ½ teaspoon Tabasco sauce
  3 cans (6½-7 ozs. each) tuna, drained, flaked

Beat ingredients together until smooth and chill before serving.

SPICY HAM BITES   *Four* SERVINGS

Here's an unusual idea from California.

  1 cup ginger ale
 ½ cup brown sugar
  1 teaspoon prepared mustard
 ¼ cup salad oil
  1 pound cooked ham, cut in 1½ inch cubes
   Whole cloves

Mix ginger ale, brown sugar, mustard, and oil. Stick each cube of ham with a whole clove. Place cubes on skewers. Marinate in ginger ale mixture for at least 30 minutes. Broil until brown and heated through, about 10 minutes.

◼

□ ✗ □ ✗ □

SOUPS

Wittth ALL of the canned, frozen, and dried soups and soup mixes available to the modern homemaker, would you think we'd need soup *recipes?*

Well, of course! We're more imaginative (at times) than to accept a soup exactly as it comes out of the can. We like to mix it with another soup, or add a vegetable or a few shrimps, or some wine. We like to season it with curry. We think it's great fun to imitate a famous soup such as Vichyssoise or Gazpacho, starting with a ready-made tomato soup or a combination of instant mashed potatoes and onion dip! And there are soups we'd like to make that can't be found in the can or packet.

Soup is the perfect beginning for dinner. Soup and salad or sandwich make a good lunch. Some soups must be eaten; others can be drunk from a cup or a glass and therefore may be carried about and enjoyed like a cocktail before dinner. There are as many different kinds of crackers at hand to eat with soup as there are soups. They are flavored with cheese or bacon or sesame seeds. They are crisp or crunchy, and they are shaped in rounds and ovals, octagons and rectangles.

I hope you will enjoy making these very special soups. You may think of a little variation of your own here and there which will make this soup or that one uniquely yours.

AVOCADO CHICKEN SOUP   *Four* SERVINGS

*Be sure to use a fully ripe, fairly soft, and buttery avocado
for best flavor and texture.*

2 cups chicken stock (page 181) or canned chicken broth
1 cup cream
1 tablespoon lemon juice
1 cup puréed avocado
  Salt to taste

Heat stock and cream gently. Add lemon juice to avocado and stir it into
the soup stock. Add salt as necessary and serve at once. Don't cook the
soup after adding avocado. A twist of lemon may garnish the bowl.

Half clam broth (bottled) and half chicken stock may be used as
the base.

This is an intriguing beginning for a dinner party featuring leg of
lamb or loin of pork.

◼

CARAWAY CHEESE SOUP   *Six* SERVINGS

*Strain out the caraway seeds, if you wish; they leave their
flavor.*

2 tablespoons minced onion
2 tablespoons butter
3 tablespoons flour
1 teaspoon salt
  Dash pepper
1 tablespoon caraway seeds
3 cups milk
1 cup shredded sharp Cheddar cheese
½ cup dry white wine
2 tablespoons chopped parsley
  Paprika

*Dottie Holland's Hot Crabmeat Dip, page 22;
Guacamole, page 23; Beth's Meat Balls, page 27*

Sauté onion in butter 5 minutes. Remove from heat. Add flour, salt, and pepper and stir until smooth. Add caraway. Add milk and stir while heating until thickened. Add cheese and stir until melted. Just before serving add wine. Garnish with parsley and paprika.

Serve this soup preceding an omelet with bacon, and a small green salad.

△

CHICKEN AND SEAFOOD GUMBO

Twelve SERVINGS

For informal entertaining this dish has it; the recipe can be expanded to suit the number of guests.

2 large onions sliced and sautéed in ¼ cup oil
2 cans Manhattan style clam chowder
2 cans condensed tomato soup
2 cans chicken gumbo soup
2 cans condensed chicken consommé
1 can or package frozen okra
2 cans or packages (6-7 ozs. each) frozen crabmeat, broken apart
2 jars chicken (6-7 ozs. each) or 2 cans tuna, broken up
½ cup sherry or Madeira
6 cups cooked rice

Heat everything together but rice and bring to a simmer. Keep covered over low heat until serving time (up to an hour). Pack rice into half-cup measure, unmold one in each soup plate, and ladle gumbo mixture around it.

Go WITHS: Garlic bread.

WINE: California Rosé or Zinfandel.

CHICKEN AND ONION BISQUE   *Four* SERVINGS

Shrimps or crabmeat, even salmon or tuna, can take the place of chicken in this kind of soup.

1 package (9 ozs.) frozen small onions with cream sauce
1 cup diced cooked chicken or turkey
1 cup water
1 cup light cream
1 tablespoon butter
3 sprigs parsley
½ teaspoon salt
⅛ teaspoon thyme

Put all ingredients together into electric blender. Blend until smooth, about 1 minute at high speed. Pour into saucepan and bring just to a boil. Remove from heat and serve. Garnish with minced parsley, if you wish.

Serve as a luncheon soup with a bacon, lettuce, and tomato sand-wich.

CLAM CHOWDER   *Four* SERVINGS

You don't always need fresh clams to make chowder!

2 slices bacon, cut fine
1 medium potato, shredded
1 medium onion, chopped
3 cups milk
1 can (7 ozs.) minced clams, with liquid

1 cup cream-style corn
½ teaspoon salt
⅛ teaspoon pepper
½ teaspoon Worcestershire sauce
Parsley (optional)

Fry bacon. Remove from pan. Sauté potato and onion until tender in bacon fat. Heat milk, clams, corn. Add bacon, potato, onion, and season-ings. Bring just to boiling point and serve in bowls with parsley garnish.

Plenty of crackers usually are required for chowder. Plus a salad of as many greens as one may find.

CRABMEAT BISQUE
Four SERVINGS

A rich and distinguished soup, simple combination that it is.

  1 can condensed tomato soup
  1 can condensed pea soup
1½ cups milk and cream
  1 teaspoon Worcestershire sauce
  1 can crabmeat (6½-7 ozs.) or 1 cup frozen crabmeat, flaked

Combine all ingredients and heat thoroughly.

A handful of carrot sticks and crusty rolls are all you need as an accompaniment.

▲

CRAB STEW WITH LEMON
Four SERVINGS

The ground lemon gives it the most intriguing flavor!

  2 tablespoons butter or margarine
  2 tablespoons flour
 ½ teaspoon salt
 ¼ teaspoon pepper
     Dash of paprika
2½ cups milk
  1 lemon, ground (skin and all)
 12 ounces fresh, frozen, or canned crabmeat (or 2 cans)
  1 tablespoon Worcestershire sauce
 ¼ cup dry white wine

Melt butter, stir in flour and seasonings, and blend. Stir in milk and cook, stirring constantly, until smooth and thickened. Add lemon and cook for about 15 minutes longer over low heat, stirring occasionally. Add crabmeat and heat through. Add Worcestershire and wine and serve.

Serve with mixed greens, herb dressing, and garlic bread.

35

FRESH CORN CHOWDER   *Four* SERVINGS

My family is very fond of this soup. Although "from scratch," it is very easy to make.

3 medium potatoes, pared, diced
¼ pound salt pork or bacon, diced and cooked crisp
1 medium onion, chopped
2 cups corn cut from cob, or 1 can corn or 1 package frozen
     whole kernel corn
1 quart milk and cream
    Salt, pepper

Cook potatoes in 1 cup water until tender. Sauté onion in pork or bacon fat. Combine and add corn, milk, and seasonings, including plenty of pepper. Heat thoroughly and serve in bowls. Minced parsley may be sprinkled on top.

Serve with crackers and a green salad for lunch or supper.

LETTUCE SOUP   *Six* SERVINGS

This is an unusual and interesting soup with excellent flavor.

2 tablespoons chopped onion
2 tablespoons butter
2 tablespoons flour
½ teaspoon salt
⅛ teaspoon pepper
2 cups beef broth or 2 bouillon cubes dissolved in 2 cups
    hot water
2 cups light cream or evaporated milk
1½ cups chopped lettuce

Cook onion in butter until tender. Add flour and seasonings and blend. Add broth gradually and stir constantly until thick and smooth. Cook slowly for 10 minutes. Add milk, heat well; add lettuce, and serve immediately.

This is a good dinner beginner. Follow with a roast and a fruit salad.

GAZPACHO
Four SERVINGS

*Since America discovered this cold summer soup it has be-
come more popular here than in southern Spain, its home!*

1 can condensed tomato soup
1 soup can water
1 cup chopped cucumber
½ cup chopped green pepper
¼ cup chopped green onions
1 clove garlic, minced

¼ cup olive oil
2 tablespoons red wine vinegar
Dash Tabasco sauce
Salt, pepper
Paper-thin slices lime

Combine ingredients and chill overnight. Stir gently and serve bedded in
crushed ice or with an ice cube in each serving. Place a slice or two of
lime in each serving.

Serve this soup-salad with crusty rolls or a chicken sandwich. Or
make it the first course at dinner on a warm evening, and skip salad.

FRENCH ONION SOUP
Six SERVINGS

*Large sweet onions and beef bouillon are the essential
ingredients.*

4 to 5 large sweet onions, sliced very thin
¼ cup butter
4 to 5 cups well-seasoned beef stock or bouillon
Dash Worcestershire sauce (optional)
Salt, pepper
½ cup sherry (optional)
Parmesan toast

Sauté the peeled onion slices (separate them into rings, if you wish)
in butter gently until yellow, about 10 minutes. They should not brown.
Sprinkle them with coarse black pepper as they cook, if you wish. Add
stock and seasonings and simmer 20 to 30 minutes. Add sherry, if
you use it, and ladle into bowls. Top each portion with a slice of
Parmesan toast. To prepare it, butter slices of French bread, sprinkle
thickly with the grated cheese, and brown and dry out in a moderate
oven.

KORBEL'S GREEN CHAMPAGNE SOUP

Four SERVINGS

This delight is straight from California champagne vine-yards.

    1 can condensed green pea soup, undiluted
  1/2 cup consommé
  1/4 teaspoon oregano
  1/8 teaspoon tarragon
  1/2 cup heavy cream, whipped (not stiff)
    1 cup California champagne
      Paprika
      Minced parsley

Heat together the soup, consommé, herbs. Fold the cream into the soup and heat, but do not boil. Add champagne and serve at once, garnished with paprika and parsley.

Serve the soup in mugs to begin a happy backyard party with chickens on the rotisserie spit. Double or triple the recipe after counting appetites.

△

OYSTER-MUSHROOM STEW

Five SERVINGS

This soup has a little more body than the usual oyster stew.

  3 tablespoons butter
  1 pint oysters, picked over for shell bits
  1 teaspoon salt
  1 can cream of mushroom soup
  3 cups milk
    Few drops Worcestershire

Simmer oysters in butter about 5 minutes. Add salt. Combine soup and milk and add. Heat to scalding, add Worcestershire, and serve.

You'll want oyster crackers and a Chef's Salad (page 240), or Caesar Salad (page 219), with this good soup.

OYSTER STEW
Four SERVINGS

Here's a flavorsome version of a favorite American dish.

    1 small onion, sliced
  1/2 cup chopped celery leaves
    1 bay leaf
    1 quart milk
    1 pint oysters, picked over
  1/4 cup fine dry bread crumbs
  1/4 cup butter
    1 teaspoon salt
      Dash black pepper

Heat onion, celery leaves, bay leaf, and milk together in the top of a double boiler for 20 minutes. Strain. Cook oysters in their own liquor until edges curl. Add oysters and liquid to strained milk and stir in remaining ingredients. Serve piping hot. Do not let an oyster stew boil.

With it you'll want a big salad with lots of vegetables in it, and crackers or toast.

RUBY-TONED CONSOMMÉ
Five SERVINGS

A relative of borscht, this soup is an excellent appetizer.

    2 cans condensed consommé
  1 1/2 soup-cans water
  1/2 cup canned beets, minced
    2 tablespoons beet juice
    2 tablespoons lemon juice
      Sour cream

Combine soup, water, beets and juices. Simmer 5 minutes to blend flavors. Serve garnished with sour cream.

Lead into dinner with this soup. It would be good before a roast.

SPLIT PEA SOUP WITH HAM BALLS

Eight or More SERVINGS

Except for the green pea garnish, this dish may be made several days early.

1 ham bone with some ham on it
1 pound split peas
2 quarts water
1 can (1 lb. 12 ozs.) tomatoes
1 onion, minced
2 small potatoes, pared, diced
3 carrots, diced
1 cup chopped celery

¼ cup minced parsley
1 teaspoon salt
1 bay leaf
Pepper
1 egg for ham balls
2 tablespoons minced parsley
2 tablespoons flour
1 package frozen peas

Put the ham bone in a big kettle after removing enough ham to make 2 cups, ground. Add split peas, water, tomatoes, and onion. Cover and simmer 2 hours. Add vegetables and seasonings; simmer 30 minutes more. Meanwhile add to the ground ham the beaten egg, parsley, and flour. Shape into 1-inch balls. Add to soup and simmer 10 minutes. Add frozen peas last 5 minutes.

GO WITHS: Crusty rolls, crisp toast or crackers, and a big fruit salad.

WINE: California Rosé.

CREAM OF PEA SOUP

Four to Five SERVINGS

The cream soup base may be used with other frozen, canned, or cooked vegetables in the very same way.

¼ cup (½ stick) butter
¼ cup flour
1 teaspoon instant onion
1 teaspoon salt
⅛ teaspoon pepper
1 quart milk

1 package (10 ozs.) frozen peas, cooked, puréed
Fresh, frozen, or freeze-dried minced parsley, chives, or
   mint

Melt butter, stir in flour, add onion, salt, and pepper and the milk, gradually. (Use 1 cup cream in place of 1 cup milk for a richer soup; or use
equal parts milk and chicken broth for a different flavor.) Add sieved
peas with their cooking liquid, plus more salt, if needed. Serve hot with
garnish of parsley, chives or mint.

Or leave out a cup of milk to make a thicker soup, chill it and serve
cold. Half a teaspoon of curry may be mixed with the flour, if the soup
is to be served cold.

Excellent as a first course before a lamb dinner, or for lunch with a
sandwich.

ROQUEFORT SOUP SUPREME *Four* SERVINGS

If you like the famous cheese, you'll love the soup!

2 tablespoons butter
2 tablespoons cornstarch
¾ teaspoon salt
¼ teaspoon pepper
3½ cups milk
1 package or wedge (3 ozs.) Roquefort or blue cheese,
   crumbled
¾ teaspoon Worcestershire sauce
1 pimiento, chopped fine

Melt butter in saucepan, blend in cornstarch, salt, and pepper and add
half the milk, and the cheese. Heat to simmering and simmer for 2 minutes, stirring constantly. Add rest of milk, Worcestershire, and pimiento.
Mix well. Reheat and serve immediately.

This unique soup could be the beginning of a steak dinner, or serve
as companion for a lettuce and tomato sandwich (toasted) at lunch.

SALMON BISQUE   *Four* SERVINGS

Creamy and flavorsome, this may become a favorite soup.

¼ cup minced onion
2 tablespoons minced green pepper (if desired)
2 tablespoons butter or margarine
3 tablespoons flour
¾ teaspoon salt
   Black pepper

½ teaspoon dry mustard
3 cups milk
1 can (8 oz.) salmon or 1 cup
   cooked flaked salmon
¼ teaspoon Worcestershire sauce
   Minced parsley
   Paprika

Sauté onion and green pepper lightly in butter. Stir in flour and season-ings, the milk, and liquid from salmon. Cook until thickened. Place over hot water. Add fine flaked salmon, heat again. Add Worcestershire sauce and parsley. Sprinkle each portion with paprika.

Serve with warm rolls and a coleslaw-stuffed tomato.

SCOTCH BROTH   *Eight* SERVINGS

This soup smells wonderful cooking! Make a heartier dish by increasing the amounts of vegetables, if you like. Prepare a day early and reheat this to save time.

2 quarts lamb stock (see below)
½ cup pearl barley
½ cup chopped onion
½ cup diced carrots
½ cup chopped celery

½ cup diced white turnips
1 cup shredded cabbage
1 cup finely diced lamb
   Salt, pepper
1 tablespoon minced parsley

To MAKE STOCK: Simmer 2½ pounds neck, breast, or shank of lamb 2½ to 3 hours with 2½ teaspoons salt, 1 onion, 1 bay leaf, 1 slice lemon, 1 stalk celery, a few peppercorns, and 2½ quarts water. Strain, skim fat. Dice meat fine.

Simmer stock, barley, and vegetables about 2 hours, add the lamb, season to taste and serve hot with parsley.

Serve the soup to begin a meal of roast turkey or duck; or serve it as lunch with crusty bread and a fruit salad.

SHERRIED SHRIMP SOUP   *Five or Six* SERVINGS

This is one of my favorites; it's elegant but easy, and people love it.

2 cans frozen condensed shrimp
   soup
2 soup-cans water
1 teaspoon curry powder

1 cup cooked shrimps or 1 can
   (6 ozs.) shrimps, rinsed in
   cold water
¼ cup sherry

Heat soup and water until soup is thawed. Add curry, shrimps, and sherry and heat just to boiling point, stirring now and then. Do not allow soup to boil.

Serve with melba toast and a big salad for lunch.

MODERN VICHYSSOISE   *Seven* CUPS

The real thing is made with leeks, but this imitation is delicious, leeks or no leeks.

3 cups water
¼ cup chopped fresh parsley
4 chicken bouillon cubes
2 tablespoons butter
2 cups milk
1 envelope instant whipped potato flakes
2 cartons (8 ozs. each) French onion dip
   Chopped chives, fresh, frozen, or freeze dried

Place water, parsley, bouillon cubes, and butter in a large saucepan. Cover and bring to a boil. Remove from heat. Add milk, then stir in potato flakes. Cool 15 minutes and fold in the dip. Chill well and serve garnished with chives.

Serve as a luncheon soup with toast and a salad, or to introduce a ham or chicken dinner.

SPRING SOUP   *Four* SERVINGS

Watercress is good in this soup if you're not too fond of spinach.

1 medium onion, sliced
1 tablespoon butter
1 medium potato, sliced
1 sliced carrot
¾ teaspoon salt, or to taste
3 cups water

1 can (6 ozs.) tomato paste
1½ cups chicken broth
2 tablespoons rice, uncooked
1 cup fresh spinach, coarsely
  shredded, packed tight

Cook onion slowly in butter until delicately browned. Add everything but spinach. Simmer, stirring occasionally, for 45 minutes. Add spinach and boil 5 minutes longer.

Serve to begin a roast beef dinner.

COLD WATERCRESS SOUP   *Two or Three* SERVINGS

Save out a sprig of watercress to garnish the bowl.

1 can frozen condensed cream of potato soup
1 soup can half-and-half
1 cup chopped watercress
¼ cup chopped celery
½ teaspoon grated lemon rind
1 green onion with top, minced

Heat ingredients together gently, then chill for 4 or 5 hours and serve in chilled bowls. Electric blender may be used to purée the vegetables.

Serve as a luncheon soup with a fruit salad and warm rolls.

◻ ◇ ◻ ◇ ◻

BREADS

THE KINDS and varieties of breads one can buy these days are astonishing. No longer can it be said that Americans live on squishy white bread. They don't. They are showing decided preference for crusty breads and rolls, French, Italian, Scandinavian types, and dark breads as well as light ones.

Today's young homemaker, although she can buy any kind of loaf her family likes, is showing an increasing interest in baking her own bread, at least part of the time. When she doesn't bake her own, she likes to do something special with one of the kinds she can buy—make garlic and herb bread with a French loaf, perhaps, or turn refrigerated biscuits into a coffee cake.

This chapter is filled with recipes for the kinds of breads modern families enjoy, some of them far removed from the varieties we were eating five or ten years ago, all of them completely removed from that soft white stuff other people think Americans still eat!

"COOLRISE" WHITE BREAD   *Two* LOAVES

This new method is great for the working wife, who mixes when she has time, and refrigerates the loaves to bake two or twenty-four hours later.

$5\frac{1}{2}$–$6\frac{1}{2}$ cups flour
　　$\frac{1}{2}$ cup warm water (105°–115° F.)
　　 2 packages or cakes yeast (dry or compressed)
　 $1\frac{3}{4}$ cups warm milk (105°–115° F.)
　　 2 tablespoons sugar
　　 1 tablespoon salt
　　 3 tablespoons oil

Spoon flour into cup to measure. Level off and pour flour onto wax paper. Place water in large warm bowl and sprinkle or crumble yeast into it; stir to dissolve. Add milk, sugar, salt, and oil. Stir in 2 cups flour. Beat with mixer or rotary beater until smooth, about 1 minute. Add 1 cup flour. Beat vigorously with wooden spoon until smooth, about 150 strokes. Add enough more flour to make a soft dough. Turn onto lightly floured board and knead until smooth and elastic, 5 to 10 minutes. Cover with plastic wrap, then a towel, and let rest 20 minutes.

Punch down dough; divide in half. Roll each portion with a rolling pin into an 8x12-inch rectangle. Roll from upper 8-inch edge toward you and seal with thumbs or heel of hand after each complete turn. Seal final seam and edges well. Place in two oiled $8\frac{1}{2}$x$4\frac{1}{2}$-inch loaf pans, brush with oil, and cover pans loosely with oiled wax paper, then top with plastic wrap. Refrigerate 2 to 24 hours. Dough rises in the refrigerator. When ready to bake, remove loaves, carefully uncover dough, and let stand 10 minutes at room temperature. Puncture any surface bubbles with an oiled toothpick. Bake at 400° F. for 30 to 40 minutes.

"COOLRISE" WHOLE WHEAT BREAD

Two LOAVES

It takes only forty-five minutes to prepare the dough, and baking may be done at a convenient time.

3–4 cups flour
2½ cups stone-ground whole
    wheat flour
½ cup warm water (105–
    115° F.)
2 packages or cakes active dry
    or compressed yeast

1¾ cups warm milk (105–
    115° F.)
2 tablespoons sugar
1 tablespoon salt
3 tablespoons oil

Measure water into large warm bowl. Sprinkle or crumble in yeast; stir until dissolved. Add milk, sugar, salt, oil. Stir in 1 cup flour. Beat with mixer or rotary beater until smooth, 1 minute. Add whole wheat flour and beat vigorously until smooth, about 150 strokes with a wooden spoon. Add enough more white flour to make a soft dough. Turn out onto lightly floured board and knead until smooth and elastic, 5 to 10 minutes. Cover with plastic wrap, then a towel. Let rest on board for 20 minutes. Proceed as directed for coolrise white bread.

BOHEMIAN BREAD

Two SMALL LOAVES

The loaf is very tender, egg-yellow, and buttery in flavor.

1 cup butter
¼ cup sugar
¾ cup cream, heated to lukewarm
2 packages active dry or com-
    pressed yeast

¼ cup warm water (105°–115°
    F.)
2 eggs, plus 2 yolks
½ teaspoon salt
4 cups flour

Cream butter and sugar. Dissolve yeast in water Add cream. Add to butter mixture and beat well. Add eggs, and yolks, then flour sifted with salt. Mix well. Turn out on floured board and knead until smooth and elastic. Round into a ball and place in greased bowl. Cover and let rise until doubled. Shape into loaves, place in greased pans about 8½x4½ inches, cover and let rise until doubled. Bake at 375° F. 50 to 60 minutes.

BUTTERMILK BREAD   *Two* LARGE LOAVES

Sounds good, doesn't it? Well, it is good!

2 packages active dry or compressed yeast
¼ cup warm water (105°–115° F.)
¼ cup sugar

1¾ cups buttermilk, lukewarm
6 cups flour (about)
2 tablespoons shortening, melted
1 tablespoon salt
½ teaspoon soda

Dissolve yeast in water. Add sugar, buttermilk, and 3 cups sifted flour and beat well. Let stand in warm place until light and bubbly, about ½ hour. Add remaining 3 cups flour, shortening, salt, and soda. Knead until smooth and elastic. Let rise until doubled in bulk; shape into loaves and place in 2 large (9x5 inches) greased loaf pans. Let rise until doubled again. Bake at 400° F. 15 minutes. Reduce heat to 375° F. and bake 30 minutes longer.

◼

CASSEROLE BREAD   *One* LOAF

This may be the simplest way to produce a good, crusty loaf of homemade bread.

1 cup milk, scalded
3 tablespoons sugar
1 tablespoon salt
1½ tablespoons shortening

1 cup warm water (105°–115° F.)
2 packages active dry or compressed yeast
4½ cups sifted flour

Stir sugar, salt, and shortening into the scalded milk; cool to lukewarm. Measure water into a bowl and sprinkle or crumble in the yeast. Stir until yeast is dissolved. Add lukewarm milk mixture. Add flour and stir until well blended, about 2 minutes. Cover and let rise until dough is triple in bulk, about 40 minutes. Stir down. Beat vigorously about ½ minute. Turn into greased 1½-quart casserole (preferably one with straight sides) and bake at 375° F. for about 1 hour.

ITALIAN CHEESE-POTATO BREAD
One LARGE LOAF

Do try this, for the texture is perfect and the flavor is interesting.

1 package active dry or compressed yeast
¼ cup warm water (105°–115° F.)
3 cups flour (about)
1 teaspoon sugar

1 teaspoon salt
⅔ cup mashed potatoes
⅓ cup butter, melted
1 cup grated Swiss cheese
2 eggs, unbeaten
¼ cup milk, scalded

Dissolve yeast in water and let stand 5 minutes. Sift flour, sugar, and salt. Combine potatoes, butter, cheese, and eggs in a large bowl. Add yeast and cooled milk. Add dry ingredients gradually and mix thoroughly. Turn out on a floured board and knead until smooth and elastic. Place in a greased bowl and cover. Let rise until doubled in bulk. Turn out and shape into a roll, about 16 inches long. Place in a buttered 10-inch tube pan. Pinch ends together to seal. Let rise until doubled. Bake at 375° F. for 35 minutes.

△

EASY YEAST ROLLS
Sixteen ROLLS

You'll want to bake these often.

1 package active dry yeast
¾ cup warm water (105°–115° F.)
2½ cups biscuit mix
2 tablespoons butter, melted

Dissolve yeast in water. Add mix and beat hard. Sprinkle more biscuit mix on the pastry cloth or counter and knead dough on it until smooth. Pat out dough and divide into 16 pieces. Shape into rolls and place on buttered cooky sheet. Cover with a cloth and let rise in a warm place for about an hour. Brush rolls with butter and bake at 400° F. for 10 to 15 minutes.

SOUR CREAM TWISTS   *Five dozen* SMALL ROLLS

These are flaky and delicious. You may roll them in cinnamon and sugar before baking, if you wish.

1 package active dry or compressed yeast
¼ cup warm water (105°–115° F.)
¾ cup sour cream (lukewarm)
1 teaspoon salt

About 3½ cups flour
1 cup shortening
2 eggs, beaten
1 teaspoon vanilla
Sugar

Dissolve yeast in water. Add cream. Cut shortening into salt and flour as for pastry, add yeast, eggs, vanilla. Mix thoroughly with spoon, then with hands. Cover and chill several hours or overnight. This makes dough easy to roll. Divide into 2 parts and roll each on sugar-sprinkled board into rectangle 8x16 inches. Fold the 2 ends to the center, overlapping, sprinkle with sugar, and roll again to the same size. Repeat 3 times, then roll ¼-inch thick. Cut into strips 1x4 inches. Twist ends of strips in opposite directions and curl into horseshoe shapes on greased baking sheet. Bake at 375° F. for 15 minutes.

SWEDISH LUCIA COFFEE BUNS   *Two* DOZEN

These are traditional at Christmas in Sweden, from whence came this recipe.

2 packages active dry or compressed yeast
¼ cup warm water (105°–115° F.)
1¼ cups scalded milk
½ cup sugar
½ cup butter or margarine

¼ teaspoon salt
3 to 4 cups flour
¼ teaspoon saffron steeped in 1 tablespoon hot water, strained
1 teaspoon cardamom, ground
½ cup raisins

Dissolve yeast in warm water. Pour hot milk over sugar, butter, salt, and cool to lukewarm. Add yeast, flour, strained saffron, cardamom. Knead until smooth and add raisins. Shape buns and place on buttered cooky sheet. Let rise until doubled, then bake at 375° F. for 15 to 20 minutes.

RICH REFRIGERATOR ROLLS   *Thirty-two* ROLLS

The dough is soft and sticky at first—don't add too much flour.

2 packages active dry or com-
    pressed yeast
¼ cup warm water (105°–115°
    F.)
¾ cup milk, scalded

¼ cup sugar
1 teaspoon salt
½ cup butter
3 eggs
5 cups flour (about)

Dissolve yeast in water. Pour milk over sugar, butter, and salt. Cool to lukewarm. Add yeast and beaten eggs. Add flour, mixing thoroughly. Turn out on a lightly floured board and knead until satiny. Place in a greased bowl, cover, and let rise until doubled, about 2 hours. Punch down and form into smooth ball. Grease the surface lightly, cover with a plate and a towel, and place in the refrigerator. Remove from refrigerator a day or two later and divide dough into fourths. Roll each piece while cold into a circle, brush with butter and cut into 8 pie-shaped wedges. Roll from wide side, tucking "tail" under each roll. Place on greased baking sheet or in pans, brush over lightly with butter, cover with a clean cloth, and let rise until doubled, about 2 hours. Bake at 425° F. for 15 to 20 minutes.

ONION BUNS   *One* DOZEN

Hamburgers are flattered to be sandwiched in these!

1 cup chopped onions
2 tablespoons butter
1 package hot roll mix

Cook onions in butter until they look transparent. Cool. Prepare roll mix according to package directions, but add onions to the dry portion. Let dough rise until doubled, then shape into buns, place on oiled cooky sheet and flatten slightly. Cover and let rise 30 to 45 minutes. Bake at 375° F. for 20 minutes.

GOOD VARIATION : Add 6 crisp-cooked, crumbled bacon strips, for bacon-onion buns.

51

ONION POPOVERS

Six LARGE

*Serve these with a pot roast of beef and vegetables. They're
full of flavor for being nothing but empty shells!*

3 eggs
1 cup milk
2 tablespoons dry onion soup mix
1 tablespoon oil
1 cup flour

Blend together eggs, milk, soup mix, and oil. Mix in flour until smooth,
then beat at least 1 minute on electric mixer, or 3 minutes with rotary
beater. Fill preheated well-oiled popover pan or 6 custard cups half full.
Bake at 400° F. for 40 to 45 minutes or until dark golden brown and
firm to touch. For extra crispness prick sides with a fork; reduce temperature to 350° F. to dry them out for 20 minutes more. Serve at once.

HONEYMOON BISCUITS

One DOZEN

Feather light, not flaky, a modern bride's pride.

2 cups sifted flour	3 tablespoons shortening
3 teaspoons baking powder	1 teaspoon grated orange rind
1 tablespoon sugar	1 egg, beaten
¾ teaspoon salt	½ cup milk

Sift dry ingredients; cut in shortening. Add orange rind. Combine egg
and milk and add to flour mixture. Stir until soft dough is formed. Turn
out on lightly floured board and knead 30 seconds. Shape dough into a
long roll and cut in 12 pieces. Roll each piece into a ball. Arrange in
greased 8-inch layer pan. Bake in hot oven, 450° F., for 15 minutes, or
until puffed and browned.

STIR-AND-ROLL BISCUITS   *One* DOZEN

Here's an easy way to make baking powder biscuits.

2 cups sifted flour
3 teaspoons baking powder
1 teaspoon salt
1/3 cup salad oil
2/3 cup milk

Sift dry ingredients together. Put oil and milk in measuring cup but don't mix. Dump at once into flour mixture and stir with a fork until dough "cleans" the sides of the bowl and rounds up into a ball. Knead about 10 times (no extra flour) with the hands and place on waxed paper. Press out 1/4-inch thick, and cut with biscuit cutter. Bake 10 to 12 minutes on ungreased cooky sheet, at 475° F.

CHEESE STRAWS   *Forty-five* STRAWS

With soup or with salad, they're a crisp and elegant touch.

1 cup instant flour
1/2 teaspoon salt
1/2 cup shredded sharp Cheddar cheese
1/3 cup plus 1 tablespoon shortening
2 tablespoons water
  Salt
  Caraway or poppy seed
  Paprika

Stir flour, salt, and cheese together in large mixer bowl. Add shortening; mix at low speed about 1 minute, scraping bowl constantly. Add water; mix until all flour is moistened, about 1 minute, scraping bowl constantly. Gather dough together, adding a teaspoon or two more of water if it is needed. Press firmly into a ball. Roll on baking sheet into an oblong 13 x11 inches. With a sharp knife, cut dough lengthwise into three strips. Cut crosswise to make 15 straws of each strip. Do not separate on the sheet as they will bake apart. Sprinkle with salt, caraway or poppy seed, and paprika. Bake 8 to 10 minutes at 475° F.

CALICO CORNBREAD Eight SERVINGS

Speckled with bacon and black olives, it's a flavorsome treat.

- 6 strips bacon, cooked, crumbled
- 2 eggs, well beaten
- 1 cup buttermilk
- 3 tablespoons bacon drippings
- 1 cup flour
- ¾ cup cornmeal
- 1 teaspoon salt
- 2 tablespoons sugar
- ½ teaspoon soda
- 1½ teaspoons baking powder
- ½ cup sliced ripe olives

Set bacon aside and combine eggs, buttermilk, and bacon drippings. Mix flour, cornmeal, salt, sugar, and leavenings. Mix in liquid ingredients, just to blend. Stir in bacon and olives. Turn into a greased 7x11 inch pan and bake at 425° F. for 25 minutes.

☐

BLUEBERRY WHEAT GERM MUFFINS Twelve to Fifteen

They're a delight with a salad luncheon.

- 2 cups biscuit mix
- ½ cup wheat germ
- ¼ cup sugar
- 1 egg, slightly beaten
- 1 cup milk
- 2 tablespoons oil
- 1 cup blueberries

Combine biscuit mix, wheat germ, and sugar. Mix egg, milk, and oil. Add to dry ingredients and beat for half a minute. Fold in blueberries. Fill greased muffin pans two-thirds full. Sprinkle tops with extra wheat germ. Bake at 400° F. for 20 to 25 minutes or until golden brown.

OATMEAL MUFFINS *One* DOZEN

Grade A flavor is what they are famous for.

1 cup rolled oats
½ cup brown sugar
1 cup buttermilk
1 egg, beaten
¼ cup melted butter

1 cup flour
½ teaspoon salt
2 teaspoons baking powder
½ teaspoon soda

Pour buttermilk over oats and sugar and let stand 5 minutes. Add egg and butter and blend well. Add sifted dry ingredients and stir only enough to blend. Bake in greased muffin pans at 375° F. for 25 minutes.

MAPLE SIRUP ROLLS *One* DOZEN

They're sticky-sweet and good to eat!

1 recipe Stir-and-Roll Biscuits (page 53)
2 tablespoons butter
½ cup chopped nuts
1½ cups maple sirup or maple blended sirup

Roll biscuit dough ¼-inch thick, into a rectangle. Spread with butter and half the nuts. Roll jelly-roll fashion and cut in slices. Pour sirup into well-buttered pan or skillet, add rest of nuts, and arrange slices in pan. Bake at 425° F. about 25 minutes.

DELICATE BUTTERMILK PANCAKES *Four* SERVINGS

They're delectable with crushed fresh strawberries.

2 cups biscuit mix
1 teaspoon soda
2 eggs

1 cup buttermilk
1 cup sour cream

Beat or shake ingredients until just mixed. Drop from a large spoon onto a lightly greased griddle and brown on both sides.

HOLIDAY BANANA TEA BREAD   One LOAF

Frost it and make it Christmas morning's treat.

1¾ cups sifted flour
2 teaspoons baking powder
¼ teaspoon soda
½ teaspoon salt
⅓ cup shortening
⅔ cup sugar
2 eggs, well beaten

1 cup mashed bananas (2 to 3)
½ cup walnuts or pecans, broken
¼ cup (2 ozs.) each, finely cut
    candied pineapple,
    cherries, citron, orange
    peel*
¼ cup raisins

Sift together flour, baking powder, soda, and salt. Beat shortening and sugar together until light; add eggs and beat well. Add flour mixture alternately with bananas, a small amount at a time, beating after each addition until smooth. Add fruit, stirring only enough to mix evenly. Bake in well-greased pan (8½x4½ inches) at 350° F. for 1 hour 10 minutes, or until done.

* Or 1 cup mixed candied fruit, finely cut.

△

CARAWAY NUT BREAD   One SMALL LOAF

It has a real caraway flavor—mighty good!

2 cups flour
½ teaspoon soda
¾ teaspoon salt
2 teaspoons baking powder
½ cup chopped nuts

1 tablespoon caraway seeds
1⅓ cups evaporated milk
1⅓ tablespoons vinegar
3 tablespoons molasses
1 tablespoon oil

Measure and sift dry ingredients together. Add caraway seeds and nuts and stir to distribute rather evenly. Combine milk and vinegar, then add molasses. Stir until milk and molasses are well blended, then add oil. Make a well in the flour mixture, stir in the liquid ingredients until flour is just moistened. Bake in greased pan, 7½x4½ inches, at 350° F. for 50 minutes.

CHERRY-NUT LOAF

One LARGE LOAF

Make it the day before you serve it; it's wonderful with cream cheese.

1 cup canned sour cherries, drained
1 cup sugar
3 cups flour
3 teaspoons baking powder
1/4 teaspoon soda
1/2 teaspoon salt
1 egg
1 1/2 tablespoons grated orange rind
2 tablespoons melted butter or oil
1 cup milk
1/2 cup chopped nuts

Cut cherries in half. Add 1/4 cup of the sugar to them. Sift flour, baking powder, soda, and salt. Combine remaining sugar with beaten egg, orange rind, butter, and milk. Pour into dry ingredients and stir just enough to mix. Fold in cherries and nuts. Bake in greased 9x5-inch loaf pan, 350° F., for 1 hour.

COCONUT TEA BREAD

One SMALL LOAF

It's ever so easy and really unusual and delightful.

1 cup shredded coconut
2 cups pancake mix
1/3 cup sugar
1/2 cup chopped nuts
1 egg, beaten
1 1/4 cups milk
2 tablespoons oil

Place coconut in shallow pan in a 350° F. oven. Stir occasionally until delicately browned. Mix together pancake mix, sugar, nuts, and the toasted coconut. Add beaten egg and milk; stir in oil. Bake in a greased, waxed-paper-lined pan (8 1/2 x 4 1/2 inches) 1 hour at 350° F.

LEMON-NUT BREAD
One LARGE LOAF

There's a whole lemon in the loaf, and what it does to the flavor is something marvelous!

3 cups flour
4½ teaspoons baking powder
½ teaspoon soda
1½ teaspoons salt
1½ teaspoons nutmeg
¾ cup sugar

¾ cup chopped nuts
1 egg, beaten
1 cup milk
3 tablespoons oil
1 medium lemon, ground or chopped fine in blender

Sift flour, baking powder, soda, salt, nutmeg, and sugar. Add nuts and mix well. Combine egg, milk, and oil. Add lemon. Add to egg and milk mixture. Add to flour mixture and stir to moisten flour. Do not overmix. Bake in greased pan (9x5 inches) for 1 hour at 350° F.

△

CRANBERRY HOLIDAY BREAD
Two LARGE LOAVES

Bake one to freeze or give as a gift, one to eat. You'll love this bread!

2 eggs, well beaten
1 cup fresh orange juice
¼ cup water
Grated rind of 2 oranges
¼ cup butter (½ stick) melted
4 cups sifted flour
1 teaspoon salt
3 teaspoons baking powder

1 teaspoon soda
2 cups sugar
1 cup chopped nuts
1 cup chopped dates
1 cup chopped mixed candied fruit
¼ cup flaked coconut
2 cups cranberries, cut in half

Combine eggs, orange juice, water, rind, and butter. Sift dry ingredients into a large bowl. Add liquids and stir until blended. Add fruits and nuts and mix well. Turn into 2 greased, wax-paper-lined pans, 9x5 inches, and bake at 325° F. for 40 minutes. Lower heat to 300° F. and bake 40 minutes more. Remove bread from pans, peel off paper and cool on racks. When cold, wrap in plastic or foil and refrigerate overnight. Bread slices better when cold.

X

BARBECUE BREAD   *Twelve* SERVINGS

There's never enough of this!

4 or 5 small brown-and-serve loaves French bread
1 cup (2 sticks) butter, melted
1 can (3 ozs.) Parmesan cheese
2 tablespoons prepared mustard
¼ cup or more chili sauce
¼ cup instant onion
Garlic salt
1 teaspoon oregano

Make crosswise cuts in the bread, but leave slices attached. Combine all other ingredients and spread lavishly between slices and over loaves. Brown and crisp in 375° F. oven and serve very hot.

◇

WINE-GARLIC BREAD   *Six* SERVINGS

Variations include substituting Cheddar for Parmesan cheese.

1 long loaf French bread
½ cup (1 stick) soft butter
1 clove garlic, crushed
½ cup grated Parmesan cheese (or more)
3 tablespoons red table wine

Gash bread into thick slices, cutting almost through the loaf. Mix butter, garlic, cheese, and wine and spread between slices and over top of bread. Sprinkle with more cheese and bake at 400° F. for about 10 minutes.

FRENCH TOAST
Four to Six SERVINGS

Breakfast is always a treat when French toast is served.

4 eggs, slightly beaten
1 teaspoon sugar
½ teaspoon salt

¼ teaspoon nutmeg
1½ cups milk
8 slices day-old bread

Mix eggs, sugar, salt, nutmeg, and milk. Pour mixture into a flat, shallow dish. Place bread slices in mixture and let stand until they absorb as much liquid as possible. Turn them with a spatula. Transfer to a buttered skillet over moderate heat and brown well, turning once. Cut in halves and serve hot with butter, preserves, or sirup, and sausage or bacon. French toast may be baked in a waffle iron, if you like.

CRUNCHY BREAD STICKS
Sixteen STICKS

You'll never miss the hot dogs!

4 frankfurter buns
¼ cup softened butter
¼ cup grated Parmesan cheese
¼ cup poppy seeds

Split rolls in two; spread with butter. Dip into cheese, then in poppy seed. Cut each half bun in two the long way. Place on cooky sheet and bake at 350° F. for 10 to 12 minutes, or until golden brown.

CHEESE STICKS
Sixteen STICKS

Foot-long cheese sticks are fun!

1 package plain or buttermilk biscuits
1 cup shredded sharp natural Cheddar cheese
2 tablespoons butter, melted
Coarse salt
Caraway, poppy, celery, or anise seeds

60

Place biscuits on lightly floured board; press together with hands. **Pat** into a rectangle and sprinkle cheese over half the dough. **Fold** other side over cheese. Pinch edges together to seal in cheese and roll to an 8x12-inch rectangle (dough should not be more than ⅜-inch thick). With pastry wheel or serrated knife, cut into 16 ½-inch-wide strips. Place 4 strips on ungreased baking sheet with sides lightly touching. Repeat this procedure three times more. Brush strips with melted butter, sprinkle with the coarse salt, and any one of the seeds. Bake at 450° F. about 10 minutes, or until crisp and golden brown. With wide spatula carefully remove each group of four strips from baking sheet and place on cooling rack. When cool, separate with serrated knife. To serve, stand in a tall glass.

CLOTHESPIN TWISTS   *Ten* TWISTS

You'll need ten nice clean clothespins. . . .

1 package refrigerated biscuits
1 can (4½ ozs.) deviled ham
2 tablespoons chopped stuffed olives or pickle relish

Roll each biscuit flat and wrap around a greased clothespin. Place on a cookie sheet and bake at 450° F. for about 10 minutes, or until golden brown. Cool slightly, remove clothespin from each roll, slit open, and fill with deviled ham mixed with olives or relish.

ORANGE ROLLS   *Five or Six* SERVINGS

They're delectable!

1 package refrigerated biscuits or brown-and-serve rolls
3 tablespoons frozen orange juice concentrate
¼ cup sugar
2 tablespoons butter

Warm orange concentrate, sugar, and butter in a small saucepan until sugar is dissolved and butter melted. Dip tops of rolls into mixture and bake as usual.

Lemonade concentrate may also be used. Omit the sugar.

COFFEE-TIME FRUIT LOAF

Eight to Ten SERVINGS

Serve this delectable preserve-decked treat while it is warm.

2 cans (8 ozs. each) refrigerated biscuits
½ cup strawberry, raspberry, apricot, or peach preserves
¼ cup chopped pecans
2 tablespoons butter, melted

FROSTING: 1 cup confectioners' sugar plus 4 teaspoons milk.

Dip each biscuit into a mixture of preserves, nuts, and butter and fold in half. Place, folded side down, in rows crosswise in buttered 9x5-inch loaf pan. Bake at 350° F. about 30 minutes. Let stand in pan 5 minutes and turn out on cooling rack. Combine sugar and milk for frosting and drip it over loaf while warm.

△

PICNIC CHICK-A-BUNS

Eight or Ten SERVINGS

Serve them warm or cool, in the park or on the porch!

1 can refrigerated buttermilk biscuits
1 can (4¾ ozs.) chicken spread
½ cup chopped celery
¼ cup chopped ripe olives
1 hard-cooked egg, chopped
2 tablespoons mayonnaise

Stretch biscuits to double their size. Mix chicken spread with remaining ingredients. Put two biscuits together, sandwich fashion, with generous amount of filling between. Press edges together with tines of fork. Brush tops with beaten egg yolk and bake on an ungreased cooky sheet at 475° F. for 10 minutes.

VARIATION: Make the spread with the chicken-spread base, pickle relish, and mayonnaise.

SAVORY BISCUIT LOAF   *Ten* SERVINGS

Serve the loaf hot and pick it apart, biscuit by biscuit.

  2 packages refrigerated biscuits
¼ cup chopped onion
¼ cup chopped green pepper
¼ cup butter
¼ cup grated Parmesan cheese
  8 bacon strips, cooked crisp and crumbled

Sauté the onion and green pepper in the butter; add the cheese and bacon. Cut each biscuit into quarters. Coat the pieces of dough with the mixture and place in an oiled 9x5-inch loaf pan. Bake at 400° F. for 30 to 35 minutes.

CLUB SANDWICH   *One* SERVING

A popular favorite wherever sandwiches are ordered.

  3 slices white bread, lightly toasted, crusts trimmed
    Sliced chicken or turkey or ham
    Lettuce, mayonnaise
    Sliced tomato
    Crisp bacon

Put the sandwich together with chicken and lettuce on the first slice of bread, coating generously with mayonnaise; tomato and bacon on the second deck. The 3-layers are then cut into triangles (corner to corner, each way), and each little sandwich is held together with a toothpick. Set the sandwiches on end and serve garnished with pickles and radishes.

OTHER CLUB SANDWICHES: Use chicken salad, tomato and bacon, or add Swiss cheese to one layer.

CARROT AND PEANUT SANDWICHES

Four SERVINGS

Small fry always enjoy these; try them and you'll see why.

    2 large carrots, ground or grated
    ½ cup salted peanuts, ground
    ¼ cup salad dressing
      Crisp lettuce
    8 slices bread, buttered

Mix carrots, peanuts, and salad dressing. Spread on 4 slices of bread. Top with lettuce and remaining bread. Cut sandwiches into quarters and serve.

◣

HOT CHICKEN or TURKEY SALAD SANDWICHES

Six SERVINGS

With tomato soup, here's a perfect lunch.

    1 cup chopped cooked chicken or turkey
    1 cup finely diced celery
    1 tablespoon sweet pickle relish
    ⅓ cup mayonnaise or salad dressing
      Salt and pepper
    3 split toasted hamburger buns or 6 slices buttered toast
    1 cup grated process cheese

Combine chicken or turkey, celery, pickle relish, and mayonnaise. Season to taste with salt and pepper. Spread on split buns. Sprinkle cheese over each. Broil until cheese melts, 2 to 5 minutes.

Swedish Lucia Buns, page 50; Coolrise White Bread, page 46; Cheese Sticks, page 60; Broiled Ham, Chicken, and Pickle Sandwich, page 66

WILLIAMSBURG CHICKEN SANDWICH
Four to Six SERVINGS

Add leaf lettuce, too, if you can.

1½ cups diced cooked chicken
¼ cup crumbled blue cheese (about 1¼ ozs.)
½ cup chopped celery
3 tablespoons mayonnaise
Buttered bread slices

Combine chicken, cheese, celery, mayonnaise; mix well and sandwich with buttered white, whole wheat, or rye bread slices.

FRENCH-TOASTED HAM AND CHEESE SANDWICHES
Four SERVINGS

Try these in your electric skillet—they make an excellent lunch.

4 slices ham
4 slices Cheddar or Swiss cheese
8 slices buttered bread

BATTER COAT: 2 eggs, slightly beaten, ½ cup milk, ½ teaspoon salt.

Place a slice of ham and a slice of cheese between two slices of bread. Mix eggs, milk, salt. Dip sandwiches in the mixture and brown on both sides in a hot skillet in which you've melted about 3 tablespoons butter.

OTHER FRENCH-TOASTED SANDWICHES
Use the same egg coating for plain cheese sandwiches, plain ham, chicken, or other meat; for sandwiches filled with applesauce and cinnamon sugar, and others. An electric skillet can brown these sandwiches beautifully for you, then keep them warm almost indefinitely without loss of character.

runch featuring Eggs Benedict, page 75

HAM, SWISS, AND PINEAPPLE SANDWICH
One SERVING

Try this also with cranberry sauce in place of pineapple.

1 slice buttered bread
2 thin slices baked or boiled ham
   Mustard

1 slice pineapple
1 slice Swiss cheese

Toast one or both sides of bread and lay ham on the buttered side. Spread lightly with prepared mustard and top with pineapple. Lay cheese over the pineapple and broil until hot and browned.

BROILED HAM, CHICKEN, AND PICKLE SANDWICHES
Four SERVINGS

Smoked tongue or corned beef might be used in place of ham.

4 slices bread, toasted on one side, buttered
4 slices cooked chicken or turkey

4 slices cooked ham
Thin sliced dill pickles
4 slices process cheese

Place slice of chicken, then slice of ham on each slice of bread. Cover with a layer of pickle, then slice of cheese. Broil until cheese melts and serve hot.

POW-WOW SANDWICHES
Six SERVINGS

Heat them on the outdoor grill if you wish.

½ pound sliced bacon, fried crisp
¾ cup shredded dried beef
¾ cup chili sauce

⅓ cup sweet pickle relish
6 slices Cheddar cheese, diced
6 buttered round buns

Crush bacon. Mix with remaining ingredients. Spread between buns, and wrap in foil or waxed paper. Bake at 350° F. for 20 minutes.

EGG AND ONION SANDWICH   *One* SERVING

Man sized, it's bound to please a man.

2 slices buttered bread
1 fried egg
   Thin slices Bermuda onion
   Salt, pepper

Fry the egg soft and sandwich with onion, salt, pepper. You may need a bib for this. The runny egg yolk makes a sauce of a sort.

EGG SALAD SANDWICHES   *Three* SERVINGS

Remember these after the Easter bunny calls.

3 hard-cooked eggs, chopped
¼ cup fine chopped celery
¼ teaspoon salt; dash pepper
½ teaspoon minced onion, optional
3 tablespoons mayonnaise
6 slices buttered bread

Combine chopped eggs, celery, salt, pepper, onion, and mayonnaise. Make sandwiches.

PEEKABOO SANDWICH ROLLS

They're a novelty, and most attractive.

Fan tan rolls (bakery, or refrigerated rolls, baked)
Butter
Deviled ham, cheese, or any favorite spread

Partly separate layers of rolls and spread with butter and sandwich spread. Press back together with filling showing at the top. Heat in 350° F. oven 5 minutes or so. These can be foil-wrapped and kept warm.

MIDNIGHT SANDWICHES   *Four* SERVINGS

They taste best at the witching hour!

8 slices white bread
8 slices Cheddar cheese
8 thick slices tomatoes
8 green onions, fine minced
  Dash salt
8 strips bacon, cut in halves, cooked limp

Toast bread on one side only. Place cheese slices on untoasted side. Cover with tomato slice and fine minced onion. Season with salt. Criss-cross 2 pieces bacon on each sandwich. Broil until bacon is crisp, cheese bubbly.

TEAROOM SPECIAL SANDWICH   *One* SERVING

This one has variations, but many restaurants find it keeps customers happy.

Slice rye bread, buttered
Lettuce leaves
Slice ham
Slice chicken or turkey
Slice Swiss cheese
Slice tomato
Thousand Island dressing
Celery curls, radishes, olives for
  garnish

You don't get butter in a restaurant, but do put some on the bread at home. Arrange several crisp lettuce leaves over the bread, then the ham, chicken, cheese, with tomato on top. Be generous with the dressing, letting it cascade down the sides of the sandwich, add garnish, and this is it.

P.S. Sometimes there are bacon curls.

▼ △ ▼ △ ▼ △ ▼ △ ▼

EGGS, CHEESE, AND LUNCHEON DISHES

A S LONG as you have eggs in your refrigerator, there's
food in the house. Scrambled eggs and omelets make
many a quick supper for a modern family on the go. When
there's cheese to supplement the eggs, and the pantry shelf
yields macaroni, spaghetti, noodles, or rice, possibilities for
quick and interesting meals are limitless.

Scrambled eggs, for example, are more versatile than
you'd think. A very delicate dish can be produced by dicing
cream cheese into the eggs just before they begin to set.
Even a small amount of ham, diced fine and folded into the
eggs, adds substance and flavor. Instant onion, dried parsley
flakes, chives, catsup, or chili sauce, cooked peas or green
beans, crumbled cooked bacon, diced chicken livers, drained
oysters, clams or other seafood—these are only a beginning
in a list of possible additions for a dish of scrambled eggs.
Water or cream, tomato juice or stock, or even white wine
may be used as the liquid.

Omelets are even more versatile. They can have a
hundred fillings, many of which could be used "as is," right
from your pantry shelf: deviled ham, tomato sauce or
stewed tomatoes, cherry pie filling, to name several.

Poached and hard-cooked eggs offer other possibilities.

69

EGG COOKERY

In cooking with eggs, remember that too much heat toughens the protein. Gentle heat must be the rule.

HOW TO HARD COOK OR SOFT COOK EGGS

Place the eggs in a deep saucepan and add enough cold water to cover them (hot water will crack cold eggs). Set over moderate heat and bring fairly rapidly to the boiling point. Then turn off heat and cover for 2 minutes (soft eggs), 4 minutes (medium soft), or 15 minutes (hard cooked). Remove eggs from the water with a slotted spoon. When you cook more than four eggs at once, do not turn off the heat, but keep water just below simmering for 4 minutes (soft eggs), 6 minutes (medium eggs), or 20 minutes (hard cooked).

Eggs that are actually boiled to hard cook them develop an ugly green sulphur ring around the yolk, and the white becomes rubbery. Plunging them into cold water immediately after cooking helps prevent the green ring and makes them easier to shell. It is, unfortunately, the very fresh egg that is difficult to peel, once cooked.

HOW TO POACH EGGS

Poached eggs are the foundation of many famous dishes, but they are also a favorite breakfast dish.

Bring about two inches of water in a shallow pan to boiling. Turn down heat to hold at simmering. Break an egg at a time into the pan, or break into a saucer first and slip quickly into the water. Wait a moment for the next egg, until the water returns to the simmer. Cook 3 to 5 minutes, depending upon the firmness you like. Remove eggs from water with a slotted spoon. Serve on toast, on slices of ham, on corned beef hash, spinach, or in any other way you enjoy poached eggs. You may do the poaching in chicken broth, meat stock, bouillon, tomato juice, or even wine or sauce, if you wish.

HOW TO SCRAMBLE EGGS

Eggs may be scrambled directly in a skillet after cooking bacon, sausage, ham, or other meat, and they brown nicely on the bottom and taste marvelous—out-of-doors. But the truth is, they are usually more than a little tough. For most purposes, the fluffy, tender scrambled eggs are far more palatable.

Allow 1½-2 eggs per person and beat them a few turns of the rotary beater or with a fork, adding a tablespoon of water, milk, or cream per egg. Turn into a butter-rubbed pan or a teflon-lined one, over moderate heat, and stir from the bottom, using a wooden spoon as soon as eggs begin to coagulate. Turn them onto a hot plate as soon as they firm up. They should still be a little wet, soft textured, and tender. Scrambled eggs may be salted and peppered before, during, or after cooking.

Cooked vegetables, all kinds of cheese, diced meats, seafoods, dried and smoked beef, chicken livers, and many other foods may be added to eggs as they scramble. Minced parsley, dried herbs, green pepper, onions, and fresh or drained cooked tomatoes are all excellent possibilities for seasoning and extending the eggs.

HOW TO MAKE AN OMELET

There are two kinds of omelet: the slim or French kind, and the puffy one made by folding beaten egg whites in last. The first is quicker, the second a little more glamorous at times. Either type may be filled with anything from asparagus tips to sautéed chicken livers.

Plain or French Omelet. For each omelet allow 2 eggs, 1 tablespoon water, ¼ teaspoon salt and a little pepper. Use a pan, teflon-lined or not, 7 or 8 inches in diameter. Heat it with butter to coat the bottom until a drop of water will sizzle. Meanwhile mix eggs, water, and seasonings with a fork until yolks and whites are blended. Pour at once into the hot omelet pan, and lift cooked egg away from edges with a fork, to allow uncooked portion to run underneath. Slide pan back and forth rapidly across heat to keep mixture in motion. When set but still creamy and moist on top, fold or roll omelet and serve on a hot platter. The technique for making this kind of omelet is perfected with practice.

Fill with a sauce, creamed chicken, meat, or seafood, with preserves or warmed pie filling, or anything else you like. Or serve plain.

Puffy Omelet. For 2 or 3 servings, separate 4 eggs. To whites add ¼ cup water and ½ teaspoon salt and whip until stiff but not dry. Add a dash of pepper to yolks and beat until thick and lemon colored. Fold yolks into whites. Turn into hot, buttered skillet and cook over low heat about 5 minutes or until puffy and browned on the bottom (lift edge with spatula to look). Slip into a 325° F. oven and bake until set, 12 to 15 minutes. Fold and serve on a warm platter with any filling you like, or none. A sauce often is added, which may be slightly thinned canned soup, White Sauce or Cheese Sauce (page 254), tomato sauce, or something else.

SCRAMBLED EGGS SUPREME   *Four* SERVINGS

They'd be nice for luncheon with a garnish of watercress and slice of ham.

4 eggs, separated
1/4 cup milk
1 tablespoon chives

1/2 teaspoon salt
1/8 teaspoon pepper
1/2 can condensed mushroom soup

Beat egg yolks slightly and mix with remaining ingredients except egg whites. Beat egg whites stiff and fold into yolks. Cook over low heat, stirring constantly until firm.

GO WITHS: Ham or sausage. At lunch, a tossed salad, in addition.

WINE, LUNCHEON: California Grey Riesling.

OMELET WITH CREAM CHEESE   *Four* SERVINGS
AND CHIVES

Delicate flavor, delicate texture—it's a very nice omelet for Sunday breakfast.

1/4 pound cream cheese
3 tablespoons chopped chives
3 eggs, separated
2 tablespoons milk
1/4 teaspoon each salt, pepper
Parsley

Soften cream cheese; blend in chives, then egg yolks, one at a time. Add milk and seasonings. Fold into stiffly beaten egg whites. Pour into a well-buttered heavy 10-inch frying pan and cook over low heat until the bottom begins to brown. Then place in a 325° F. oven or under low broiler heat until the top is dry and the texture is firm. Fold and serve with a garnish of parsley.

GO WITHS: Blueberry Wheat Germ Muffins (page 54).

WINE, LUNCHEON: California Chablis.

INDIVIDUAL CHEESE OMELETS

Four to Six SERVINGS

They're baked on a griddle, like pancakes.

6 eggs, separated
2 tablespoons hot water
¾ teaspoon salt

⅛ teaspoon pepper
½ pound process cheese, shredded

Beat the egg yolks, add hot water, salt and pepper, then fold into stiffly beaten egg whites. Make omelets by pouring the mixture in individual portions onto a hot, well-greased griddle. Cook slowly until firm, then place in a 300° F. oven a few minutes to dry the tops. Sprinkle each omelet with shredded cheese and return to the oven just long enough to melt the cheese. Fold and serve immediately.

GO WITHS: Country sausage. At lunch, add peas and Stir-and-Roll Biscuits (page 53).

WINE, LUNCHEON: California Rosé.

ORANGE OMELET

Four SERVINGS

Beautifully light—sauce it with fresh sweetened strawberries for a gustatory treat.

6 eggs, separated
¼ teaspoon salt
3 tablespoons sugar
2 tablespoons lemon juice

¼ cup orange juice
Grated rind of 1 orange
2 tablespoons butter or
    margarine

Beat egg whites and salt until stiff. Beat yolks with sugar, fruit juices, and rind until very thick and yellow. Fold into whites carefully. Melt butter in large omelet pan or 12-inch skillet. Pour in omelet mixture and bake at 300° F. for about 20 minutes. Serve immediately.

GO WITHS: At brunch, bacon, fruit juice, or melon, Danish pastry.

WINE: New York State champagne (brut).

SHRIMP OMELET WITH LEMON BUTTER

Four to Six SERVINGS

Start with the uncooked seafood for an exquisite omelet.

1 pound raw shrimps, peeled, deveined and sliced
½ cup chopped celery
1 cup chopped green onions
¼ cup butter

6 eggs, beaten well
½ teaspoon salt
¼ cup lemon juice
¼ cup butter, melted

Sauté shrimps and vegetables in 2 tablespoons of the butter until seafood turns pink and vegetables look transparent. Melt the other 2 tablespoons butter in a large skillet. Mix beaten eggs and salt with shrimp mixture and pour into pan. Cook over low heat until eggs are set on bottom, lifting mixture occasionally with a spatula to let the uncooked egg run underneath. When omelet is set on the bottom, place under broiler a minute or so to set top. Fold over on a hot plate and pour mixture of lemon juice and melted butter over omelet.

Go withs: Broccoli, crusty rolls.

Wine: California Sauvignon Blanc.

x

EGGS WITH FRESH DILL GRAVY

Four SERVINGS

Dill and sour cream make harmony with eggs as well as vegetables.

¼ cup fresh dill, chopped
¼ teaspoon salt
⅛ teaspoon pepper
2 tablespoons flour
1½ cups sour cream
1 tablespoon butter, melted
8 hard-cooked eggs, cut in half

Simmer dill in ¾ cup water for 10 minutes. Add salt and pepper. Blend flour with sour cream and butter and add to dill mixture. Stir over low heat until mixture is smooth and slightly thickened. Serve hot over eggs on toast or in casseroles.

GO WITHS: Cold cuts, tossed salad.

WINE: California Chablis.

EGGS BENEDICT   *Four* SERVINGS

An expensive restaurant might garnish each portion with a slice of truffle—you could use pieces of ripe olive, or pimiento.

4 thin slices ham
4 poached eggs (page 70)
2 split English muffins, buttered and toasted
1 packet hollandaise sauce mix, prepared as directed, or
   1 small jar prepared hollandaise, warmed

Fry the ham, if you wish, or use ready-to-eat canned or "boiled" ham. Have eggs ready, poached soft. For each serving, place a hot slice of ham on a toasted muffin half, park a poached egg on the ham, and spoon the warm hollandaise sauce over the egg. Run the combination under the broiler for a moment or heat through in a 400° F. oven, just to be certain the combination is served hot. A hot plate helps.

If you are having this classical dish for brunch, precede it with melon. You may want to double the recipe to have two eggs per portion.

GO WITHS: At lunch, a branch of broccoli.

WINE: California Grenache Rosé.

EGGS BOMBAY STYLE (CURRIED) *Six* SERVINGS

If you're really hungry or haven't much else on the menu, make it three servings for these!

6 eggs, poached (page 70)
3 tablespoons butter
2 teaspoons curry powder
2 tablespoons flour

1½ cups chicken or veal stock, consommé or bouillon
1 egg yolk, beaten lightly
2 tablespoons heavy cream
6 rounds toast, buttered

Begin the sauce before cooking the eggs. Melt butter, blend in curry powder and flour, and add stock, stirring to make a smooth sauce. Keep hot in the top of a double boiler while poaching the eggs. When eggs are about ready to serve, stir into sauce beaten egg yolk and cream and remove at once from heat. Place poached eggs on toast and pour sauce over them.

GO WITHS: Asparagus and Peas with Herbs (page 256).

WINE: Ohio State Rosé.

EGGS IN BACON RINGS *Four* SERVINGS

Breakfast is more appealing when something attractive like this is served.

4 strips bacon, half cooked
4 eggs

4 tablespoons cream
Salt, pepper

Rub muffin cups or custard cups with the half-cooked bacon to grease them well, then wind a strip of bacon around inside each. Break the eggs into these cups. Pour a tablespoon of cream over each. Bake in a 350° F. oven until egg yolks are as firm as you like them, 12 to 15 minutes, usually. Season with salt and pepper before serving, or let each season his own.

Grated cheese may be sprinkled over the eggs, if you wish.

GO WITHS, AT LUNCH: Frozen spinach soufflé, rye rolls.

WINE: California Chablis.

76

BAKED LUNCHEON EGGS   *Four* SERVINGS

*The foundation may be changed to suit your fancy. Ham,
cooked spinach, or corned beef could be the casserole liner.*

8 eggs
½ cup toasted buttered crumbs
2 teaspoons minced chives
2 teaspoons minced parsley
½ cup or more light cream

Butter individual casseroles and sprinkle crumbs in them. Break two eggs
into each and sprinkle with chives and parsley. Pour 2 tablespoons or
more of cream around each set of eggs. Bake at 350° F. for about 15
minutes or until eggs are as done as you like them. Salt and pepper may
be added at the table.

GO WITHS: Canadian bacon, broccoli.

WINE: California Grey Riesling.

RANCH STYLE EGGS   *Four* SERVINGS

*The appetite appeal of this attractive combination is tre-
mendous.*

1 can or jar (about 2 cups) spaghetti sauce without meat,
    or stewed tomatoes
4 or 8 eggs
½ cup or more shredded or grated sharp cheese

Heat the sauce and distribute it among 4 individual baking dishes. Break
eggs into center and sprinkle with cheese. Bake at 350° F. until eggs are
as firm as you like them, 10 to 15 minutes.

GO WITHS: Fresh or frozen asparagus spears with pimiento, mixed green
salad, rye bread.

WINE: California Sylvaner.

SHIRRED EGGS FLORENTINE
Two or Four SERVINGS

When you get home late from the office and are going out at eight, try this speedy supper!

1 package boil-in-a-bag creamed spinach
2 or 4 eggs
   Salt, pepper
¼ cup grated or shredded Cheddar or Swiss cheese

Boil spinach 6 minutes and spoon into two or four individual casseroles. Break 1 or 2 eggs into each casserole, season with salt and pepper and sprinkle cheese on top. Bake at 350° F. for 12 to 15 minutes, or until egg whites are set.

GO WITHS: Buttered whole wheat toast, Waldorf Salad (page 239).

WINE: California Chablis.

EGGS CONTINENTAL
Four to Five SERVINGS

These make a perfectly delicious luncheon entrée.

¾ cup fine soft bread crumbs
4 hard-cooked eggs, sliced
3 slices bacon, diced
¼ pound fresh mushrooms, sliced, or 1 medium can mushrooms, drained

1 cup sour cream
2 tablespoons minced parsley or chives
¼ teaspoon each, salt, paprika
½ cup grated Cheddar cheese
   Paprika

Line shallow individual casseroles or an 8-inch pie pan with crumbs. Place sliced eggs in a layer over the crumbs. Fry bacon crisp, adding mushrooms about 5 minutes before you finish the bacon, sautéing them lightly. Drain off fat and add bacon and mushrooms to sour cream, parsley, or chives, seasonings. Mix and spread over eggs. Top with grated cheese and sprinkle with paprika. Bake at 375° F. for 15 to 20 minutes or until cheese is melted and sauce bubbly. Serve promptly.

GO WITHS: Green beans, Calico Cornbread (page 54).

WINE: New York State Delaware or Niagara.

DEVILED EGGS IN MUSHROOM SAUCE

Six SERVINGS

If you want cold deviled eggs for a picnic, forget the mush-room sauce and chill the filled eggs.

12 hard-cooked eggs	Few drops Tabasco sauce
2 teaspoons grated onion	¼ teaspoon pepper
2 teaspoons Worcestershire sauce	¼ cup mayonnaise
1 teaspoon each: dry mustard, salt, and paprika	1 tablespoon wine vinegar

SAUCE:

¼ cup butter	¼ cup flour
½ pound mushrooms, sliced	1 teaspoon salt
4 green onions and tops, sliced thin	¼ teaspoon pepper
	2 cups milk, scalded

Cut eggs into halves lengthwise. Sieve yolks and mix with onion, season-ings, mayonnaise, and vinegar. Blend thoroughly. Refill whites with yolk mixture, using decorating tube.

TO PREPARE SAUCE: Melt butter, add mushrooms and onions, and cook for 5 minutes. Blend in flour and seasonings. Add milk and cook until sauce is thick and smooth. Arrange eggs in serving dish and add sauce. Serve from chafing dish, or warm the combination in oven at 325° F. for 15 minutes before serving. If you wish, serve the preparation over toast points.

GO WITHS: Shoestring potatoes, Bibb lettuce salad with cherry tomatoes.

WINE: California Chenin Blanc.

CURRIED EGGS IN SHRIMP SAUCE

Four SERVINGS

Basically, these are just hot deviled eggs with a sauce.

    6 hard-cooked eggs, cut in half lengthwise
    1/4 cup mayonnaise
    1/2 teaspoon curry powder
    1 can frozen condensed cream of shrimp soup
    1/2 soup-can milk
       Split, toasted, buttered English muffins
       Paprika

Scoop out egg yolks, mash them, and mix with mayonnaise and curry. Refill whites. Combine soup and milk and heat until soup is thawed. Stir now and then. Place eggs in the hot soup sauce and cover. Heat gently a few minutes until eggs are hot. Place eggs on English muffin halves and spoon sauce over them. Sprinkle with paprika.

GO WITHS: Shoestring potatoes, peas, lima beans, or asparagus.

WINE: California Rosé.

CHEESE-AND-ONION PIE

Six SERVINGS

A close relative of the popular quiche Lorraine, this delicacy makes an excellent luncheon dish.

    6 slices bacon, cooked crisp, crumbled
    2 cups thinly sliced onion
    1/2 pound sharp Cheddar or Swiss cheese, shredded
    3 eggs, slightly beaten
    2 cups milk
    1 teaspoon salt
    1/8 teaspoon pepper
    1/4 teaspoon nutmeg
    1 tablespoon butter for top
       Unbaked 9-inch pie shell

Set aside the bacon and sauté onions in a little of the bacon fat, just until transparent. Place bacon, onions, and cheese in pie shell. Mix eggs, salt, and pepper and pour over bacon mixture. Top with nutmeg and dot with butter. Bake at 375° F. for 50 minutes, or until custard is set.

GO WITHS: Broccoli or another green vegetable, sliced beet and orange salad.

WINE: California Pinot Chardonnay.

EARLY AMERICAN FONDUE

Six to Eight SERVINGS

*This isn't the Swiss dish, but it is almost as good, and per-
haps easier to make.*

12 ounce can or bottle beer or ale
½ pound Swiss cheese, grated (about 2 cups)
½ pound Cheddar cheese, grated (about 2 cups)
3 tablespoons flour
¼ teaspoon salt
¼ teaspoon Tabasco sauce
  Nutmeg
1 loaf French bread

Heat beer in fondue dish, chafing dish, or skillet. Combine cheeses and flour; add in small amounts to beer, stirring to melt. When mixture starts bubbling, add salt and Tabasco sauce. Sprinkle with nutmeg. Spear bread cubes on long-handled forks and dip in fondue to eat. If mixture thick-ens, stir in a small amount of warm beer.

GO WITHS: A big mixed green salad with lots of tomatoes and cu-cumber.

WINE: Make it beer.

BABY PIZZAS   One DOZEN

Fix these up some late evening when everyone's watching television.

½ pound pork sausage or Italian sausage
¼ small onion, chopped fine
6 English muffins, split and toasted
1 can (6 ozs.) tomato paste
Dried parsley flakes
Oregano
¼ cup Parmesan cheese
12 thin slices Mozzarella cheese

Cook sausage in skillet, keeping it loose and broken up. Drain off fat. Spread muffins with tomato paste, dot with sausage and onion, and sprinkle with parsley and oregano. Sprinkle on Parmesan cheese and top with cheese slices. Broil or bake about 8 minutes in a very hot oven, 500° F. Serve hot.

GO WITHS, FOR LUNCH: Cups of vegetable soup.

WINE: California Zinfandel. Or beer.

TOMATO RABBIT   Four SERVINGS

Crisp bacon slices may be used to garnish this cheese dish.

1 can (8 ozs.) tomato sauce
1 package (10 ozs.) sharp Cheddar cheese, grated or
        shredded
8 slices buttered toast

Heat tomato sauce over moderate heat. Add cheese gradually and stir until smooth. Cut 4 slices toast into triangles. Pour rabbit over uncut slices, placed on warm plates, and garnish with the triangles, placing them crust sides against the toast, points outward.

GO WITHS: Molded vegetable salad.

WINE: New York State claret or Burgundy.

KIDNEY BEAN RABBIT *Six* SERVINGS

Here's excellent refreshment after an evening of cards, or a good lunch.

2 tablespoons chopped onion
1 green pepper, chopped
2 tablespoons butter
1 can (1 lb.) kidney beans, well drained
2 tablespoons catsup

2 teaspoons Worcestershire sauce
½ teaspoon salt
⅛ teaspoon pepper
Speck cayenne
½ pound Cheddar cheese, cubed

Sauté onion and green pepper in butter for 5 minutes. Add other in-gredients. Heat in top of double boiler and serve on toast.

GO WITHS: Orange and grapefruit salad, corn bread.

WINE: California mountain red.

◧

ASPARAGUS-CHEESE SOUFFLÉ *Four* SERVINGS

Take a can of soup, 4 eggs, some cheese—

1 can condensed asparagus soup, undiluted
¾ cup grated sharp cheese
4 eggs, separated

Heat soup and cheese until cheese is melted. Stir in the well-beaten egg yolks and mix. Fold in egg whites, beaten stiff. Bake in greased casserole at 350° F. for 1 hour.

GO WITHS: Cold cuts, Orange Rolls (page 61).

WINE: California dry Semillon.

CAULIFLOWER, BACON, AND CHEESE SOUFFLÉ

Four to Six SERVINGS

All the cheese is in the soup ingredient—no need to shred or grate.

1 can condensed cheese soup
2 tablespoons milk
2 tablespoons butter
1 tablespoon minced onion
4 eggs, separated
½ teaspoon salt

1 cup cooked chopped cauliflow-er (or asparagus tips or broccoli tips)
6 slices bacon, cooked crisp and crumbled

Blend soup, milk, butter and onion. Heat but do not boil. Add well-beaten egg yolks. Beat egg whites and salt until stiff and glossy. Fold into first mixture with cauliflower and bacon. Turn into an ungreased 1½-quart casserole, set in a shallow pan of water, and bake at 325° F. for an hour. Serve at once.

GO WITHS: Broiled tomatoes, corn sticks, green salad.

WINE: New York State Rosé.

CHEDDAR CHEESE SOUFFLÉ

Six SERVINGS

Practice makes perfect with cheese soufflé. This one's worth mastering.

1 cup Thick White Sauce (page 254)
½ teaspoon dry mustard
Dash Tabasco sauce or cayenne pepper
5 eggs, separated
½ pound sharp aged Cheddar cheese, shredded or grated

Add mustard and pepper sauce to white sauce while hot. Remove from burner while you beat egg yolks until very thick and light. Beat them into the sauce with a wire whisk, blending well. Beat in the cheese. Cool the mixture somewhat, then fold into the egg whites which have been beaten until stiff and glossy. Cut and fold until mixture is well blended but do not overmix or soufflé will not be light. Pour into an ungreased 2-quart casserole. With a teaspoon draw a circle through the mixture, an inch from the edge, to make a crown on the soufflé. Bake at 300° F. for 1 hour and 15 minutes. Have everything else in your menu waiting on the table, and the diners assembled. Rush the soufflé from the oven to the table before it has a chance to shrink.

GO WITHS: Asparagus with Almond-Lemon Butter (page 257), poppy-seed rolls.

WINE: California Gamay or claret.

MACARONI AND CHEESE BAKE

Twelve SERVINGS

Easy and economical for a luncheon, this dish could go off to a potluck supper as well.

1 pound elbow macaroni, cooked
2 cans cream of chicken soup diluted with ¾ cup milk

4–5 tomatoes, sliced
12 slices process Cheddar cheese or Swiss cheese
Oregano or chives (optional)

Cook macaroni according to directions on package. Heat soup and milk, mix with macaroni, and place in buttered 9x12-inch baking dish. Alternate overlapping slices of cheese and tomatoes over the top of the dish and sprinkle with oregano or chives, if you wish. Bake 25 minutes at 350° F.

GO WITHS: Green Beans with Mushrooms and Soy Sauce (page 259), molded fruit salad.

WINE: California claret, or mountain red.

NOODLE RING WITH CHEESE

Six to Eight SERVINGS

Makes a well-seasoned nest for creamed chicken, shrimps.

1 package wide noodles (8 to 9 ozs.), cooked
2 cups Medium White Sauce (page 254)
¾ teaspoon dry mustard
2 eggs, slightly beaten
¼ pound grated sharp cheese
1 medium onion, grated

Add mustard to white sauce. Stir sauce slowly into slightly beaten eggs. Add cheese and onion. Add noodles and pour into well-greased ring mold. Place in a pan of hot water. Bake at 350° F., about 40 minutes, or until inserted knife comes out clean. Cool slightly before turning onto platter or chop plate. Fill center with creamed fish or chicken or buttered vegetables.

GO WITHS: Big salad of mixed greens and crisp vegetables.

WINE: California crackling Rosé.

x

MACARONI CASSEROLE

Eight SERVINGS

Could be your contribution to "pot luck."

8 ounces macaroni, cooked
2 cans mushroom soup
1 cup milk
3 hard-cooked eggs, chopped
¼ pound dried beef

½ pound Cheddar cheese, shredded
1 small onion, chopped
½ cup buttered bread crumbs

Mix ingredients except crumbs; place in a buttered casserole. Top with crumbs and bake at 350° F. for 40 minutes.

GO WITHS: Sliced tomato and cucumber salad, bread sticks.

WINE: New York State Rosé.

ITALIAN MACARONI CASEROLE

If you need color in your meal, add some minced parsley.

8 ounces shell macaroni, cooked
1 cup thin onion slices
2 teaspoons salt
¼ teaspoon pepper

8 ounces Mozzarella cheese, sliced
½ cup mayonnaise
1 cup light cream

Place one-half of the cooked macaroni and onions in a 12x8-inch buttered baking dish. Sprinkle with half the salt and some pepper. Cover with one-half of the cheese. Repeat layers. Blend mayonnaise and cream and pour over macaroni. Cover and bake at 350° F. for 35 minutes.

GO WITHS: Broccoli or green beans, crusty rolls or pumpernickel bread, tomato salad.

WINE: California Chablis.

△

SPAGHETTI-MUSHROOM LOAF

Turns out nicely, slices prettily.

1½ cups Thin White Sauce (page 254)
    Pinch of nutmeg
½ teaspoon salt
1½ cups chopped mushrooms
2½ cups chopped cooked spaghetti
1 pimiento, minced
3 eggs, beaten slightly

Add nutmeg, salt, mushrooms, spaghetti, pimiento, then eggs to sauce. Bake in small buttered loaf pan set in a pan of hot water, for about 1 hour at 350° F. Serve hot with tomato sauce. Good cold, too.

GO WITHS: Artichokes, carrots, Barbecue Bread (page 59).

WINE: California or New York State Rosé.

SPEEDY SPAGHETTI
Six SERVINGS

Chopped parsley might top this lovable combination to add color.

8 ounces spaghetti, cooked
2½-ounces dried beef, cut in small pieces
1 can (4 ozs.) mushrooms
1 can (8 ozs.) whole kernel corn
1 can (8 ozs.) peas

¼ cup butter or margarine
¼ cup flour
1 cup liquid from vegetables
1 tall can (1⅔ cups) evaporated milk
½ teaspoon salt
¼ teaspoon pepper

Combine cooked and drained spaghetti with dried beef. Drain mushrooms, corn, and peas, reserving liquids. Combine liquids and add water if necessary to make 1 cup. Melt butter in saucepan, stir in flour, then stir in vegetable liquid and evaporated milk. Cook, stirring constantly, until smooth and thickened. Add salt and pepper and vegetables. Add to spaghetti and toss lightly. Heat thoroughly and serve. Mixture may be turned into greased casserole, topped with grated cheese, and baked at 350° F. for 30 minutes.

GO WITHS: Pineapple salad, Wine Garlic Bread (page 59).

WINE: California mellow red.

NOODLES WITH COTTAGE CHEESE AND SOUR CREAM
Six SERVINGS

Divine! That's what people call 'em!

6–8 ounce package noodles, cooked
1 cup sour cream
1 cup cottage cheese
½ cup milk
2 teaspoons Worcestershire sauce

1 small onion, grated
1 minced garlic clove
1 teaspoon salt
⅛ teaspoon pepper
Dash cayenne
Coarse bread crumbs
3 tablespoons butter

Combine noodles with everything except butter and crumbs. Turn into a shallow buttered baking dish. Sprinkle crumbs on top and dot with butter. Cover dish and bake for 10 minutes at 350° F.; remove cover and bake about 10 minutes longer, or until browned lightly on top. Serve directly from baking dish.

GO WITHS: Sweet-Sour Red Cabbage (page 263), or broccoli and a tossed salad.

WINE: California Chenin Blanc or Riesling

DIPPY NOODLES   *Four to Six* SERVINGS

You'll love these noodles with minute steaks. An onion soup mix plus sour cream may be substituted for the onion dip, if it's easier.

      8 ounces medium noodles, cooked, drained
    ½ teaspoon salt
        Dash pepper
      1 clove garlic, minced
      1 egg, slightly beaten
  1–2 tablespoons melted butter
      2 cartons (8 ozs. each) French onion dip
        Grated Parmesan or Parmesan and Romano cheese

Mix noodles, seasonings, egg, butter, and dip together. Place in buttered 1½-quart casserole and sprinkle generously with the cheese. Bake at 350° F. for 30 minutes.

GO WITHS: Minute steaks, peas or zucchini, Calico Cornbread (page 54).

WINE: California Emerald Riesling.

RICE AND CHEESE CUSTARD   *Six* SERVINGS

If you like onion, add a little of the instant kind.

        2 eggs, slightly beaten
        1 tablespoon melted butter or margarine
    1½ cups milk
        1 teaspoon salt
    ⅛ teaspoon pepper
        2 cups cooked rice
        1 cup grated Cheddar cheese

Add melted butter to eggs. Mix in milk, salt, pepper, rice, and ¾ cup cheese, blending well. Pour into greased baking dish and sprinkle remaining cheese over top. Place in pan of hot water and bake at 350° F. for 50 minutes.

GO WITHS: Frankfurters, chicken, or ham; green beans, Perfection Salad (page 224).

WINE: New York State or Ohio Rosé.

BURMESE FRIED RICE   *Four* SERVINGS

Cooked pork or beef could be substituted for shrimps or ham in this savory mixture.

4 cups cold cooked rice
3 tablespoons oil
1 cup shredded shrimp or cooked
    ham

2 eggs, slightly beaten
6 green onions, chopped
2 tablespoons soy sauce
½ teaspoon sugar

Cook rice in hot oil for 10 minutes, stirring frequently. Add shrimp or meat. Pour eggs over mixture. Cook slowly for 5 minutes, stirring frequently with fork. Add onions, soy sauce, and sugar. Heat through.

GO WITHS: Sautéed Escarole (page 268), tomato, pineapple, and avocado salad.

WINE: California Rhine wine.

GREEN RICE
Six SERVINGS

Bake this well-seasoned mixture in a ring mold, if you wish.

1 green pepper, ground
1 clove garlic, ground
2 medium onions, ground
1 cup parsley, ground
1 pound Cheddar cheese, ground
1 teaspoon salt
⅔ cup oil
2 cups cooked rice
1 cup milk

Combine ingredients and bake in greased casserole at 350° F. for 40 minutes, or until firm.

GO WITHS: Ham or hamburgers, carrots.

WINE: California Gamay or Grey Riesling.

JAVANESE RICE WITH SHRIMPS
Four SERVINGS

This could be a side dish with a chicken dinner or be given more importance at lunch.

¼ cup butter
2 teaspoons curry powder
1 cup uncooked rice
½ cup finely chopped celery
½ cup finely chopped onion
2 cups chicken broth
1 teaspoon salt
⅛ teaspoon pepper
½ cup chopped-cooked or canned shrimps
½ cup diced cooked ham
1 cucumber, pared and cut lengthwise in strips

Melt butter in a skillet, stir in curry powder, and add rice, celery, and onion. Cook over low heat, stirring, until rice is golden. Turn into a 2-quart casserole. Add chicken broth, salt, and pepper. Cover and bake at 350° F. about 30 minutes, or until rice is tender. Stir in shrimps and ham. Bake 15 minutes more to heat through. Serve garnished with cucumber strips.

GO WITHS, AT LUNCH: French-fried Eggplant (page 267), broccoli with hollandaise.

WINE: California sauterne.

BAKED RICE RING
Six SERVINGS

Serve this filled with meat balls or creamed chicken or sea-food. It's nice also with a curry.

¼ cup minced onion
¼ cup butter or margarine
¼ cup flour
2 cups milk
1½ teaspoons salt
¼ teaspoon pepper

2 teaspoons baking powder
2 eggs, slightly beaten
¼ cup minced parsley
3 cups cooked rice (use 1½ cups pre-cooked kind)

Cook onion in butter until soft but not browned. Blend in flour. Add milk and cook to smooth sauce. Add seasonings, baking powder, eggs, and parsley. Stir in rice and turn into well-oiled 6-cup ring mold. Bake at 350° F. for 1 hour. Loosen around edges with knife, turn out onto hot platter, and serve with whatever you wish to put in the center.

GO WITHS: Beets, molded fruit salad.

WINE: California crackling Rosé

△

FIVE-MINUTE PAELLA
Four or Five SERVINGS

Spain has hundreds of recipes for its favorite rice dish—but probably not this one! See page 206 for another.

1⅓ cups packaged pre-cooked rice
2 tablespoons minced onion
1½ cups bouillon
⅛ teaspoon saffron

1 can (7½ ozs.) minced clams
1 can (5–6 ozs.) boned chicken
½ teaspoon salt
4 pimientos, quartered
1 package frozen peas (optional)

Combine all ingredients in a saucepan. Cover and bring to a boil. Simmer 5 minutes.

GO WITHS: Sliced orange salad on curly endive, Italian style dressing.

WINE: California Rosé.

◎ ◎ ◎ ◎ ◎ ◎ ◎ ◎ ◎

FISH AND SHELLFISH

FISH COOKERY is easy if we remember two words among the F's in the culinary dictionary: Fast and Fresh. Fish and shellfish cook very quickly, and they are moist and tender when eaten at the end of the few minutes it takes for heat to penetrate. If cookery is prolonged, however, fish toughens. Two or three minutes can make the difference.

Only fresh fish is worth cooking. This isn't much of a problem any more, with commercial freezing holding our fish in perfect condition and fresh-fish markets handing us firm-fleshed, bright-eyed, clean-smelling products for the skillet, oven, and grill. Out of the water, into the skillet, onto the table is the sing-song to remember.

Frozen fish is better if thawed before cooking. We never refreeze fish, once thawed. To do so impairs quality.

Frozen fish comes in a bewildering array of shapes and sizes. Sometimes you don't have an idea what kind of fish you are buying in the fillets, portions, sticks, or cakes you pluck from the frozen food cases. But if you follow package directions in preparing them, you'll have a good meal.

All fish and seafoods love lemon, and most are better if there is butter in the sauce served with them or in the skillet in which they are cooked. Many good commercial tartar sauces are available for use with fish cooked in a simple manner. Mayonnaise with lemon juice and pickle relish in it makes an excellent fish sauce.

Canned fish are a great convenience, the favorites being salmon and tuna, crab and shrimps. These and others available may be creamed or casseroled in dozens of combinations.

Fish belongs on the menu once a week or more often. Some tasty and speedy recommendations for luncheons and dinners follow. I have one small suggestion: For those times when you can't find a fresh lemon in the refrigerator, keep on hand lemon juice in the bottle.

COURT BOUILLON   *One* QUART

All we have here is beautifully seasoned water in which to cook shellfish or "poach" any kind of fish, giving it a delicate flavor.

   1 quart water or chicken, fish, or veal stock or bouillon
   2 cups dry white wine (optional)
   1 onion, sliced
   1 bay leaf
   A few whole black peppers (peppercorns)
1½ teaspoons salt (adjust salt to suit basic stock used)
   1 rib celery with leaves
   1 carrot
   2 or 3 sprigs parsley

Bring ingredients to a boil and simmer for half an hour to season and reduce quantity, if you have time.

To poach any kind of fish, put a rack in your kettle, wrap the fish in cheesecloth which will allow seasonings to reach it but prevent it from breaking apart. Simmer covered in the bouillon for 6 to 10 minutes per pound for fillets or steaks, about 8 minutes per pound for whole fish. Serve the fish hot with a sauce, or chill it for salads or casseroles.

Cook shrimps from 2 to 5 minutes in the broth, only until they turn pink.

Cook lobster tails 1 minute per ounce plus 1 minute "for the pot"; i.e. cook a 6-ounce lobster tail 7 minutes. Do not boil, just simmer.

FRIED FISH
Six SERVINGS

Indoors or out, the heavy iron skillet seems to do the best job of frying fish.

6 panfish, ready to cook, or 2
   pounds fresh or frozen
      (thawed) fillets
   Milk or evaporated milk
½ cup flour

¼ cup cornmeal
1½ teaspoons salt
¼ teaspoon pepper
   Paprika, if you wish
   Butter or oil for frying

Dip fish into milk, then into mixture of flour, cornmeal, salt, pepper and paprika. Heat butter or oil until hot but do not let butter brown or oil smoke. Put the fish in the pan and fry about 4 minutes to the side, turning carefully. Flesh should flake easily when fish is done. Drain on paper toweling and serve with lemon wedges, immediately. On the barbecue grill, keep the skillet 4 inches from the coals.

Go WITHS: French fries, Coleslaw (page 229).

WINE: California or New York State Rhine wine.

FISH FILLETS EXTRA SPECIAL
Four SERVINGS

Red wine is unusual with fish, but then there's the cheese . . .

1 pound fish fillets, fresh or frozen and thawed
1 bottle (12 ozs.) chili sauce
¼ cup California Burgundy
¼ cup finely chopped onion
1 cup shredded Cheddar cheese

Place fillets in a single layer in a buttered baking dish, spread with other ingredients, cheese on top and bake at 450° F. for 10 to 12 minutes or until fish flakes easily with a fork.

Go WITHS: Parsley buttered potatoes, broccoli with hollandaise.

WINE: California Burgundy.

CREOLE FILLETS   *Four* SERVINGS

Use this method for any fillet—haddock, cod, halibut, mackerel, ocean perch, or what have you.

1 pound fillets, cut in serving portions
1/4 cup chopped green pepper
1 chopped onion
1/4 cup butter or margarine

1 cup diced celery
3/4 teaspoon salt; dash pepper
2 cans (8 ozs. each) tomato sauce
1/2 cup sliced stuffed olives

Place fillets in greased baking dish. Sauté onion and green pepper in butter, add celery, seasonings, tomato sauce. Simmer 20 minutes. Add olives. Pour half the sauce over fillets and bake 20 minutes at 375° F. Serve on hot platter with the remaining sauce.

Go WITHS: Fluffy rice, peas, crusty bread.

WINE: California or New York State dry sauterne.

FILLETS OF PERCH CARIBBEAN   *Four to Six* SERVINGS

An excellent dish for company, the combination has an exotic appeal.

1 1/2 pounds perch fillets
Juice of 1/2 lime
1/2 cup thinly sliced peeled cucumber
1/2 cup seedless grapes

1/2 cup white wine
1/2 cup cream
1/2 teaspoon anchovy paste
Parsley for garnish

Rub baking dish with cut clove of garlic, if you wish, and arrange fillets in the dish. Sprinkle with lime juice, and top with cucumber and grapes. Add wine. Cover and bake at 450° F. for 15 minutes. Uncover and add cream and anchovy paste blended together. Continue baking uncovered for another 5 minutes. Serve garnished with parsley.

Go WITHS: Potato puffs, fresh asparagus.

WINE: California Emerald Riesling.

FISH SQUARES WITH CRABMEAT SAUCE

Six SERVINGS

Crisply browned fish squares or portions seem the plainest of food, until you dress them up with crab sauce!

6 breaded fish squares, cooked according to package directions
1½ cups Medium White Sauce (page 254)
1 egg yolk, lightly beaten
1 can (6 ozs.) crabmeat or ¾ cup lump crabmeat, flaked

Keep cooked fish squares warm while preparing sauce. Beat in egg yolk and add crabmeat. Taste and add more salt and pepper, if you need it. Serve hot over hot fish squares.

Go WITHS: Green beans cooked whole, hot buttered French bread.

WINE: New York State or Ohio sauterne.

FROGS' LEGS PROVENCALE

Six SERVINGS

Here's a famous French method for "a-wooing" your palate.

3 pounds frogs' legs, thawed if frozen
Milk, flour
Salt, pepper
½ cup butter or butter and olive oil
Lemon juice, minced parsley
Garlic butter

Wipe frogs' legs with damp cloth. Dip in milk, then in flour, and sauté until golden brown in butter, about 4 minutes to each side. (Don't crowd the skillet; do this in instalments, or 2 skillets.) Transfer to hot platter and sprinkle with salt, pepper, lemon juice, and minced parsley. Add 2 minced garlic cloves to ¼ cup butter in the skillet, let the butter turn brown (don't burn it!) and pour the garlic butter over the frogs' legs.

Go WITHS: Potatoes au Gratin (page 274), whole green beans, relish tray.

WINE: California Emerald Riesling.

FISH FILLETS MORNAY   *Four* SERVINGS

If possible, use fish or veal stock in place of half the milk in the white sauce. Makes it more authentic.

1½ pounds fish fillets, browned in butter, salted and
      peppered
1½ cups Medium White Sauce (page 254)
 ½ teaspoon prepared mustard
 1 teaspoon minced onion
 ½ teaspoon Worcestershire sauce
 ¼ cup grated Parmesan cheese

Add seasonings and cheese to hot white sauce, pour over browned fillets and place under broiler 2 minutes, or until sauce bubbles. Or start with the raw fish fillets, sprinkled with salt and pepper, cover with sauce and bake at 450° F. for 10 minutes or until sauce bubbles and browns and fish flakes.

GO WITHS: Potatoes with dill, Brussels sprouts, cornmeal muffins, sliced tomatoes.

WINE: California mountain white.

X

HADDOCK IN CREAM   *Six* SERVINGS

The fish comes to table in its own savory sauce.

1½ pounds haddock or other fillets
    Salt, pepper
 2 tablespoons lemon juice
 1 teaspoon prepared mustard
 ½ teaspoon Worcestershire sauce
 3 small onions, sliced
 1 cup cream

Wipe haddock with damp cloth, season with salt and pepper and place in 2-quart baking dish. Mix lemon juice, mustard, and Worcestershire, and spread over fillets. Top with onions and pour cream over the combination. Bake 25 minutes at 400° F.

GO WITHS: Browned potato cakes, asparagus tips, green salad.

WINE: New York State Chablis.

BAKED HALIBUT AU GRATIN *Four* SERVINGS

A regal dish. Bacon may be omitted if it's a "fish" day.

    4 small halibut steaks (about 1¼ lbs.)
    4 slices bacon, cut in squares
    1 small onion, sliced thin
      Piece bay leaf
      Salt, pepper
    2 tablespoons butter or margarine
    2 tablespoons flour
    1 cup buttered bread crumbs
    ¼ cup grated Parmesan cheese

Place half the bacon in bottom of shallow baking dish. Cover with sliced onion. Add bay leaf. Lay fish steaks, seasoned with salt and pepper, on onions, and coat with paste of melted butter and flour. Sprinkle with crumbs and cheese, top with rest of bacon. Bake at 400° F. for 30 minutes.

GO WITHS: Hashed brown potatoes, baked crumbed tomato halves, avocado salad.

WINE: California Riesling.

BAKED HALIBUT WITH DILL SAUCE

Four SERVINGS

The cream thickens nicely for a sauce.

4 halibut steaks
1 small onion, chopped fine
1 tablespoon chopped fresh dill
    or 1 teaspoon dried dill
    Salt, pepper
    Dots of butter
½ - ¾ cup half-and-half

Place halibut steaks side by side in buttered 7x11-inch pan and sprinkle with onion, dill, salt, and pepper. Dot with butter. Cover with the cream and bake at 350° F. for 30 to 40 minutes.

GO WITHS: Mashed potatoes, peas or green beans, radish, tomato and cucumber salad.

WINE: California dry sauterne or Semillon.

SCARLET SINNERS

Six SERVINGS

New England codfish balls with cranberry sauce are different and so good!

1 cup flaked cooked codfish
2 cups hot cooked mashed potatoes
    Salt, pepper as needed
1 egg
1 can jellied cranberry sauce
1 teaspoon or more grated horseradish

Combine fish, potatoes, seasonings, and egg. Shape into balls and brown in a skillet or fry in deep hot fat at 375° F. until golden brown. Mash cranberry sauce, heat to boiling, and add horseradish. Serve as sauce.

GO WITHS: At breakfast or brunch, melon and assorted sweet rolls.

WINE: California Rosé.

GRILLED RED SNAPPER STEAKS   *Six* SERVINGS

This method may be applied to other kinds of fish as well.

2 pounds frozen red snapper
    steaks, thawed
½ cup oil
¼ cup lemon juice
2 teaspoons salt

½ teaspoon Worcestershire sauce
¼ teaspoon white pepper
Dash Tabasco sauce
Paprika

Cut fish into serving-size portions and place in well-greased hinged wire grills. Blend oil and lemon juice with seasonings, baste fish with sauce, and cook about 4 inches from well-burned-down coals for about 8 minutes. Turn and baste again and cook 7 to 10 minutes more or until fish flakes easily with a fork.

GO WITHS: French fried potatoes, sliced tomatoes, buttery French bread heated in foil.

WINE: California Johannisberg Riesling.

SALMON CAKES   *Six* SERVINGS

Ever so easy, ever so good !

1 can (1 lb.) salmon, flaked
1 tablespoon each, grated onion,
    chopped parsley
½ cup bread crumbs

½ cup finely chopped celery
2 eggs, slightly beaten
½ teaspoon salt
Pepper

Combine ingredients, form into cakes, sauté until brown in butter or margarine. Serve with mushroom or cheese sauce (use mushroom soup or the prepared cheese sauce to make it speedy).

GO WITHS: Mashed potatoes, broccoli.

WINE: New York dry Catawba or Niagara.

BAKED SALMON-MACARONI SURPRISE

Six SERVINGS

The cucumbers and tomatoes make it an interesting combination.

1 can (1 lb.) salmon drained
2 cans (about 1 lb. each) macaroni with cheese sauce
2 medium tomatoes, thinly sliced
¾ cup sliced peeled cucumber
⅓ cup soft bread crumbs
2 tablespoons melted butter or margarine
½ cup grated process Cheddar cheese

Flake salmon, after removing skin and bones. Arrange macaroni, salmon, cucumber, and tomatoes in alternate layers in baking dish or 2-quart casserole. Mix bread crumbs, butter, and cheese; arrange over top. Bake at 375° F. for 45 minutes.

GO WITHS: Crusty bread, green salad.

WINE: New York State Rosé.

BROILED SALMON WITH AVOCADO SAUCE

Six SERVINGS

The color combination here is most interesting.

6 salmon steaks
1½ cups Medium White Sauce (page 254)
½ teaspoon Worcestershire sauce
Few drops Tabasco sauce
1 large avocado, peeled, diced
2 tablespoons chopped pimiento

Broil salmon steaks (five minutes each side). Add Worcestershire and Tabasco sauce to White Sauce. Remove from heat and add avocado and pimiento. Arrange salmon on hot serving platter and top with sauce. Sprinkle with paprika and serve.

GO WITHS: Mashed potatoes, peas with tiny onions, escarole salad.

WINE: New York or Ohio Rosé.

SALMON-SPINACH SOUFFLÉ   *Four* SERVINGS

You'll find this a colorful luncheon dish of good flavor.

½ cup Thick White Sauce (page 254)
½ cup grated Cheddar cheese
½ teaspoon salt
  Dash pepper
3 eggs, separated
1 package (12 ozs.) frozen chopped spinach, thawed, drained
1 can (6½ ozs.) salmon, flaked

Add cheese and seasonings to White Sauce. Add beaten egg yolks, spinach and salmon. Fold in egg whites, beaten stiff. Taste and add more salt if needed. Turn into a buttered casserole and set it in a pan of hot water. Bake at 350° F. for 1 hour or until firm in center.

GO WITHS: Small baked potatoes, Harvard beets.

WINE: California Chablis, or mountain white.

ROSY SALMON LOAF
Six SERVINGS

All that catsup provides a perky flavor as well as color. Easy, pretty and good!

1 pound can salmon, flaked
1 egg, beaten
2 tablespoons minced onion or 1 tablespoon instant onion
1 tablespoon lemon juice
1 cup soft bread crumbs
1 cup catsup

Combine ingredients and pack into a small greased loaf pan. Bake at 375° F. for about 45 minutes. If you'd like a sauce, try 1 cup White Sauce (page 254), adding 1 tablespoon lemon juice, 1 tablespoon minced parsley, and 2 tablespoons mayonnaise.

Go WITHS: Cottage fried potatoes, green lima beans.

WINE: California Rosé.

X

SALMON SOUFFLÉ
Six SERVINGS

Texture and flavor are delicate in this easily made dish.

1 can (1 lb.) salmon
1 tablespoon lemon juice
½ teaspoon salt
¼ teaspoon pepper

1 can cream of celery soup, undiluted
4 eggs, separated

Drain salmon, remove bones and skin, add lemon juice and seasonings, and mash fine. Stir in soup and heat through. Beat in egg yolks, one at a time. Fold in egg whites, beaten stiff. Turn into buttered casserole and place the casserole in a shallow pan of water. Bake at 350° F. for 1 hour or until firm in center.

Go WITHS: Broccoli with hollandaise, potatoes with dill.

WINE: New York State dry Catawba or Riesling.

CURRIED SARDINES ON TOAST Six SERVINGS

This is a nice breakfast dish if you're hungry.

    2 cups Medium White Sauce (page 254)
    ⅛ teaspoon paprika
    ¾ teaspoon curry powder
    4 hard-cooked eggs
    2 cans sardines
    6 slices toast

Add seasonings to sauce. Stir in sliced whites of eggs and 2 chopped yolks. Heat through. Broil sardines 5 minutes or until piping hot. Place on toast and cover with sauce. Top with remaining egg yolks, grated.

Go WITHS: At lunch, a cup of vegetable soup.

WINE: California Sauterne.

△

TROUT AMANDINE Four SERVINGS

One of the most delicate of fish, trout is also among the easiest to cook.

    4 trout, ½–¾ pound each
    ½ cup melted butter
    ½ cup slivered almonds
    1 tablespoon lemon juice
      Minced parsley

Thaw trout if frozen. If they come in a plastic bag, leave them in it to thaw at room temperature about 4 hours. Wipe dry, then brush with butter. Brush broiler pan with butter also. Broil about 8 minutes 4 inches from heat. Do not try to turn. Meanwhile, brown almonds lightly in remaining butter, add lemon juice and parsley. Transfer fish to a very hot platter and pour the sauce over them.

Go WITHS: French fries, zucchini with tomatoes, crusty rolls.

WINE: California Gewürztraminer or Johannisberg Riesling.

FILLET OF SOLE, HAWAII   *Four* SERVINGS

Try other delicate fish fillets in this same manner, with or without the finishing touches of avocado and nuts.

    4 large sole fillets, about 1–1½ pounds
    1 teaspoon grated lemon peel
    2 tablespoons lemon juice
      Salt, pepper, flour
    ¼ cup butter
    ⅓ cup light cream or evaporated milk
    1 avocado, peeled, sliced
    ¼ cup chopped macadamia nuts or cashews

Place fillets in a shallow dish and sprinkle with grated lemon peel, 1 tablespoon of the juice, and salt and pepper. Let stand 10 minutes. Coat fish with flour. Melt half the butter in a large skillet. Sauté fish until well browned on one side, about 3 minutes. Turn fish. Add remaining butter and sauté 3 to 5 minutes more, just until fish is tender. Remove to hot platter and sprinkle with remaining lemon juice. Add cream to skillet. Bring to a boil, scraping browned particles from pan. Spoon over fish. Top with avocado slices and sprinkle with nuts. Serve with lemon quarters.

White wine may be used instead of cream.

Go WITHS: Shoestring potatoes, frozen spinach soufflé.

WINE: California Rhine wine or Grey Riesling.

BAKED TUNA CASSEROLE   *Eight* SERVINGS

Everything in the dish comes from a can!

    1 can (14½ ozs.) evaporated milk
    1 can cream of mushroom soup
    1 can (4 ozs.) mushroom pieces (don't drain)
    1 can (4 ozs.) pimiento, chopped
    2 cans (7 ozs. each) tuna, drained, flaked
    2 cans (4 ozs. each) shoestring potatoes

Blend milk, soup, mushrooms, pimiento. Stir in tuna and potatoes. Turn into a buttered casserole and bake at 375° F. for 30 minutes.

GO WITHS: Fruit salad, oatmeal bread.

WINE: New York State Rosé.

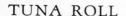

TUNA ROLL   *Four to Six* SERVINGS

Use salmon, if you'd rather, a one-pound can; filling, appealing.

    2 cans (6½–7 ozs. each) tuna
    ½ teaspoon salt
    ¼ teaspoon pepper
    1 pimiento, chopped
    2 tablespoons chopped chives
    3 or 4 sprigs watercress, chopped
      Grated rind ½ lemon
    2 cups biscuit mix
      Juice of ½ lemon plus water to make ½ cup
    1 egg yolk plus 2 tablespoons milk

Empty tuna into large mixing bowl, flake and season with salt and pepper. Add pimiento, chives, and watercress. Add lemon peel to biscuit mix. Prepare biscuit dough according to directions, using mix and liquid. Roll into rectangle ¼-inch thick. Spread with tuna mixture. Roll up from long side. Place seam side down in greased baking pan. Pinch ends together. Brush top with egg yolk and milk. Bake at 400° F. 25 to 30 minutes. Slice and serve hot. Add a sauce or not, as you wish.

GO WITHS: Carrots and peas, Mint Julep Salad (page 234).

WINE: California mountain white.

BAKED TUNA
WITH STUFFING

Six to Eight SERVINGS

Prepared stuffing is handy for more than turkey and chicken!

2 cans (6½–7 ozs. each) tuna, drained, flaked
1 cup prepared herb seasoned stuffing
¼ teaspoon pepper
¼ teaspoon paprika
2 tablespoons butter, melted
1 cup tomato juice
3 eggs, separated

Mix tuna with stuffing, seasonings, butter, and tomato juice. Add slightly beaten egg yolks. Beat egg whites until stiff and fold into tuna mixture. Bake in a buttered casserole 40 minutes at 350° F. Serve with hot White Sauce (page 254).

Go WITHS: Baked potatoes, peas and corn, celery hearts.

WINE: California Rosé.

TUNA-CHEESE PIE

Six SERVINGS

Rim this attractive luncheon dish with wedge slices of tomato for the last ten minutes in the oven, if you like.

3 eggs, well beaten
1 cup milk
½ teaspoon salt
1 can (6½ ozs.) tuna, flaked

½ pound grated Swiss cheese
1 tablespoon flour
2 teaspoons minced onion
Unbaked 9-inch pie shell

Mix eggs, milk, and salt. Stir in tuna, cheese, flour, and onion. Turn into pie shell and bake at 425° F. for 40 to 45 minutes. Serve warm.

Go WITHS: Relishes or a green salad, and a fruited dessert.

WINE: Ohio dry Catawba or New York State Rhine wine.

WHITEFISH FLORENTINE   *Six* SERVINGS

Fish, dressing, and spinach—now you need a salad and you're all set!

1½ pounds whitefish fillets
1 cup chopped fresh or frozen spinach
1 cup soft bread crumbs
2 tablespoons minced onion
Salt, pepper

Milk or water to moisten dressing
Melted butter or margarine
⅔ cup mayonnaise
⅓ cup water
½ cup grated Cheddar cheese

Sprinkle fish with salt and pepper. Place half in bottom of a greased baking dish and cover with dressing made by combining spinach, crumbs, onion, seasonings, and liquid to moisten. Top with rest of fish and brush with melted butter. Bake uncovered at 375° F. for one-half hour. Stir water into mayonnaise and brush over fish. Sprinkle with cheese and brown about 5 minutes under broiler. Serve at once with lemon wedges.

GO WITHS: Cabbage salad.

WINE: New York State Rhine wine.

SHERRIED CRAB CASSEROLE   *Eight* SERVINGS

Two cans of frozen potato soup, two cans of crabmeat, and not much else is required.

2 packages frozen or 2 cans (about 6 ozs. each) crabmeat
2 cans frozen potato soup, thawed
½ cup cream
2 tablespoons sherry

¼ cup minced parsley
1 tablespoon lemon juice
½ teaspoon salt
½ teaspoon curry powder
1 cup coarse fresh buttered crumbs

Combine ingredients except crumbs. Bake in individual dishes or a larger casserole, with the crumbs on top, at 350° F. for 25 minutes.

GO WITHS: Broccoli, Jellied Olive and Grapefruit Salad (page 234).

WINE: California Chablis.

SAVORY DEVILED CRAB   *Six* SERVINGS

You'll find this a delicious luncheon with crunchy green salad and hot rolls.

2 packages frozen crab (6 ozs. each), thawed,
    or 2 cans (6½ ozs. each) crabmeat
2 hard-cooked eggs, chopped
1 cup mayonnaise
1 teaspoon each: minced onion, parsley, Worcestershire,
    prepared mustard
2 teaspoons lemon juice
½ teaspoon salt
¼ cup sherry
1 cup Buttered Crumbs (page 255)

Mix crabmeat, eggs, mayonnaise, and seasonings. Fill 6 buttered ramekins and top with crumbs. Bake at 375° F. 15 to 20 minutes. Or bake in a casserole 25 minutes.

GO WITHS: Peas, Bibb lettuce and cucumber salad, brown-and-serve rolls.

WINE: California Rosé.

DEVILED CRAB, RECTOR   *Eight* SERVINGS

This is a rich, Lucullan dish, but a simple one to prepare.

2 tablespoons butter or marga-
    rine
2 tablespoons flour
2 cups light cream
2 egg yolks
½ teaspoon salt
    Dash of cayenne
1 teaspoon dry mustard

1 teaspoon Worcestershire
    sauce
1½ pounds fresh or 3 6-ounce
    packages frozen crabmeat
¼ pound mushrooms, sliced and
    sautéed
    Buttered Crumbs (page 255)

Melt butter, stir in flour, then stir in cream and cook until thickened, stirring constantly. Beat egg yolks with salt, cayenne, mustard, and Worcestershire. Stir into hot mixture, blending well. Remove from heat and add crabmeat and mushrooms. Mix well and fill individual shells with mixture. Sprinkle with buttered crumbs. Bake 15 to 20 minutes at 375° F.

GO WITHS: Fresh artichokes, lemon mayonnaise, sliced tomatoes.

WINE: California Pinot Chardonnay.

CRAB CASSEROLE WITH VEGETABLES

Six SERVINGS

There are peas for color, water chestnuts for crunch.

1 can (7½ ozs.) Alaskan king crab
2 cans cream of celery soup
1 package (10 ozs.) frozen peas, thawed
1 jar (2 ozs.) pimiento, chopped
1 can (8 ozs.) water chestnuts, drained, sliced
1 can or jar (4½ ozs.) mushrooms, drained
½ cup minced green onion with tops
1 cup buttered croutons

Mix ingredients and turn into 6 small or one larger casserole, topping with the croutons. Bake at 350° F. for 30 minutes.

GO WITHS: Avocado Garnet Salad (page 230), cornbread from a mix.

WINE: California Emerald Riesling.

CRAB IMPERIAL   *Four* SERVINGS

Mayonnaise is used here as a sauce; it should have a lemon tang.

1 pound lump crabmeat or 2 cans (about 7 ozs. each) Alaskan king crab
½ cup lemony mayonnaise
½ teaspoon dry mustard
1 pimiento, chopped

1 egg, slightly beaten
Salt, pepper
Dash Worcestershire sauce
Dash Tabasco sauce
Mayonnaise to top each portion
Paprika

Mix ingredients and place in shells or buttered ramekins. Top each with a teaspoon of mayonnaise and sprinkle with paprika. Bake at 350° F. for 20 minutes.

GO WITHS: Zucchini, shoestring potatoes, tossed greens.

WINE: New York State Rhine wine.

□

CRABMEAT IN SKILLET

This dish is famous in a Chicago restaurant.

¼ cup butter
1 pound fresh or frozen crabmeat, lump style
1 tablespoon chopped chives or finely sliced green onion
2 tablespoons tarragon vinegar
½ teaspoon freshly ground black pepper
1 teaspoon salt
1 teaspoon Worcestershire sauce

Melt butter in skillet. Add crabmeat and sauté a few minutes. Add remaining ingredients and heat through. Serve immediately in covered skillet.

GO WITHS: Homemade White Bread (page 46), relishes.

WINE: California Johannisberg Riesling.

CURRIED ROCK LOBSTER   *Six* SERVINGS

The shells make attractive containers for this well-seasoned blend.

6 rock lobster tails, 5 or 6 ounces each
¼ cup butter
3 onions, diced
½ clove garlic, minced
¼ teaspoon ginger
3 tomatoes, peeled, diced
2 tablespoons curry
1 small cinnamon stick
1 bay leaf
3 cloves
1 teaspoon salt

Drop lobster tails while frozen into boiling salted water. When water returns to boil, lower heat and simmer 6 to 7 minutes. Drain, drench with cold water, and cut away underside membrane with kitchen shears. Remove meat, keeping shells intact for serving. Dice lobster. Heat butter in heavy pan, add onions, and cook soft. Add garlic, ginger, and tomatoes. Stir in curry, cinnamon, bay leaf, and cloves. Simmer for 30 minutes, adding more butter if mixture becomes dry. Add salt and lobster, mix well, heat through and spoon into lobster shells. Serve with rice and curry condiments such as chopped nuts, chutney, currants or raisins, and flake coconut.

GO WITHS: Chinese snow peas or Italian green beans, steamed parsley-potatoes, Bibb lettuce salad.

WINE: California Pinot Chardonnay.

DEVILED LOBSTER TAILS   *Four* SERVINGS

They are epicurean, but any amateur can prepare them easily.

4 lobster tails (about ½ lb. each) cooked
¼ cup butter
½ teaspoon dry mustard
1 small onion, minced
1 teaspoon Worcestershire sauce
2 cups Medium White Sauce (page 254)
   Salt, pepper, dash of cayenne
   Grated Parmesan or Swiss cheese

Melt butter, add mustard, onion, Worcestershire; simmer 5 minutes and add White Sauce. Season as desired with salt, pepper, and cayenne. Add diced lobster-tail meat and return mixture to shells. Dot with butter, sprinkle with cheese, and broil until brown and bubbly. Do not overcook.

GO WITHS: Asparagus, shoestring potatoes, Bibb lettuce salad.

WINE: California Pinot Chardonnay.

△

LOBSTER NEWBURG   *Four* SERVINGS

Rock lobster tails are meatier than the expensive New England lobster and are recommended for such preparations as this.

¼ cup (½ stick) butter
3 tablespoons flour
1 pint half-and-half
1 egg, beaten
1 teaspoon salt
2 tablespoons sherry
2 packages (9 ozs. each) frozen lobster tails, cooked
   (page 113), and cut in pieces

Melt butter, stir in flour, and add the half-and-half, stirring to a smooth sauce. Add a little of the hot mixture to the egg, blend egg into sauce, and add salt and sherry. Taste and add more salt, if you wish. Heat lobster tails gently in sauce and serve in warmed frozen puff-paste shells or on toast.

Go WITHS: Artichokes with mustard butter; curly endive, leaf lettuce, green onion and tomato slice salad.

WINE: California Johannisberg Riesling or Emerald Dry Riesling.

x

LOBSTER-STUFFED MUSHROOMS *Six* SERVINGS

You'll want mushrooms all of a size for this elegant company dish.

2 cups Thick White Sauce (page 254)
2 cups fresh cooked lobster or lobster tail meat, or 2 cans
(6–7½ ozs. each) crab, diced
2 teaspoons minced parsley
½ teaspoon paprika
3 hard-cooked eggs, sieved
1 pound medium to large mushrooms (caps only)
3 tablespoons butter
1 teaspoon dry mustard
½ cup sherry
½ cup cream
⅓ cup grated sharp cheese

Combine half the lobster with half the white sauce and add parsley, paprika, eggs. Sauté mushroom caps in butter (save stems and chop them for some other dish) about 3 minutes. Fill with lobster mixture and arrange in shallow baking dishes. Add mustard, sherry, cream, and cheese to remaining sauce, stir well and add rest of lobster. Pour over filled mushrooms and bake 20 minutes at 400° F.

Go WITHS: Ambrosia Salad (page 229), hot rolls.

WINE: California Pinot Chardonnay or Sauvignon Blanc.

SEAFOOD IN A CHAFING DISH   *Eight* SERVINGS

Where would one find an easier company supper or a more charming one?

> 1 package (1 lb.) frozen deveined shrimps
> 2 packages (6 ozs. each) frozen crabmeat
> 2 cans frozen shrimp soup
> 2 cans mushroom soup
> 1¼ cups half-and-half
> ½ cup minced parsley
> 2 teaspoons curry

Cook shrimps according to package directions; drain. Thaw crab, drain well, pressing moisture out with paper towel. Heat soups in a chafing dish or heavy saucepan. Blend in half-and-half, parsley, curry, and then seafood. Heat gently and serve over toast points or on rice.

Go WITHS: Asparagus tips on sliced tomatoes with Bibb lettuce, Italian style dressing, crusty rolls.

WINE: California Chablis.

SEAFOOD RICE CASSEROLE *Eight to Ten* SERVINGS

Sunday supper out of cans may be delicious, n'est ce pas?

2 cups cooked rice	1 cup mayonnaise
½ cup chopped green pepper	1 cup tomato juice
1 cup chopped celery	¼ teaspoon salt
½ cup finely chopped onions	⅛ teaspoon pepper
1 can (4½ ozs.) water chest-nuts, drained, sliced	½ cup sliced almonds
2 cans (4½ ozs. each) shrimps	1 tablespoon butter, melted
1 can (6½ ozs.) crab	1 cup shredded Cheddar cheese
	Paprika

Combine rice, green pepper, celery, onion, water chestnuts, seafood, mayonnaise, tomato juice, and salt and pepper. Mix well. Pour into a buttered 2½-quart casserole. Toast almonds in butter and sprinkle on casserole with cheese and paprika. Bake 25 minutes at 350° F.

Go WITHS: Olives, pickles, carrot sticks; toasty French bread.

WINE: Ohio Rosé.

❑

OYSTERS ROCKEFELLER *Four* SERVINGS

Antoine's in New Orleans made them famous.

> 2 dozen oysters in their shells
> ⅔ cup minced fresh spinach
> ⅔ cup minced green onions, with tops
> 2½ tablespoons minced parsley
> ⅓ cup butter, creamed with 1 teaspoon Worcestershire
>   sauce
> ½ teaspoon salt
>   Dash pepper, cayenne, Tabasco sauce
> ¼ cup fine dry bread crumbs

Open and shuck oysters, saving shells and liquid. Or have your fish dealer do this job for you—it's difficult, if you're inexperienced. Combine minced vegetables with butter and seasonings, crumbs and oyster liquid. Place oysters back in their shells and lay shells on a bed of rock salt in a large baking pan. Place a spoonful of vegetable mixture on each oyster. Slide pan under the broiler and broil 5 minutes. Serve at once.

If you can't buy oysters in the shell, place shucked oysters in heatproof casseroles, add topping, and broil or bake at 450° F. for 10 minutes.

Go WITHS: Baked Stuffed Potatoes (page 272), relishes.

WINE: New York State Rhine wine.

BROILED OYSTERS   *Four* SERVINGS

Simply scrumptious! Do them the same way in the half-shell.

2 dozen large oysters, rinsed and dried on towel
Prepared mustard
Salt, pepper
12 strips bacon, cut fine, fried crisp
Fine dry bread or cracker crumbs
1/4 cup melted butter or margarine

Spread oysters thinly with mustard, sprinkle with salt and pepper, and roll in crisp bacon, then in crumbs. Place in shallow buttered pan, pour butter over them, and broil 3 to 4 minutes.

GO WITHS: Chef's Salad (page 240), without meat.

WINE: California Chablis.

■

OYSTERS BENEDICT   *Four* SERVINGS

Even easier to prepare than Eggs Benedict, this dish can be described as gourmet food.

4 thin slices baked ham, preferably "hammy" ham
16 large oysters, drained
2 English muffins, split and toasted
1 small jar hollandaise sauce, warmed
Parsley for garnish

Sauté ham lightly in its own fat (add a bit of butter if you need to) and cook oysters 1 minute in the same fat. Place a slice of ham and 4 oysters on each toasted muffin half and cover with warm hollandaise. Serve garnished with parsley.

GO WITHS: Precede at breakfast with melon or grapefruit. If for lunch, add a green salad.

WINE (FOR LUNCH): California dry Semillon or Pinot Chardonnay.

OYSTERS CASINO

Four SERVINGS

It is extremely simple, but one of the best of all oyster dishes.

1 pint oysters, drained, picked over
¼ cup finely minced green pepper
1 tablespoon minced onion
½ cup finely cut bacon
1 tablespoon lemon juice
Dash of pepper

Place oysters in 4 individual casseroles. (Better yet, in their own shells, using 6 oysters per serving.) Sprinkle with green pepper, onion, bacon, lemon juice, and pepper and bake about 10 minutes at 450° F. Or broil 6 to 8 minutes.

Clams often are done this way, too. In restaurants, either shellfish would be baked on a bed of rock salt, but at home you can simply use a shallow baking pan.

Go WITHS: Au gratin potatoes, tomato aspic, French bread.

WINE: California Chablis.

SCALLOPED CORN AND OYSTERS

Six SERVINGS

Here's an affinity of flavors!

1 can (1 lb.) cream style corn
1 pint oysters, drained
1½ cups Medium White Sauce (page 254)
Salt, pepper
1 cup Buttered Crumbs (page 255).

Make 2 layers of corn, oysters, and sauce in a buttered baking dish, sprinkling corn and oysters with salt and pepper; top with crumbs. Bake at 375° F. for 20 minutes, or until hot and browned on top.

Go WITHS: Celery and radishes, molded fruit salad.

WINE: California Rosé.

OYSTERS POULETTE

Four SERVINGS

A little practice and you'll be doing this dish in front of guests.

1 bouillon cube dissolved in ¾ cup hot water
2 tablespoons butter or margarine
3 tablespoons flour
¼ cup Chablis or other white table wine
⅓ cup cream
2 eggs yolks, slightly beaten
½ teaspoon salt
Pepper
Dash of cayenne
1 pint oysters

Melt butter in top of double boiler or chafing dish over direct heat; blend in flour; add bouillon and wine. Cook, stirring constantly, until sauce boils and thickens. Place over hot water. Mix cream and egg yolks; add to sauce, stirring constantly. Add salt, pepper, and cayenne. Heat oysters in their liquid until edges curl; drain thoroughly. Add to sauce. Serve at once in patty shells, or on toast.

GO WITHS: Stuffed tomato salad (with peas, celery).

WINE: California Chablis.

⚠

SCALLOPED OYSTERS

Four SERVINGS

Here's a dish that hasn't changed much over the years—it was simple to prepare from the very beginning!

1 pint medium-size oysters, drained and picked over
1 cup strained oyster liquid and cream
1½ cups plain or cheese crackers, crumbled
Salt, pepper
3 tablespoons melted butter

Make two layers of oysters in a casserole, topping each with crumbs (you may double or triple the recipe for more people). Sprinkle each layer also with salt and pepper; then pour oyster liquid and cream around the edges of the dish, letting it come up under the top layer of crackers. Use more cream, or milk, if you need to. Drip the butter over the top and bake at 400° F. for 20 minutes.

GO WITHS: Barbecue Bread (page 59), Easy Caesar Salad (page 219).

WINE: California Pinot Chardonnay or Chablis.

□

HANGTOWN FRY   *One* PORTION

This is a famous dish dating from the gold rush days of the west.* It is a perfect late night "breakfast."

5 bluepoints or 15 Olympia oysters	2 large eggs, slightly beaten
⅓ cup fine crumbs	1 tablespoon water
3 tablespoons flour	2 strips bacon, cooked crisp
Butter	Salt, pepper

Drain oysters well, coat with mixture of crumbs and flour, and sauté until golden brown in butter. Pour off excess butter. Mix eggs and water. Crumble bacon into skillet and increase heat a little as you pour in eggs. Season well with salt and pepper and cook until eggs have set but remain moist on top. Fold over like an omelet and serve on a warm plate with parsley and a wedge of lemon.

Two portions may be cooked together, but it is better to prepare the portions by ones and twos than to try to make a larger omelet. If everything is ready, including the cooked bacon, making the dish is speedy.

GO WITHS: Sourdough bread; a green salad if you wish.

WINE: California sauterne or Rhine wine.

---

* Hangtown later became Placerville. Legend has it that a miner condemned to hang for murder demanded for his last meal tiny Olympia oysters from Puget Sound scrambled with eggs and bacon. His executioners, obeying the principle of granting the last gastronomical wish, sent for the oysters, which were so long coming that the canny miner's pals were able to rescue him.

BAKED NEW BEDFORD SCALLOPS

Four SERVINGS

The smaller bay scallops would be used whole in this de-licious blend.

1 pound (1 pt.) sea scallops, quartered
2 teaspoons lemon juice
¼ cup butter
⅔ cup dry bread crumbs
¼ cup chopped green pepper
¼ cup catsup
1 teaspoon freeze-dried chopped shallots
1 teaspoon Worcestershire sauce
½ teaspoon salt
⅛ teaspoon pepper

Sprinkle scallops (thaw frozen ones) with lemon juice. Melt butter and add crumbs, green pepper, catsup, shallots (if you can't find them, use chopped green onions), Worcestershire sauce, salt and pepper. Mix well. Spoon scallops into individual baking dishes or shells and sprinkle with crumb mixture. Bake at 350° F. for 25 minutes.

GO WITHS: Braised zucchini, baked or broiled tomato halves, muffins.

WINE: California Rhine wine.

⋈

SAUTÉED SCALLOPS

Four SERVINGS

They take only five minutes to cook, and are a great delicacy!

1 pound scallops
¼ cup flour
¼ teaspoon salt
⅛ teaspoon pepper
¼ cup butter

Wipe scallops with damp paper towel. Roll in flour seasoned with salt and pepper. Melt butter in skillet. Add scallops. Cook 5 minutes only over high heat, turning constantly to brown evenly. Serve immediately. If you use the large sea scallops, cut in small pieces. Serve with tartar sauce or cocktail sauce. If you'd rather, dip scallops in fine bread crumbs, then in beaten egg (2 eggs), again into crumbs, and sauté. Sprinkle with salt and pepper.

GO WITHS: Artichokes, carrots, creamed new potatoes.

WINE: California Pinot Chardonnay.

BAKED SHRIMPS
Four SERVINGS

It's all done in the oven—no preliminary cooking of the shellfish.

- 1 pound uncooked shrimps, peeled, veined
- 2 eggs, well beaten
- ½ cup fine dry bread crumbs
- 1 large onion, chopped fine
- ¼ cup butter, melted
- 3 tablespoons chopped parsley
- ¼ cup grated sharp cheese
- 1 small clove garlic, minced
- 1 8-ounce can tomato sauce

Dip shrimps in eggs and then in bread crumbs. Place in shallow baking dish. Sauté onion in butter for 5 minutes. Sprinkle over shrimps. Top with parsley and cheese. Mix garlic with tomato sauce and pour over all. Bake at 350° F. for 30 minutes.

GO WITHS: Frozen baby lima beans in butter sauce, Parkerhouse rolls.

WINE: California Gamay Rosé.

BUTTERFLY SHRIMPS   *Six* SERVINGS

Everybody loves these; better fix plenty!

2 pounds raw shrimps
½ teaspoon salt
¼ teaspoon pepper
2 eggs, slightly beaten with 2 tablespoons water
1 cup fine dry bread crumbs

Remove shells from shrimps, keeping tails intact for handles. Cut about two-thirds through the center of each and flatten out. Remove the sand veins as you do this. Season with salt and pepper, dip in crumbs, then in egg, and again in crumbs. Fry in deep oil heated to 350° F., about 3 minutes. Drain on paper toweling. Serve with cocktail sauce or tartar sauce.

Go WITHS: Coleslaw, baked potatoes, green beans.

WINE: California sauterne.

x

QUICK SHRIMP CURRY   *Four* SERVINGS

Curries do not have to be elaborate to be good!

2 cups cooked shrimps or 2 cans shrimps rinsed well in
    cold water
4 green onions, minced
1 tablespoon butter
1 can frozen shrimp soup, undiluted
1 teaspoon or more curry powder
1 cup sour cream

Cook onion in butter 2 or 3 minutes, add soup and heat to boiling point. Stir in curry, cream, and shrimps. Heat through but do not boil. Serve on rice accompanied with chutney.

Go WITHS: Sesame seed bread sticks, Chinese Bean Salad (page 222).

WINE: California Grey Riesling

SHRIMP GUMBO
Six SERVINGS

Colorful and appetizing, this dish is a good and easy party concoction.

1 clove garlic, minced
2 onions, chopped
2 tablespoons butter
1 can okra or 1 package frozen okra, sliced

3 cups chicken stock or bouillon
3 medium tomatoes, skinned, chopped
1½ cups diced cooked ham
1½ pounds cooked shrimps

Sauté garlic and onions in butter for a few minutes. Add okra and cook about 3 minutes. Add stock, tomatoes, and ham. Simmer for 30 minutes. Add shrimps and heat through. Add salt and pepper, if necessary, and serve over fluffy rice.

Go WITHS: Crusty French bread.

WINE: California Gamay Rosé.

SHRIMPS IN BEER
Six SERVINGS

Planning a picnic or a party? Serve shrimps in the shell—everyone shells his own portion.

1 clove garlic crushed with 1 teaspoon salt
2 bottles or cans beer
2 tablespoons dry mustard
4 tablespoons celery seed

½ teaspoon cayenne pepper
½ cup wine vinegar
3 pounds raw shrimps in the shell

Put everything but the shrimps in a saucepan, bring to a boil, add shrimps (slit on outside curve of shell to let more flavor seep in, if you like) and simmer 5 minutes. Cool in stock, chill, drain, rinse and serve.

Go WITHS: Any informal party fare such as potato salad, cold cuts, hard-boiled eggs or deviled eggs, coleslaw.

WINE: No wine. Beer this time.

125

LITTLE SHRIMP AND CELERY PIES

Four SERVINGS

Easily made from cans, these pielets are filling and good.

1 can cream of celery soup
½ cup milk
2 hard-cooked eggs, chopped
2 cans (5¾ oz. each) or 2 cups cooked shrimps
1 cup cooked peas
1 teaspoon curry powder
Pastry or biscuit dough from a mix

Mix milk with soup and add other ingredients. Place in four individual casseroles and top with circles of pie pastry or biscuit dough. Bake at 400° F. for 20 minutes.

GO WITHS: Mixed greens salad.

WINE: California Rhine wine or Chablis.

SPANISH SHRIMPS

Four to Six SERVINGS

Try to find fresh sweet red peppers to use for this dish.

2 pounds shrimps, fresh or frozen
4 green or red peppers, or 2 of each
1 clove garlic, minced
¼ cup olive oil
¼ cup dry white wine
Salt, pepper

Shell and vein shrimps. Wash and dry peppers and remove stems and seeds. Cut lengthwise into strips. Add garlic to oil and heat. Add peppers and cook over high heat 1 minute. Add shrimps and wine. Reduce heat, cover, and cook 5 minutes. Serve hot with fluffy rice.

GO WITHS: Artichoke bottoms, crusty rolls, Jellied Olive and Grapefruit Salad (page 234).

WINE: New York State Rhine wine.

MEATS

MOST menu planning begins with the meat. If the meat is tender and succulent, the dinner is very likely to be good. Fortunately meat cookery is simple if you know the basic cuts, buy from a reliable market, and follow directions in the cooking.

You need a good meat thermometer for roasts. Otherwise the cooking can only be guesswork. A meat thermometer tells you exactly when to take the rib roast or leg of lamb from the oven. It is well worth its price.

Other equipment should include a shallow roasting pan with a rack for oven roasts, and a dutch oven or heavy pot with a tight cover for pot roasts, the meats you cook with water or other liquid added. These are the "less tender" cuts such as chuck or shoulder roasts, rump and round.

"Oven" roasts are the tender cuts such as beef ribs, pork loin, leg of lamb. They are cooked in the open roaster without any added moisture, except for an occasional basting sauce.

It doesn't make much difference when you season the meat, but it usually is more convenient to do it before cooking. However, steaks should not be salted (with a few exceptions such as when a marinade is used) until after cooking, as salt tends to draw the juices.

127

There are seasoning mixtures for every kind of meat. Try them for variety now and then, even if you're just a salt and pepper cook. Onion and garlic and their many jarred and bottled forms are helpful in seasoning meats. Wine, especially red wine, may be used to baste meat or season the gravy.

A few general principles apply: A teaspoon of salt seasons a pound of meat as a rule. Ground chuck is the best choice for hamburgers as it contains more fat than the round, and is of better quality than "hamburger," ground from trimmings. You need some fat for juiciness and tenderness.

All cuts of lamb are tender and may be cooked without the moisture required to break down connective tissue in less tender meats. Veal is tender, but also tends to be dry, therefore a large cut is often cooked as a pot roast, and braising is sometimes employed for the smaller cuts.

The recipes in this section are explicit enough to give you all the help you need in preparing the various meats in savory fashion, I think.

◆

HOW TO ROAST BEEF

Rub the roast with salt and pepper and place it fat side up on a rack in a shallow roasting pan. Place your meat thermometer in the middle of the thickest muscle, the tip resting in meat, not in fat or against bone. Only by checking the temperature will you be able to serve perfectly cooked beef, done to a turn. Otherwise, timing is only a guess.

Roast at 325° F. uncovered, with no water in the pan. Basting is not necessary. Timing for a 6-pound standing rib roast which will serve six to eight at a dinner party is 2 to 2¼ hours for rare meat, 2½ hours for medium, on the average. Boned, rolled roasts may take longer. Thermometer readings are 140° F. for rare meat; 160° F. for medium; 170° F. for well done. A roast can change a few degrees in the center while it waits for carving—many cooks like to roast beef to 135° F., expecting it to rise to 140° F. while the meat "sets" for the usual 10 to 20 minutes which make it easier to carve.

128

Oysters Rockefeller, page 117;
Rolled Fillets of Sole; Baked Striped Bas

MAKING THE GRAVY

Remove the roast to a hot platter and keep it in a warm place while you make gravy. Pour off all but 2 tablespoons drippings for each cup of gravy you want to make. Add to the drippings 2 tablespoons flour for each cup, then stir over moderate heat to brown flour lightly and scrape up all the good cooked-on scraps of meat. Add 1 cup water; cook and stir to smooth, thickened brown gravy, and season with salt and pepper.

If you think your gravy needs more flavor, add a beef bouillon cube or a teaspoon of brown gravy base, or a can of beef gravy.

BARBECUED POT ROAST   *Six* SERVINGS

Serve mashed potatoes as a base for the tasty gravy.

3 to 4 pound pot roast
2 tablespoons drippings
Salt, pepper
2 tablespoons sugar
½ teaspoon each: dry mustard, paprika, black pepper
1 teaspoon salt

½ cup water
3 tablespoons vinegar
3 tablespoons Worcestershire sauce
1 cup catsup
1 medium onion, chopped
½ cup chopped celery

Brown roast on both sides in hot drippings in a heavy pan. Season with 1 teaspoon salt and ¼ teaspoon pepper. Add 1 cup water, cover pan tightly, and simmer about 1 hour. Combine remaining ingredients and pour over meat. Cover pan again and simmer about 1½ hours longer or until meat is tender.

GO WITHS: Mashed potatoes, carrots, lima beans.

WINE: California mellow red.

TOP—*Fried Fish, page 95*
BOTTOM—*Onion-dip Burgers, page 145*

ROAST BEEF TENDERLOIN

Eight to Twelve SERVINGS

Tenderest but most expensive of beef cuts, the tenderloin is for special occasions.

1 beef tenderloin, 4 to 6 pounds
Garlic
¼ cup bacon drippings
6 mushroom caps, sautéed in butter

Rub cut clove of garlic over meat, from which surface fat has been re-moved. Place beef on rack in a shallow pan. Tuck narrow end of meat under, so roast will be of even thickness. Brush with drippings; roast at 450° F. for 45 to 60 minutes, or until thermometer inserted in center of thickest part of meat registers 140° F. Top with mushroom halves.

Go WITHS: Browned potatoes, green beans, molded fruit salad.

WINE: California Pinot Noir.

BURGUNDY POT ROAST

Eight SERVINGS

Unusually delicious, this meat is even tastier reheated for a second meal.

5 pounds beef chuck, rolled and tied
Flour, salt, pepper
2 tablespoons bacon drippings or other fat
1 can (8 ozs.) tomato sauce

1 cup Burgundy
½ cup finely chopped onion
½ cup celery
¼ cup finely chopped parsley
¼ teaspoon oregano
¼ teaspoon sweet basil

Dredge meat with flour seasoned with salt and pepper. Brown slowly on all sides in fat. Add all remaining ingredients; season to taste with salt and pepper. Cover and simmer gently 3 to 4 hours, or until meat is tender, turning meat occasionally. Transfer to hot platter.

Measure liquid in kettle and add water if necessary to make 4 cups; heat to boiling. Blend ¼ cup flour with ½ cup cold water to make a smooth paste; stir slowly into boiling liquid; cook, stirring constantly, for 2 or 3 minutes. Thin with a little additional water, if you wish. Taste and add salt and pepper, if necessary. Serve with meat. Meat may be sliced and reheated in gravy.

GO WITHS: Mashed potato patties, lima beans, crabapple pickles.

WINE: California or New York State Burgundy.

SAUERBRATEN
Eight SERVINGS

This is the authentic version, not difficult, and what flavor!

1½ cups cider vinegar
½ cup red wine
1 cup water
12 peppercorns
2 tablespoons sugar
2 large onions, peeled, and sliced
4 bay leaves
12 whole cloves
1 teaspoon mustard seed
2 teaspoons salt

4 pounds round or rump beef
2 tablespoons flour
1½ teaspoons salt
Dash pepper
¼ cup shortening
1 onion, peeled, sliced
½ teaspoon mustard seed
6 whole cloves
½ teaspoon peppercorns
⅓ cup flour
⅓ cup crushed gingersnaps

Two to four days before serving, combine first 10 ingredients in a large bowl. Place beef in this mixture and let stand two to four days, covered, in refrigerator, turning each day. At end of marinating period, remove meat and dry on paper toweling.

Combine salt, pepper, and 2 tablespoons flour. Coat meat on all sides with seasoned flour. Brown on all sides in shortening in Dutch oven. Strain marinade; add to meat with sliced onion, mustard seed, cloves, and peppercorns. Cover, simmer 3½ to 4 hours or until meat is tender. Remove meat to heated platter; slice it.

Strain liquid. Mix ⅓ cup flour and gingersnaps in Dutch oven; slowly add liquid. Simmer, stirring constantly until thickened. Pour some of this gravy over meat, serve remainder at table.

GO WITHS: Boiled or baked potatoes, carrots, relishes.

WINE: California Chianti or Zinfandel.

QUICK SAUERBRATEN   *Six to Eight* SERVINGS

A good German cook would not acknowledge this dish, but it isn't bad at all!

3–4 pound beef pot roast
    Salt, pepper
  1 bottle (8 ozs.) Italian
      dressing

Flour, oil
1 large onion, sliced

Salt and pepper the meat lightly and pour the dressing over it. Cover and refrigerate overnight. Drain meat, pat dry, flour, and brown in a small amount of oil or drippings. Add onion and the marinade. Cover and simmer very gently 3 to 4 hours, or until meat is very tender. Thicken liquid for gravy.

GO WITHS: Parsley potatoes, cauliflower, Cinnamon Apple Salad (page 230).

WINE: Beer might be more appropriate.

SAVORY POT ROAST AND SPAGHETTI   *Eight* SERVINGS

Try this wonderful cure for brisk weather hunger!

5 pound round-bone pot roast
1 tablespoon salt
1 teaspoon garlic salt
¼ teaspoon pepper
¼ cup drippings
1 cup chopped celery
2 cups chopped onions

1 green pepper, chopped
1 No. 2½ can tomatoes
    (3½ cups)
3 tablespoons minced parsley
1 pound spaghetti, cooked
    Grated Parmesan cheese

Rub roast with seasonings. Brown on all sides in hot fat. Remove from pan. Sauté celery, onion, and green pepper in drippings 5 minutes. Add tomatoes and parsley. Return meat to pan. Cover tightly, cook slowly 3 to 3½ hours, or until tender. Serve sauce with spaghetti and meat, sliced thin. Accompany with cheese.

GO WITHS: Crusty, hot French bread, relishes.

WINE: A California vino rosso.

SPIT·ROASTED BEEF   *Eight to Ten* SERVINGS

It's heaven just to smell it cooking!

> 4–6 pounds beef (ribeye, rolled rib, or high quality sirloin
>   tip or rump)
> Salt, pepper
> Barbecue sauce

Rub meat with salt and pepper, also with a cut clove of garlic, if you like. Run spit through center of meat, making sure it is evenly balanced. Insert meat thermometer if you have one, placing it in the center of the meat, but avoiding fat. It should not touch the rod. Adjust spit to holder and start it revolving. Time is variable, hence the thermometer is a good idea. The meat continues to cook after removal from heat, so remove it when the meat is 5 degrees underdone. Rare meat registers 140° F.; medium, 160° F.; and well done, 170° F. On the average, time will be 18 to 20 minutes per pound for rare meat, 20 to 22 minutes per pound for medium, 22 to 24 minutes per pound for well done.

Brush the roast with barbecue sauce frequently as it turns.

Coals should be covered with a gray ash during rotisserie roasting.

GO WITHS: Corn cooked on grill, Potato Salad (page 226), garlic bread, relishes.

WINE: California Burgundy.

GUIDE TO STEAKS AND THEIR COOKERY

CHUCK STEAK: From the shoulder section of beef. Contains either a round or a blade bone. Usually braised (browned, then cooked gently with a little liquid), but often nowadays treated with meat tenderizer and charcoal grilled. A big thick steak for a crowd.

CLUB STEAK: A small individual steak, triangular in shape, with little or no tenderloin. Cut from the short loin of beef from which the T-bone also comes. Broil or grill it.

DELMONICO STEAK: A boneless club or rib steak also known as Spencer or rib-eye steak. An excellent choice for broiling or grilling.

FLANK STEAK: Not ordinarily tender enough to broil. Top quality flank steak, well seasoned, may be broiled and is known as London Broil. This is a lean, flat, boneless piece of meat with long fibers. Good stuffed and braised.

HIP or HIP BONE STEAK: Also called pinbone sirloin. This is sirloin steak with some of the hip bone in it. Broil or grill. Good choice for a family.

KANSAS CITY STEAK: Restaurant term for sirloin strip steak, a boned sirloin cut served broiled. Also known as loin strip steak or New York cut steak.

MINUTE OR CUBE STEAK: Cut from round or chuck, made tender by cutting the fibers. Sauté quickly in butter, a minute to each side.

PORTERHOUSE STEAK: Largest of the three loin steaks (club, T-bone are the others). Has a large portion of tenderloin. Luxurious choice for broiling or grilling.

RIB STEAK: Cut from the rib roast. Boned rib steaks are known as Spencer, Delmonico, or rib eye. Broil or grill.

ROUND STEAK: A less tender cut, usually braised. Swiss steak, beef birds are made from round.

SIRLOIN STEAK: Exceedingly popular steak cut from loin or hip end of beef loin. Sirloins vary in size, shape, and bone size, depending upon their position in the loin. Wedge bone sirloin is the largest steak, a good choice for family. Others are round bone, double bone, and pin bone, also called hip bone. The term "top sirloin" refers to boned sirloin. "Sirloin butt steak" on a restaurant menu indicates boneless sirloin steak. Broil or grill.

SIRLOIN STRIP STEAK: Partly or completely boned sirloin, with the tenderloin removed. New York cut and Kansas City steak are cut from the sirloin strip roast, which is a good choice for a rotisserie. Broil or grill.

T-BONE STEAK: Named for the shape of the bone, this one is larger than its next-door neighbor, the club steak, and smaller than Porterhouse, on the other side. It has some tenderloin in it (club steak has little or none, porterhouse more than T-bone). A generous individual steak, or if cut thick, will serve two or three. Broil or grill.

TENDERLOIN STEAK OR FILET: The tenderloin muscle alone; this is the expensive, luxury "filet mignon."

A steak 1½ inches thick takes 14 to 18 minutes cooked rare; 18 to 22 minutes, medium; and 22 to 30 minutes "well." You need a distance of 3 to 5 inches between surface of meat and heat. Cook half the time, turn, and finish the cooking. Salt at the turn, second side when finished.

CUBED STEAK DE LUXE   *Four* SERVINGS

They're tender and nicely seasoned.

4 cubed steaks
Salt, pepper
2 bay leaves

1 small clove garlic, sliced
½ cup French dressing

Season meat and place on a platter. Place bay leaves and garlic on meat and cover with dressing. Cover with waxed paper and place a weight on top. Let stand for ½ hour. Turn meat in dressing and cover again for ½ hour. Remove as much dressing as possible from meat. Broil a few minutes on each side.

GO WITHS: Baked potatoes with sour cream, Brussels sprouts.

WINE: California Burgundy.

ORIENTAL STEAK

Six SERVINGS

Toasted sesame seeds, onions, garlic, and soy sauce produce an intriguing flavor.

1 sirloin steak, about 3 pounds, cut 1 inch thick
2 tablespoons sesame seeds
1 teaspoon butter or oil

1 small clove garlic, mashed
4 green onions and tops, sliced
2 tablespoons soy sauce

Stir sesame seeds in butter over moderate heat until golden. Add garlic, onion, and soy sauce. Mix well and spread on steak, both sides. Let stand an hour, then scrape off mixture and broil or sauté in a small amount of butter until brown on both sides. Do not overcook. Spread sesame seed mixture on steak again for last few minutes of broiling or browning.

GO WITHS: Hot Potato Salad (page 227), frozen peas in butter sauce, celery hearts, radishes and olives.

WINE: California Burgundy.

◘

FRENCH PEPPER STEAK

Two SERVINGS

If you love pepper, this is the steak for you—if not, avoid it! This is the classical French au poivre.

2 filets (tenderloin steaks), 5 ounces each
Freshly ground coarse black pepper
¼ cup butter
1 tablespoon olive oil or salad oil
3 tablespoons brandy
Salt

Press the pepper firmly and thickly into the steaks with your hands. Brown quickly on each side in hot butter and oil. Lower heat and cook for about 4 minutes per side. Steaks should be rare within. Warm brandy in a small metal cup, ignite, and pour into the skillet with the meat and juices. Lift pan from heat and rotate it until the flames die out. Season with a little salt and serve at once.

Go WITHS: Au Gratin Potatoes (page 274), artichoke hearts with lemon, fresh pear salad on romaine.

WINE: California Cabernet Sauvignon.

▼

SWISS STEAK   *Eight* SERVINGS

A good pounding tenderizes the meat.

1 round steak (3 lbs.), about 1½ inches thick	1 can (1 lb.) tomatoes
⅓ cup flour	2 medium onions, chopped fine
1½ teaspoons salt	1 green pepper, cut julienne style
¼ teaspoon pepper	1 tablespoon cornstarch
¼ cup drippings	¼ cup cold water

Place meat on a cutting board. Cover with seasoned flour and pound with meat hammer or edge of a heavy plate. Turn steak several times, pounding until all the flour is taken up by the meat. Brown on both sides in drippings. Add tomatoes and onions; cover pan and cook to boiling. Lower heat and simmer about 2 hours or until meat is tender. Top with green pepper the last 10 minutes of cooking.

Place meat on a heated platter. Blend cornstarch and water and stir into liquid; cook until slightly thickened. Pour thickened gravy over meat and serve immediately.

Go WITHS: Mashed potatoes or parsley rice.

WINE: New York State claret.

STEAK SUKIYAKI
Six SERVINGS

This is a prize-winning version of the famous Japanese dish.

1½ pounds sirloin steak
2 tablespoons drippings
¼ cup sugar
¾ cup soy sauce
¼ cup water
2 medium onions, sliced thin
1 green pepper, cut in thin strips
1 cup celery, cut diagonally in 1-inch strips
1 10-ounce can bamboo shoots, sliced thin
1 4-ounce can sliced mushrooms
1 bunch green onions, and tops, cut in 1 inch pieces

Cut meat in thin diagonal slices, about 2 inches long and ½ inch wide. Brown lightly in drippings in a heavy skillet or electric fry-pan. Mix sugar, soy sauce, and water. Add to meat. Cover pan and bring to boiling point. Lower heat and cook about 20 minutes, or until meat is tender. Add remaining ingredients, except green onions, and cook about 5 minutes. Add green onions and cook 2 minutes longer. Serve over hot fluffy rice.

Go WITHS: Melon salad, buttermilk biscuits.

WINE: California claret.

STEAK CHOW MEIN
Six SERVINGS

Your family will enjoy this easy, flavorsome supper.

1 pound round steak, cubed
2 tablespoons butter or margarine
2 cups beef bouillon
3 tablespoons soy sauce
2 tablespoons cornstarch

2 cups sliced celery
1 cup sliced onions
1 can (1 lb.) Chinese vegetables, with liquid
Salt, pepper

Brown meat in fat; add 1½ cups bouillon and the soy sauce. Cover and simmer until meat is almost tender, 20 to 30 minutes. Combine cornstarch and remaining bouillon; mix smooth. Add to meat and cook and stir until thickened and clear. Add vegetables; cover and cook 15 minutes or until meat and vegetables are tender. Season to taste.

Go WITHS: Fluffy rice, pineapple-banana salad.

WINE: California mountain red.

BAKED CHOP SUEY   Six to Eight SERVINGS

Of all the chop sueys there are, this is probably easiest and best!

2 pounds diced beef or beef, veal, and pork, in any proportion (½-inch cubes)
2 onions, sliced thin
2 cups celery, sliced
1 small green pepper, chopped
1 can (1 lb.) chop suey vegetables
1 can (1 lb.) bean sprouts
1 can (4 ozs.) mushroom stems and pieces
1 can (8 ozs.) water chestnuts, sliced thin

1 can (8 ozs.) bamboo shoots, sliced thin
1 package onion soup mix
⅓ cup molasses
2 tablespoons soy sauce
1 teaspoon salt
⅛ teaspoon garlic powder
½ teaspoon seasoned salt
½ teaspoon pepper
2 tablespoons cornstarch

Line a 9x13-inch pan with heavy foil, leaving enough foil to cover chop suey mixture well. Drain vegetables and bean sprouts only, saving liquid. Place all ingredients except cornstarch in foil-lined pan. Add ¾ cup liquid from vegetables. Seal foil, allowing room for steam to form over mixture. Bake at 350° F. for 3 hours.

Remove meat and vegetables from pan with slotted spoon and turn into a serving dish. Pour liquid into a pan. Blend cornstarch and ½ cup cold liquid drained from vegetables and stir it into the drained liquid. Cook and stir until thick and smooth, pour over chop suey mixture and serve.

Go WITHS: Fluffy hot rice.

WINE: California or New York State Rosé.

BEEF BORDELAISE   *Six* SERVINGS

There's a surprise ingredient in this delicious dish: anchovies.

    2 pounds round steak, sliced thin
    3 hard-cooked eggs, chopped fine
    1 large onion, sliced thin
    2 teaspoons salt
      Pepper
    1/4 teaspoon nutmeg
    1/2 cup parsley, chopped fine
    3 anchovies, chopped
    2 tablespoons chopped suet or other fat
    1/4 cup fat for browning

Cut steak into 12 pieces. Combine remaining ingredients and mix well. Spread over meat and roll each carefully and tightly, fastening with skewers or string. Flour and brown all around in the 1/4 cup fat. Add 1/2 cup water, cover, and simmer gently 2 hours, or until tender. Thicken drippings for gravy and serve over meat rolls.

GO WITHS: Duchess potatoes, zucchini squash.

WINE: California Cabernet Sauvignon.

BEEF CHUNKS IN BURGUNDY   *Six* SERVINGS

There's that soup again!

1 1/2 pounds beef chuck or round, cut in 1-inch cubes
    2 teaspoons salt
      Freshly ground black pepper
    2 tablespoons fat for browning
    1 cup chopped onion
    1 cup sour cream
    1 cup grated Cheddar cheese
    1/2 cup Burgundy or other red table wine
    1 minced clove garlic
    1/4 teaspoon each, thyme, marjoram, basil
    1 can cream of mushroom soup

Season beef with salt and pepper and brown on all sides in hot fat. Add onion near end of browning time and fry until soft. Transfer to large

140

casserole or Dutch oven and add mixture of remaining ingredients. Cover and bake at 325° F. for 2 hours, or until meat is tender.

Go WITHS: Noodles or spaghetti, glazed carrots, green salad.

WINE: New York State Burgundy.

TOMATO-BEEF CURRY   *Four* SERVINGS

You'd never take this for a leftover dish.

2 cups diced leftover pot roast
1 cup or 1 can beef gravy
1 cup tomato sauce

1 teaspoon curry powder
   (or more)
Cooked rice
Chutney

Combine gravy, tomato sauce, and curry powder. Add meat and heat thoroughly. Serve over cooked rice with chutney as a side relish.

Go WITHS: Molded fruit salad, crusty bread or rolls.

WINE: New York State Rosé.

EASY BEEF STEW (OVEN)   *Six* SERVINGS

"It's great!" says every cook who has tried this recipe; it's the kind of thing you'll prepare repeatedly.

2 pounds beef stew meat in 1½
   inch cubes
1 medium onion, peeled and sliced
1 stalk celery, cut on the diagonal
6 carrots in chunks

2 teaspoons salt
1 tablespoon sugar
2 tablespoons tapioca for thick-
   ening
½ cup tomato juice

Place meat in a 7x11-inch pan. Add vegetables. Blend salt, sugar, and tapioca. Sprinkle over meat and vegetables. Add tomato juice. Cover pan with foil, sealing tight around the edges. Bake at 250° F. for 4 hours.

Go WITHS: Brown-and-serve rolls, Ambrosia Salad (page 229).

WINE: California Burgundy or mountain red.

BEEF CASSEROLE   *Three to Four* SERVINGS

Tuck it in the oven and forget it!

1 pound beef stew meat, cut into 1-inch cubes
1 cup red wine
1 can beef consommé, undiluted
¾ teaspoon salt
⅛ teaspoon pepper
1 onion, sliced
¼ cup fine dry bread crumbs
¼ cup flour

Mix beef, wine, consommé, seasonings, and onion in a casserole. Blend crumbs and flour and stir into mixture. Cover and bake at 300° F. for 3 hours. Serve over hot cooked noodles.

Go WITHS: Carrots and peas, cornbread, radishes.

WINE: California Burgundy (same as used in casserole).

SHORT RIBS DELICIOUS   *Three* SERVINGS

Short ribs are a man's dish; most men are fond of them.

2½ pounds short ribs of beef, cut into serving portions
1 tablespoon shortening
1 can beef gravy
½ cup chopped onion
2 tablespoons chili sauce
2 tablespoons vinegar
1 tablespoon brown sugar
1 tablespoon horseradish
1 teaspoon Worcestershire sauce
1 clove garlic, minced

Brown meat in shortening; cover and cook over low heat for 1 hour. Pour off excess drippings. Stir in rest of ingredients, re-cover, and cook for 1 hour more, or until tender, stirring now and then.

Go WITHS: Boiled potatoes or noodles, broccoli, tomato salad.

WINE: California or New York State Burgundy.

MINUTE-MINDED BEEF STEW

Four to Six SERVINGS

Own a good can opener?

2 cans (1-1½ lbs. each) beef stew
1 can (10¾ ozs.) beef gravy
1 can (1 lb.) peas and carrots, drained
 Sprinkling of mixed herbs

 Heat ingredients together and serve hot.

GO WITHS: Baking Powder Biscuits (page 53), cucumber and tomato salad.

WINE: California mountain red.

HUNGARIAN GOULASH (GULYAS)

Six SERVINGS

It's an authentic Hungarian recipe, though there's some dispute about the potatoes—some say "Of course," some say "Never!"

2 pounds beef round, cubed
2 or 3 large diced onions
2 tablespoons butter
2 tablespoons paprika
1 tablespoon salt

½ teaspoon caraway
2 tomatoes, diced
1 green pepper, sliced thin
 Diced potatoes, if desired

Sauté onions in melted butter until golden. Add seasonings, tomatoes, green pepper, and meat, not browned. Simmer several hours, adding water if more gravy is needed. Add diced potatoes ½ hour before done. For *gulyas levas* (soup) add more water and square noodles during the last 15 minutes of cooking.

VARIATION: Add a can of sauerkraut with potatoes, and 1 cup sour cream just before serving.

GO WITHS: Hot herbed Italian bread, fresh pear salad.

WINE: California or New York State sparkling Burgundy.

143

BEEF STROGANOFF   *Four* SERVINGS

This is one of the simpler versions of this favorite dish.

2 medium onions
½ cup butter
1 pound tender beefsteak, cut in
      ½-inch strips
1 tablespoon Worcestershire

1 jar (4 ozs.) mushrooms,
      drained
Salt, pepper
½ cup sour cream

Cut onions in half lengthwise, then slice thin crosswise and sauté in butter until golden (this can be done early in the afternoon). Add beef and cook, stirring frequently over medium heat just until browned, about 10 minutes. Add Worcestershire and mushrooms; salt and pepper to taste. Stir in cream and serve.

GO WITHS: Buttered noodles, fresh asparagus, French bread.

WINE: California Pinot Noir.

SPICY BEEF BALLS   *Four to Six* SERVINGS

These will make a hit with buffet-supper guests!

1½ pounds ground beef
⅓ cup bread crumbs
1 egg, slightly beaten
⅓ cup minced onion
¼ cup finely chopped green
      pepper
2 teaspoons curry powder
1½ teaspoons salt

Pepper
2 tablespoons oil
1 can beef gravy
⅓ cup crumbled gingersnaps
2 tablespoons vinegar
¼ cup raisins
Chopped peanuts or coconut

Combine beef, crumbs, egg, onion, green pepper, and seasonings. Shape into 24 meat balls. Brown in skillet in oil. Pour off fat. Add gravy, gingersnaps, vinegar, and raisins. Cover and cook over low heat about 20 minutes. Stir now and then. Garnish with peanuts or coconut.

GO WITHS: Rice or noodles, zucchini, Waldorf Salad (page 239).

WINE: California vino rosso.

144

CHEESEBURGERS DE LUXE   *Six* SERVINGS

Man-size burgers are for hearty appetites!

1½ pounds ground chuck
1½ teaspoons salt
¼ teaspoon pepper
6 thick tomato slices

6 strips bacon, cooked and
    crumbled
6 slices Cheddar cheese, cut with
    doughnut cutter
6 hamburger buns, split and toasted

Season meat with salt and pepper and form into 6 large patties. Broil until brown on both sides. Place a slice of tomato on each patty, sprinkle with crumbled bacon, and top with cheese slice. Return patties to broiler and heat until cheese is melted. Serve on toasted buns.

If you wish, serve the cheeseburgers open face; top each with a mushroom which has been sautéed in butter.

GO WITHS: Celery hearts, pickles, olives.

WINE: California Burgundy.

□

ONION-DIP BURGERS   *Four* SERVINGS

That onion dip surely does get around!

1 pound ground chuck
1 teaspoon salt
⅛ teaspoon pepper
1 tablespoon chopped parsley
½ cup onion dip
3 tablespoons bread crumbs

Blend ingredients well together, shape into four patties and broil until well browned and as well done as you like burgers.

GO WITHS: Buns or no buns, French fries or hash-brown potatoes, relish tray with cherry tomatoes.

WINE: California mountain red.

TOM'S CHILIBURGERS   *Eight* SANDWICHES

Here's a speedy cure for hunger pangs!

1 pound ground beef
1 cup catsup
¼ cup prepared mustard
2 teaspoons chili powder
Split toasted buns

Brown beef in a skillet, stirring with a fork to break it up as it cooks. Add catsup, mustard, and chili powder. Cover and simmer 10 to 15 minutes. Spoon into warm buns. Mixture may be served over rice or spaghetti, also.

GO WITHS: French fries, sliced tomatoes, carrot sticks, green onions.

WINE: California or New York State Burgundy.

ITALIAN MEAT LOAF   *Eight* SERVINGS

Oregano, tomato paste, and Mozzarella create the "Italian" flavor—a nice, juicy one!

2 pounds ground beef chuck
¾ cup finely chopped onion
½ cup cornflake crumbs
2 eggs
1 can (6 ozs.) tomato paste
2 teaspoons oregano

1½ teaspoons salt
½ teaspoon garlic salt
¼ teaspoon Tabasco sauce
¼ pound Mozzarella cheese, sliced

Combine ingredients except cheese and mix well. Pack into an oiled 9x5-inch pan, then turn out onto oiled shallow baking pan and finish shaping with your hands. Bake at 350° F. about 45 minutes. Remove from oven, top loaf with overlapping cheese slices, and return to oven until cheese softens. Serve plain or with catsup or tomato sauce.

GO WITHS: Creamed or scalloped potatoes, peas, Waldorf Salad (page 239).

WINE: California Chianti or Zinfandel.

SPANISH BEEF LOAF
Six SERVINGS

You'll like it sliced cold for sandwiches, if any is left!

  1½ pounds ground beef
   1 cup mashed potatoes
  1½ teaspoons salt
   ¼ teaspoon pepper
   1 can (1 lb.) tomatoes
   2 tablespoons butter, melted
   1 large onion, chopped

Mix meat, potatoes, salt, and pepper; shape into a loaf in a shallow baking pan. Combine rest of ingredients and pour over loaf. Bake, basting once or twice with the sauce, at 350° F. for 45 minutes.

GO WITHS: Brussels sprouts or broccoli, Perfection Salad (page 224) bread sticks.

WINE: California vino rosso.

AVOCADOS WITH CHILI
Six SERVINGS

For a Mexico-themed informal party, here's a great idea!

  3 avocados of ripe eating quality
    Lime juice
  1 can (1 lb.) chili con carne without beans
  1 cup soft Buttered Crumbs (page 255)
  ½ cup grated sharp cheese

Cut avocados in half and brush with lime juice. Heat chili and spoon into avocado cavities. Top each portion with crumbs and cheese. Broil 2 to 3 minutes under moderate heat to brown crumbs and melt cheese. Serve at once. Avocados should not be cooked; mere warming is sufficient.

GO WITHS: For a Mexican party, frijoles refritos and Tacos (page 148).

WINE: California Zinfandel. Or beer.

TACOS
Six to Twelve SERVINGS

You may think of other fillings, but these are a good start!

12 canned tortillas
½ pound ground beef browned in 1 tablespoon oil and mixed with 1 can (1 lb.) chili con carne
Tomato sauce
Shredded cheese
Chopped onions
Chopped hard-cooked eggs
Shredded lettuce

Fill each tortilla as you wish, perhaps with everything but lettuce, which comes later. Fold over and secure with toothpicks. Fry on both sides in hot oil until filling is hot and tortilla crisp. Remove toothpicks and insert some shredded lettuce in the opening. Serve hot as finger food.

GO WITHS: Canned frijoles refritos, Guacamole (page 23), extra fried tortillas.

WINE: California vino rosso.

SPEEDY CHILI BAKE
Four SERVINGS

Take a can of chili, a can of corn, and . . .

1 can (1 lb.) chili without beans
1 can (8 ozs.) whole kernel corn, drained
1 can (8 ozs.) tomato sauce
1 cup grated Cheddar cheese
Crushed corn chips

Arrange alternate layers of the ingredients in a casserole, topping with the corn chips. Bake at 350° F. for 25 minutes, or until hot and bubbly.

GO WITHS: Whole wheat bread, Molded Cranberry Salad (page 232).

WINE: California Zinfandel.

CHILI CON CARNE *Four* SERVINGS

*Adjust the amount of chili powder to suit your own taste—
this is a moderately "hot" mixture.*

1 package onion soup mix
½ cup diced green pepper
1 clove garlic mashed with 1 tea-
    spoon salt
¼ cup oil
1 pound ground beef

1 strip bacon, diced
1 can (1 lb.) tomatoes
1 can (1 lb.) kidney beans
2 teaspoons sugar
2 tablespoons chili powder

Sauté soup mix, green pepper, and garlic in oil for 5 minutes. Add beef
and bacon. Cook about 5 minutes, stirring frequently. Add rest of
ingredients and simmer 30 minutes more.

GO WITHS: Fluffy rice, big green salad, cornbread.

WINE: California Zinfandel.

BUSY BEE LUNCHEON *Six* SERVINGS

*A Montana rancher's wife contributes this quickie, com-
menting "It's better with Montana beef!"*

2 cups (½-inch cubes) of cooked roast beef
4 cups (1-inch cubes) pared potatoes
¾ cup chopped green pepper
2 medium onions, sliced
1 can tomato soup
1 cup water
¼ teaspoon pepper
1 teaspoon salt

Combine ingredients in a heavy skillet. Heat to boiling. Then cover
and cook on low heat for about 35 minutes.

GO WITHS: Homemade Whole Wheat Bread (page 47).

WINE: California mountain red.

LASAGNE
Eight to Ten SERVINGS

*This popular dish is a lot of work except when you make it
this way.*

> 1 package (1½ ozs.) spaghetti sauce mix
> 1 can tomato paste
> 1 pound ground beef
> 1 teaspoon salt
> ¼ teaspoon pepper
> ½ pound lasagne, cooked
> ½ pound Ricotta cheese (or dry cottage cheese)
> ½ pound Mozzarella cheese

Prepare spaghetti sauce according to package directions, adding tomato
paste. Brown beef, adding salt and pepper. Add to sauce and simmer
20 minutes. Cook lasagne as directed on package.

Place ⅓ sauce in 8x12-inch baking dish. Lay over it half the
lasagne. Add half the Ricotta and half the Mozzarella. Repeat with
sauce, lasagne, cheese. Top with last portion of sauce. Bake at 350° F.
for 30 minutes, until bubbling. Let stand for 10 minutes before cutting
to serve.

WINE: California mellow red wine or mountain red.

CORNED BEEF DINNER
Six to Eight SERVINGS

*Corned beef takes a long time to cook tender, and needs to
be sliced very thin.*

> 5 pound piece corned beef brisket
> Water
> 6 to 8 medium potatoes
> 12 to 16 medium carrots
> 1 head cabbage, cut into wedges
> Melted butter
> ¼ cup minced parsley

Wipe corned beef brisket with a damp cloth. Cover meat with water and heat to boiling. Reduce heat, cover pan tightly, and let meat simmer until tender, allowing 45 to 60 minutes per pound. About 45 minutes before end of cooking period, add potatoes. Allow 18 to 20 minutes for cooking carrots, and 10 to 15 minutes for cooking cabbage wedges.

Arrange cooked beef on large platter and surround with cabbage, carrots, and cooked potatoes that have been rolled in melted butter and then in minced parsley. Cut the cooked meat into thin slices across the grain. Use leftover meat for sandwiches or hash.

GO WITHS: Rye bread or rolls.

WINE: California Rosé.

CORNED BEEF CASSEROLE   *Six to Eight* SERVINGS

A can of corned beef is what all this fuss is about!

1 package (8 ozs.) medium noodles	1 can (12 ozs.) corned beef, broken into pieces
3 tablespoons butter	1 can condensed cream of chicken soup
½ cup chopped onion	1 cup milk
½ cup chopped green pepper	¼ cup fine dry bread crumbs
2 cups (½ lb.) cubed Cheddar cheese	1 tablespoon butter, melted

Cook noodles according to package directions; drain. In a small skillet melt 3 tablespoons butter; add onion and green pepper and sauté 5 minutes. Layer noodles, onion-green pepper mixture, cheese, and corned beef in a 2½-quart casserole, winding up with cheese on top. Combine soup and milk and pour over casserole. Mix crumbs with butter and sprinkle on top. Bake 40 minutes at 350° F.

GO WITHS: Tossed greens with tomato and cucumber, hot yeast rolls.

WINE: California mountain red.

CORNED BEEF HASH WITH EGGS

Four SERVINGS

An old-timer, always good, and it's so simple!

- 1 can corned beef hash
- 4 eggs
- 1 tablespoon minced parsley
- ½ cup grated cheese

Press hash into greased shallow baking dish and make 4 indentations in the surface with a spoon. Break an egg into each. Sprinkle with parsley and cheese, and bake at 375° F. until centers of eggs are as firm as you wish them.

GO WITHS: Corn on the cob or baked squash, cloverleaf rolls.

WINE: California Zinfandel.

JUDY'S CORNED BEEF QUICKIE

Three to Four SERVINGS

"Maybe it sounds terrible, but it's really good!"

- 1 can (12 ozs.) corned beef, chilled
- 1 teaspoon soft butter
- 1 lemon cut lengthwise in eighths
- 2 medium onions, sliced thin
- 1 cup chili sauce
- ¼ cup water

Cut corned beef in half lengthwise (it is less likely to break up if cold) and place in baking dish. Spread soft butter over it and lay slices of lemon and onions in overlapping rows over the meat. Mix chili sauce and water, pour over corned beef, and bake at 350° F. for 20 minutes.

GO WITHS: Baked Stuffed Potatoes (page 272), Pear Blush Salad (page 235).

WINE: California mellow red.

QUICK BARBECUED FRANKS   *Four* SERVINGS

They're delicious in or out of buns.

10 frankfurters (1 lb.)
 1 can condensed tomato soup
½ cup India relish
¼ cup chopped onion
 2 teaspoons Worcestershire

Brown frankfurters in a little butter or simmer 5 minutes in water. Simmer other ingredients 5 to 10 minutes and serve over the frankfurters.

GO WITHS: French fried potatoes, peas, mixed fruits with whipped cream dressing.

WINE: California mountain red. Or beer.

△

BROILED FRANKFURTERS   *Four to Six* SERVINGS
AND SAUERKRAUT

It's such a colorful, appetizing combination!

3 tablespoons minced green pepper
3 tablespoons minced onion
2 tablespoons bacon drippings
  No. 2½ can sauerkraut (3½ cups)
1 cup canned tomatoes
8 to 10 frankfurters

Sauté onion and green pepper in drippings about 5 minutes. Stir in sauerkraut and tomatoes, mixing well. Simmer 10 minutes. Remove from heat and place mixture in bottom of broiler pan. Place frankfurters on broiler grill and broil about 8 minutes on each side.

GO WITHS: Baked stuffed potatoes, green beans.

WINE: New York State sparkling Burgundy.

CONEY ISLAND SPECIAL   *Six* SERVINGS

Try these packaged toothsome treats with your next corn roast.

    6 frankfurters, sliced
    1½ cups shredded Cheddar cheese
    ⅓ cup chili sauce
    ⅓ cup Sauterne or other white wine
    2 tablespoons chopped onion
    6 frankfurter rolls

Mix ingredients and fill rolls which you've hollowed somewhat in the center. Wrap each in foil and heat on the barbecue grill for 15 to 20 minutes, turning frequently.

GO WITHS: Potato salad, corn on the cob, coleslaw.

WINE: California sauterne.

◆

VEAL CORDON BLEU   *Two* SERVINGS

A meat-and-cheese sandwich is what this epicurean specialty amounts to—and the preparation is really very simple.

    4 thin veal cutlets of equal size
      Salt, pepper
    2 slices Swiss cheese
    2 thin slices boiled or baked ham
    1 tablespoon flour
    1 egg, beaten
    ½ cup fine crumbs
    ¼ cup oil or butter

Have your meat dealer flatten the veal as thin as possible. Salt and pepper lightly, then put two slices together sandwich fashion with a slice of cheese and a slice of ham between. Cheese and ham should be cut slightly smaller than the meat. Pound edges of meat together to seal the packages. All this can be done hours early. Then flour the meat, dip into eggs and then crumbs, and fry quickly until brown in the hot oil or butter, 4 to 5 minutes to the side.

Go withs: Asparagus and tomato salad, crusty rolls.

Wine: California Gewürztraminer.

VEAL ALMOND · Four SERVINGS

Substitute chicken and you have Chicken Almond!

- ½ cup crushed pineapple
- 2 tablespoons butter or margarine
- 1½ tablespoons cornstarch
- ½ cup pineapple juice
- 2 cups meat stock or bouillon
- 2 cups cubed cooked veal
- ½ cup slivered, toasted almonds
- ½ cup chopped celery
- Chow mein noodles

Brown crushed pineapple slowly in butter 5 minutes. Combine cornstarch with pineapple juice; add meat stock or bouillon, and cook, stirring constantly, until thickened. Add veal, almonds, and celery. Heat thoroughly, adding salt if needed, and serve over noodles.

Go withs: Broiled eggplant, green salad.

Wine: California Riesling.

VEAL PARMIGIANA   *Four* SERVINGS

The meat is ever so savory—and there are two kinds of cheese!

    4 slices veal cutlet, flattened
    1 egg, beaten
      Salt, pepper
  1/2 cup fine bread crumbs
    2 tablespoons grated Parmesan cheese
    2 tablespoons olive oil
      Mozzarella or Munster cheese slices
    1 can (8 ozs.) tomato sauce

Dip thin slice of cutlet in egg seasoned with salt and pepper, then into mixture of crumbs and cheese. Brown in oil. Place in shallow baking pan. Cover with tomato sauce, then with slices of Mozzarella. Sprinkle with a little more Parmesan cheese. Bake 30 minutes at 350° F.

GO WITHS: Canned German style potato salad, crusty rolls.

WINE: California Grey Riesling.

X

WIENER SCHNITZEL   *Four* SERVINGS

The secret of flavor is a lemon-juice bath.

    4 slices veal cutlet, 1/2 inch thick, flattened (about 1 lb.)
  1/3 cup lemon juice
    1 egg, beaten
    1 cup fine bread crumbs
      Salt, pepper
  1/4 cup butter

Flatten the cutlet with the side of a cleaver or have your meat man do it. Place in a shallow pan and pour the lemon juice over it. Turn several times in the juice and let stand 1 hour. Dip in egg, then in crumbs with salt and pepper added (about 1 teaspoon salt). Let stand on wax paper 30 minutes so that coating will adhere well. Sauté until brown on each side in the hot butter.

OPTIONAL: Add sour cream or a little dry white wine to the pan after removing the meat, stir to remove cooked-on meat particles, and serve this sauce around the meat.

GO WITHS: Buttered noodles, green beans, pink cinnamon (candies) applesauce.

WINE: California Gewürztraminer or Grey Riesling.

VARIATION

Schnitzel Parma. Lay a slice of Swiss cheese over each cutlet when you turn them, and allow it to melt.

VEAL SCALLOPINE ALLA MARSALA

Four SERVINGS

An Italian favorite, the dish is easy to prepare.

    4 flattened slices veal cutlet (1½ lbs.)
      Grated Parmesan cheese
    ¼ cup butter
    ½ cup Marsala (or sherry)
      Salt, pepper
    1 teaspoon meat extract or brown sauce

Dip the cleaver-flattened, thin slices of meat into grated cheese, and sauté in butter until browned on each side. Season with salt and pepper. Transfer to hot platter. Add meat extract and wine to skillet, simmer a few minutes, and pour over meat. Serve at once.

One cup diced mushrooms sautéed in butter may be added.

GO WITHS: Fettuccini, Italian green beans, tomato salad.

WINE: California Gewürztraminer.

QUICK SPRING STEW   *Six* SERVINGS

The simmering takes about an hour.

1 pound veal, cut in 1-inch cubes
¼ cup chopped onion
2 tablespoons drippings
1 can condensed mushroom soup
¾ cup water

6 medium carrots, cut in 1-inch sticks
2 cups 1-inch pieces celery
1 cup cut green beans
1 teaspoon salt
½ teaspoon pepper

Cook onion in drippings until golden brown. Remove onion and brown meat in drippings. Add onion, soup, and water; blend. Simmer 40 minutes. Add carrots, celery, green beans, salt, and pepper. Simmer 20 minutes or until vegetables are tender. Serve over chow mein noodles.

GO WITHS: Avocado and orange salad.

WINE: California dry Semillon.

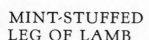

MINT-STUFFED   *Six to Eight* SERVINGS
LEG OF LAMB

Catch your butcher at a non-busy time for boning the leg of lamb.

6 pound leg of lamb, boned
Lemon juice, pepper
Mint Stuffing (see next page)
Wine Lamb Baste (see next page)

Rub lamb with lemon juice and pepper. Fill cavity with mint stuffing and tie leg into shape. Roast at 350° F. about 2½ hours, basting often with wine and herb mixture.

MINT STUFFING: Combine an 8-ounce package of stuffing mix, 3 tablespoons chopped fresh mint leaves, a pinch of rosemary, 1/4 cup melted butter, 1 minced garlic clove, 1 chopped small onion, 1/3 cup raisins, and 3 tablespoons Rosé wine.

LAMB BASTE: Simmer a few minutes 1 cup Rosé wine, 1/4 cup soy sauce, 1/2 teaspoon dried rosemary, 1/2 teaspoon dried oregano.

GO WITHS: Au gratin potatoes or saffron rice, peas.

WINE: California Grenache or Gamay Rosé.

▼

IDAHO BARBECUED LAMB

Ten to Twelve SERVINGS

Lamb is mighty succulent prepared in this manner.

6 pound leg of lamb	1 clove garlic, minced
1 teaspoon ginger	2 tablespoons chili sauce
1 teaspoon mustard	2 tablespoons Worcestershire
1 teaspoon salt	sauce
1/2 teaspoon pepper	2 tablespoons oil
Flour	1 tablespoon vinegar
2 medium onions, sliced	1 cup boiling water

Rub lamb with mixture of ginger, mustard, salt, and pepper. Sprinkle with flour. Place in baking pan and cover with onions and garlic. Roast at 350° F. about 2 1/2 hours. Mix rest of ingredients and use as a baste every 15 minutes during the last hour.

GO WITHS: Creamed potatoes, glazed carrots with parsley.

WINE: California Cabernet Sauvignon.

COMPANY MIXED GRILL   *Six* SERVINGS

An entire dinner on one platter saves some dish doing.

6 boned, skewered lamb kidney   4 thin slices bacon
   chops   6 chicken livers
  Salt, pepper   Butter
3 medium tomatoes   4 medium sweet potatoes, cooked
6 large mushroom caps   6 toast rounds

Have lamb kidney chops boned at the market, and skewered with the flank wound around the chop. Broil one side of the chops, sprinkle with salt and pepper, and turn. Then, around the edge of the rack, arrange the halved tomatoes, slices of cooked sweet potato dipped in melted butter, and mushrooms, also buttered. Wrap the chicken livers in bacon and skewer with toothpicks. Arrange near the center of the broiler rack. Return to the heat and continue cooking until the lamb chops are done and the bacon around the chicken livers is crisp. Serve on a large hot platter, livers in the center. Around the platter alternate the toast rounds, topped with the grilled tomatoes and mushroom caps and the broiled lamb chops. Pile the grilled sweet potato slices at either end of the platter, garnish with cress, and serve immediately. A lemon-parsley-butter sauce is a zestful accompaniment.

GO WITHS: Relish tray.

WINE: California Cabernet Sauvignon.

LAMB CHOP AND   *Four* SERVINGS
BANANA GRILL

What an interesting combination this is!

4 thick lamb loin chops
  Salt, pepper
4 bananas, not too ripe
4 slices bacon
2 tomatoes, cut in half
1/3 cup shredded sharp Cheddar cheese

Mint-stuffed Leg of Lamb, page 158

Broil chops on one side, about 7 minutes, season with salt and pepper, turn and place on grill with the bananas, each wrapped in a strip of bacon and skewered with wooden picks. Sprinkle tomato halves with cheese and place on rack also. Broil 6 or 7 minutes until chops are brown on second side and tomatoes and bananas are lightly browned. Turn bananas once during cooking. Season chops and serve the mixture on hot plates.

Go WITHS: Baked Green Peppers Stuffed with Corn Pudding (page 270).

WINE: California Gamay Rosé

LAMB CHOP AND KIDNEY GRILL

Four SERVINGS

I consider this one of the most appealing of all dinners.

4 lamb loin, rib, or shoulder chops
2 lamb kidneys, split
2 tomatoes, cut in half crosswise
4 whole cooked carrots
  Salt, pepper
  Oil or butter

Place chops and kidneys on broiler rack. Brush kidneys with oil or butter and broil meats about 7 minutes or until chops are well browned. Season with salt and pepper, turn, and arrange tomatoes and carrots on the grill, first seasoning with salt and pepper and brushing with oil or butter. Broil another 7 minutes and serve hot.

Go WITHS: Corn sticks, mixed greens.

WINE: California Cabernet Sauvignon.

VARIATION

Link sausages may be included in the broiling, and the vegetables may be exchanged for fruit such as peach halves or pineapple rings.

Mustard-glazed Ham, page 170

LAMB CHOPS WITH ZUCCHINI *Four* SERVINGS
ITALIAN STYLE

A can of mushroom gravy spares the saucemaking.

4 shoulder lamb chops
1 tablespoon oil or butter
1 can mushroom gravy
　Pinch oregano
1 large clove garlic, minced
2 medium zucchini, sliced
½ cup chopped canned Italian style tomatoes or fresh
　　tomatoes

Brown chops in oil and pour off fat. Add gravy, oregano, and garlic. Cover and cook over low heat 20 minutes. Add zucchini and tomatoes. Cover and cook 15 minutes more, or until meat is tender, stirring occasionally.

GO WITHS: Noodles or rice, crusty rolls, relishes.

WINE: California mountain red.

LAMB CURRY WITH BANANAS *Six* SERVINGS
AND SAFFRON RICE

A leg of lamb makes two good meals: first the roast, then the curry.

1 cup thinly sliced onion
¾ cup chopped green pepper
1 small clove garlic, minced
2 tablespoons olive oil
2 tablespoons flour
2 cups meat stock or bouillon
½ cup tomato sauce
2 tablespoons minced parsley
1 tablespoon curry powder
1 teaspoon salt
⅛ teaspoon pepper
1 large bay leaf
　Pinch of thyme, dash of mace
2 whole cloves
2½ to 3 cups cooked diced lamb
3 bananas, sliced ½ inch thick,
　　sautéed in butter
Saffron Rice (see next page)

Sauté onion, green pepper, and garlic until golden in the oil. Sprinkle on flour, stir, and add meat stock. Simmer until thickened and smooth. Add tomato sauce, parsley, and seasonings; simmer 15 minutes. Stir in the meat and let stand in the sauce overnight or for at least an hour. Shortly before serving cook banana slices in remaining oil. Heat lamb and serve over rice with the bananas.

SAFFRON RICE. Combine in a saucepan 1 cup uncooked rice, 1 teaspoon salt, 1/4 teaspoon saffron, 2 cups water and 1 tablespoon butter. Heat to boiling, stir, cover, and cook over low heat until rice is tender, about 15 minutes.

GO WITHS: Fruit salad, sesame seed rolls.

WINE: California claret.

SPICY LAMB SHANKS · *Four* SERVINGS

This economical meat is pleasingly fruited.

4 lamb shanks	1/2 teaspoon cinnamon
Flour, salt, pepper	1/2 teaspoon allspice
1 cup cooked prunes	1/4 teaspoon cloves
1 cup cooked dried apricots	3 tablespoons vinegar
1/2 cup sugar	1/4 teaspoon salt
1 cup water	

Dredge meat in seasoned flour and place in greased baking dish. Bake at 350° F. until tender, 1 1/2–2 hours. Combine remaining ingredients and simmer together 5 minutes. When meat is tender, remove from oven and drain off fat. Cover shanks with fruit mixture, and bake at 400° F. for 30 minutes. Serve immediately.

GO WITHS: Baked sweet potatoes, mixed green salad.

WINE: California vino rosso.

LAMB MOLÉ   *Six to Eight* SERVINGS

A Mexican specialty of excellent flavor, the dish has one surprise ingredient: cocoa.

1½ pounds boneless lamb shoulder
1½ teaspoons brown seasoning sauce
2 teaspoons salt
⅛ teaspoon pepper
½ teaspoon chili powder
¼ teaspoon cocoa
⅛ teaspoon cinnamon
2 tablespoons fat

1 small clove garlic, minced
½ cup finely diced onion
½ cup finely diced celery
8 ounce can tomato sauce (1 cup)
1½ cups water
1½ cups sliced raw carrots
1 cup long grain or converted rice

Cut lamb into 1½-inch cubes and place in mixing bowl. Sprinkle with seasonings. Toss lightly with fork to coat evenly. Melt fat in Dutch oven or large frying pan. Add meat and brown on all sides over moderate heat. Add garlic, onion, and celery. Cook about 5 minutes, stirring frequently. Add tomato sauce and water and bring to boil. Add carrots and rice. Cover tightly and cook over low heat until rice and carrots are barely tender, about 35 minutes.

GO WITHS: Melba toast, fruit salad.

WINE: California Rosé.

△

LAKE CITY LAMB BARLEY STEW   *Six* SERVINGS

A budget-parer, this stew gives full measure of flavor.

2 pounds cubed boned lamb shoulder
2 tablespoons oil
3 cups water
1 package onion soup mix
1 bay leaf

1 teaspoon seasoned salt
½ cup pearl barley
6 carrots, halved
1 rib celery with tops, chopped
1 medium zucchini, sliced

164

Brown lamb in oil in Dutch oven and remove excess fat. Add water, soup mix, seasonings and barley. Simmer covered for 30 minutes. Add carrots and celery; cook 30 minutes more. Add zucchini and cook 15 minutes or until meat and vegetables are tender. Add ½ cup dry red, white, or rosé wine the last 15 minutes, if you wish.

GO WITHS: Refrigerated biscuits, leaf lettuce salad, or Ambrosia Salad (page 229).

WINE: California Rosé.

■

BAKED CANADIAN STYLE BACON   *Six to Eight* SERVINGS

In one large piece, the meat makes an excellent roast.

    1 piece Canadian style bacon, about 3 to 4 pounds
    2 canned pineapple rings, cut into pieces
      Whole cloves
    ¼ cup maple sirup

Place meat, fat side up, on a rack in a shallow pan. Roast at 325° F. to an internal temperature of 170°. (A 4-pound piece will take about 2½ hours.) Score meat. On top and sides arrange pineapple pieces, speared with cloves. If necessary, secure pineapple with toothpicks. Pour sirup over garnished meat and bake 10 minutes longer. Leftover meat is good sautéed in butter for breakfast, or served cold in sandwiches.

GO WITHS: Candied sweet potatoes, broccoli, celery hearts.

WINE: New York State or Ohio Rosé.

BAKED HAM WITH GRAPES   *Four* SERVINGS

There's really nothing to fixing ham this way, and it's SO good!

1 center slice cooked ham, 1 inch thick
1 tablespoon butter
2 tablespoons brown sugar
¾ cup red wine
⅛ teaspoon ginger
½ cup seedless grapes

Melt butter in skillet over low heat, stir in sugar, and add ham. Brown ham on both sides, then transfer to baking dish and pour wine over ham. Sprinkle with ginger. Bake at 350° F. about 20 minutes. Transfer ham to hot platter and add grapes to liquid in baking dish. Heat through in oven or on surface of range and pour over ham.

Go WITHS: Parsley rice, buttered noodles or sweet potatoes, Italian green beans, relishes.

WINE: New York State claret or Burgundy.

HAM AND EGG PIE   *Six* SERVINGS

Tiny slices can be served as appetizer.

3 eggs, well beaten
1 cup milk
¼ teaspoon salt
⅛ teaspoon pepper
1 cup minced cooked ham
1 9-inch unbaked pie shell
Nutmeg

Mix eggs, milk, salt, pepper, and ham. Pour into unbaked pie shell. Sprinkle nutmeg lightly on top. Bake at 425° F. for 35 minutes.

Go WITHS: Peas, whole kernel corn, curly endive salad.

WINE: California Gamay Rosé.

HAM AND RICE AU GRATIN   *Six* SERVINGS

Just a little leftover ham will do.

1 cup minced onion
1 cup diced celery
3 tablespoons butter, melted
3 cups cooked rice
1 cup sliced stuffed olives
½ teaspoon salt

½ teaspoon pepper
1 teaspoon thyme
1 can cream of mushroom soup
2 cups sharp Cheddar cheese, diced
⅔ cup diced cooked ham

Cook onion and celery in butter until tender. Remove from heat and stir in rice, olives, and seasonings. In a saucepan heat soup and 1 cup cheese until cheese has melted. Add to rice mixture with ham. Turn into greased 1-quart casserole; top with remaining cheese. Bake at 375° F. for 15 minutes.

Go WITHS: Baked acorn squash, Molded Cranberry Salad (page 232).

WINE: New York State claret or Burgundy.

HAM AND SWEET POTATO   *Six* SERVINGS
CASSEROLE

It doesn't take much ham to yield fine flavor.

2 cups diced cooked ham
   Butter or ham fat
4 cups hot, mashed sweet potatoes
       (instant)
2 eggs, beaten

½ cup milk
2 tablespoons orange juice
   concentrate
½ teaspoon salt (or more)

Brown ham slightly in about 1½ tablespoons butter or ham fat. Whip potatoes until smooth and combine with beaten eggs, milk, orange juice, and salt, blending thoroughly. Mix with the meat and drippings and turn into 2-quart greased casserole. Bake uncovered at 350° F. for 45 minutes.

Go WITHS: Cauliflower, spinach.

WINE: California mellow red.

HAM-BANANA ROLLS WITH CHEESE SAUCE

Four SERVINGS

Here's a dish both appealing and different.

4 thin slices boiled ham
Prepared mustard
2 large or 4 small firm bananas
Melted butter or margarine
Cheese Sauce (page 255)

Spread ham slices lightly with mustard and wrap around banana halves or whole bananas. Brush tips of bananas with butter. Place rolls in greased shallow baking dish, pour Cheese Sauce over them, and bake at 350° F. for 30 minutes, or until bananas are easily pierced with a fork.

GO WITHS: Broccoli, molded vegetable salad.

WINE: California crackling Rosé.

X

HAM LOAF WITH TOMATO HORSERADISH SAUCE

Six SERVINGS

A can of soup moistens the loaf and sauces it as well.

1 pound ground lean ham
½ pound ground lean pork
1 can condensed tomato soup
½ cup fine dry bread crumbs
⅓ cup minced onion

¼ cup finely chopped celery
1 egg, slightly beaten
½ teaspoon dry mustard
Dash pepper
2 teaspoons prepared horseradish

Mix ham, pork, ½ cup soup, crumbs, onion, celery, egg, mustard, and pepper. Shape firmly into a loaf and place in a shallow baking pan. Bake at 350° F. for 1¼ hours. Blend rest of soup with horseradish; heat and serve over slices of the loaf.

GO WITHS: Parsley buttered potatoes, asparagus, pickles, raisin bread.

WINE: California Gamay or Gamay Rosé.

HAM, PINEAPPLE, AND SWEET POTATO STACKS

Five SERVINGS

These are neat packages, and so full of flavor!

      10 strips bacon
       5 slices canned pineapple
    2½ cups mashed, seasoned sweet potatoes (canned, instant,
            or cooked)
       1 pound ground "hammy" ham

Cross two strips of bacon for each portion and lay a slice of pineapple in it. Shape five patties from the sweet potatoes, five from the ham. Lay a sweet potato patty on the pineapple, then a ham patty, and fold over the ends of the bacon, fastening with picks. Bake at 375° F. for half an hour.

GO WITHS: Head lettuce, Thousand Island Dressing (page 251), bakery rolls.

WINE: New York State or Ohio Rosé.

HAM SUPREME WITH STRAWBERRIES

Four SERVINGS

Here's a real delicacy, and it's all so simple!

       1 slice ham 1 inch thick
      ½ teaspoon dry mustard
    6 to 8 whole cloves
       1 package (10 ozs.) frozen strawberries, thawed

Slash fat around edge of ham slice and spread mustard over it. Pierce with cloves. Drain thawed berries and pour juice over ham. (Extra glamorizer: add ¼ cup white or Rosé wine to juice). Bake half an hour at 350° F. Scatter berries over ham and bake 10 minutes more.

GO WITHS: Au Gratin Potatoes (page 274), artichokes, hot biscuits.

WINE: New York State Rosé.

169

MUSTARD-GLAZED HAM

    1 boneless ready-to-eat ham or canned ham (6 to 10 lbs)
    Whole cloves (optional)
    ¼ cup prepared mustard
    ½ cup packed brown sugar
    1 can (6 ozs.) frozen orange juice concentrate

Follow packer's directions in preparing ham. It needs only to be heated in most cases. The usual oven temperature is 325° F. Before cooking, or half an hour before taking ham from the oven, cut the fat in diamond pattern, and stud with cloves, if you wish. For the last half hour, apply the glaze. Spread with mixture of mustard, brown sugar, and thawed orange concentrate. Return to oven and baste several times with the mixture until ham is brown, shiny, and well spiced.

GO WITHS: For a picnic, potato salad, corn on the cob.

WINE: Make it beer, or lemonade.

GOLDEN GLAZED HAM

It's so easy to dress up a modern ham!

    Fully cooked ham, 5–10 pounds
    1 jar (12 ozs.) orange marmalade
    ½ cup orange juice
    1 tablespoon (or more) prepared mustard
    ¼ teaspoon ginger
    ¼ teaspoon cloves
    Whole cloves
    ½ cup raisins

Bake ham at 350° F. or according to package directions. Half an hour before end of heating time (2 hours for a large ham), score the fat, spoon half the marmalade mixture over ham, stud with cloves, and return to oven. Combine remaining marmalade mixture with raisins, heat, and serve with the ham.

GO WITHS: Baked Stuffed Potatoes (page 272), asparagus, celery and olives.

WINE: California mountain red.

HONG KONG PORK CHOPS   *Eight* SERVINGS

Dinner party in mind? Here's a good place to start planning!

8 pork loin chops, cut 1 inch thick
Salt, pepper
1 onion, sliced thin
¼ cup soy sauce
¼ cup sherry
2 tablespoons lemon juice
1 can (4 ozs.) sliced mushrooms, with juice

½ teaspoon ground ginger
¼ teaspoon garlic powder
½ green pepper, chopped
½ can (4 oz.) water chestnuts, sliced
1 unpeeled lemon, sliced thin
Fluffy hot rice

Sprinkle chops lightly with salt; brown in their own fat or in 1 tablespoon oil; cover with onion slices. Mix soy sauce, sherry, lemon juice, mushrooms, ginger, and garlic powder and pour over chops. Cover and bake at 350° F. for 45 minutes. Add green pepper, chestnuts, and lemon slices and bake 15 to 20 minutes more. Serve with rice.

GO WITHS: Whole green beans, crusty rolls, fruit salad.

WINE: California Cabernet Sauvignon.

HONOLULU PORK CHOPS   *Four* SERVINGS

Mushroom gravy in the can is the success secret here!

4 pork chops, 1 inch thick
⅓ cup chopped onion
1 clove garlic, minced
2 tablespoons oil
1 can mushroom gravy

1 tablespoon brown sugar
1 teaspoon lemon juice
½ teaspoon Worcestershire sauce
2 drops Tabasco sauce
4 pineapple slices

Brown chops and cook onion with garlic in oil. Pour off excess fat. Stir in gravy, sugar, lemon juice, Worcestershire and Tabasco. Cover and cook over low heat for 45 minutes or until tender, stirring now and then.

GO WITHS: Rice or baked potatoes, Italian green beans.

WINE: California claret or Gamay.

SAVORY PORK CHOPS   *Six* SERVINGS

They look attractive and taste divine!

6 medium pork loin chops	6 slices orange (do not peel)
1/3 cup flour	6 thick slices onion
1/2 teaspoon salt	6 green pepper rings
1/8 teaspoon pepper	1 can tomato soup
2 tablespoons drippings	1/2 cup water

Dredge pork chops in flour mixed with salt and pepper. Brown in fat in heavy skillet. When browned well on both sides, lay an orange slice, an onion slice and a green pepper ring on each chop. Dilute soup with water and pour over chops. Cover skillet, turn heat low, and simmer until done, about 1 hour. Arrange chops and vegetables on serving platter, using drippings in pan as gravy or as sauce for freshly cooked spaghetti.

GO WITHS: Spaghetti, noodles or rice, relish tray.

WINE: California Gamay.

BARBECUED PORK TENDERLOIN   *Four* SERVINGS

This unusual barbecue sauce has a celestial flavor.

2 pork tenderloins, about 1 1/2 pounds each	3 tablespoons honey
2 tablespoons soy sauce	1/4 teaspoon powdered ginger
2 tablespoons sherry	1 teaspoon salt

Place tenderloin in a large bowl. Combine remaining ingredients and pour over meat. Cover and chill several hours or overnight. Bake in a covered casserole at 350° F. for 2 hours. Remove cover last 30 minutes. Baste with sauce a few times during baking. Cut into thin slices.

GO WITHS: Scalloped Potatoes (page 274), or Candied Sweet Potatoes (page 275), broccoli.

WINE: California Gamay.

SAUSAGE AND APPLE RINGS   *Four* SERVINGS

*For brunch, lunch, or supper, this combination is a happy
one.*

1 pound brown-and-serve sausages
4 large apples, not pared
¼ cup brown or white sugar

Cook sausages in skillet according to package directions and place on a
warm plate or in a warm oven for a few minutes while you cook the
apples. Core apples and slice ½-inch thick. Sauté in sausage drippings
or in a little butter until tender and golden brown. Sprinkle with sugar
and let it melt. Serve on the platter with the sausage links.

Go WITHS: Onion Buns, (page 51). For brunch, scrambled eggs; for
lunch or supper, Molded Vegetable Salad (page 224).

WINE: California Zinfandel.

SAUSAGE-PEACH BALLS   *Four* SERVINGS

They're attractive and enticing!

1 pound pork sausage
2 tablespoons minced onion
1 egg, beaten
2 cups soft bread crumbs
¼ teaspoon salt

Dash pepper
8 peach halves, drained
24 whole cloves
½ cup peach juice

Combine sausage, onion, egg, crumbs, seasoning. Shape into 8 balls.
Arrange peach halves, cut side up, in shallow baking dish. Stick 3
cloves around the outer edge and place sausage ball in center of each.
Bake in an 8-inch square pan at 350° F. for 45 minutes. Remove to hot
platter, draining off fat. Pour heated peach juice over balls.

Go WITHS: Au gratin potatoes, green beans.

WINE: California Zinfandel.

SAUSAGE-PINEAPPLE STACKS   *Four* SERVINGS

For a higher stack, add a tomato slice, and cheese.

1 pound bulk pork sausage
4 slices canned pineapple
   Prepared mustard

Form sausage into four patties, a little larger than the pineapple slices. Partly cook in a skillet, browning on both sides very lightly. Spread pineapple with mustard and lay a sausage patty on each slice. Bake at 350° F. for half an hour, basting occasionally with some of the sirup from the canned pineapple.

SAUSAGE STACK VARIATION: Cross 2 strips bacon for each stack, lay a browned sausage patty on each 2 slices, top with a slice of onion, a slice of tomato. Skewer bacon across top and bake.

GO WITHS: Creamed potatoes with dill, peas, buttermilk biscuits.

WINE: California Vin Rosé.

SWEET-SOUR   *Ten to Twelve* SERVINGS
LOIN OF PORK

A bottled sauce saves time and a long list of ingredients!

6 pound pork loin, chine bone removed
¼ cup soy sauce
1 teaspoon salt
½ teaspoon freshly ground pepper
½ teaspoon ginger
¼ teaspoon nutmeg
1 bottle (8 ozs.) oriental style sweet-sour sauce or salad
   dressing
1 can (1 lb. 14 ozs.) peaches, apricots, or pineapple

Rub meat with combined soy sauce, salt, pepper, ginger, and nutmeg. Place on a rack in a shallow roasting pan and roast at 325° F., allowing

25 minutes per pound. Baste the last half hour with combination of bottled sauce and ½ cup sirup from the canned fruit. Transfer meat to a hot platter, drain off fat, and heat the canned fruit in the drippings. Use to garnish meat. Heat remainder of basting sauce and pour over meat before you serve it.

GO WITHS: Buttered noodles or scalloped potatoes or rice, green beans, Ambrosia Salad (page 229).

WINE: California Gamay Rosé.

SWEET-SOUR PORK   *Six* SERVINGS

This kind of flavor combination grows increasingly popular.

2 pounds lean pork shoulder, cut into 2x½-inch strips
¼ cup flour
½ teaspoon salt
¼ teaspoon pepper
2 tablespoons drippings
½ cup water
2 tablespoons cornstarch
¼ cup brown sugar
¼ cup vinegar
1 tablespoon soy sauce
1 can (1 lb. 4½ ozs.) pineapple chunks
1 green pepper, cut julienne style
1 small onion, sliced thin

Dredge meat in seasoned flour. Brown on all sides in drippings. Add water, cover pan, and simmer for an hour. Combine cornstarch and sugar. Add vinegar, soy sauce, and juice drained from pineapple chunks. Cook on low heat, stirring constantly, until mixture is thick and clear. Pour sauce over meat. Add pineapple, green pepper, and onion. Heat through on low heat. Serve over noodles or rice.

GO WITHS: Hot buttered French bread.

WINE: California Cabernet Sauvignon.

BARBECUED SPARERIBS   *Six* SERVINGS

Ribs may be cooked ahead and reheated if it is any easier.

3 pounds spareribs
1 large onion, chopped
½ cup water
1 cup chili sauce
¼ cup vinegar
2 tablespoons brown sugar

1 tablespoon Worcestershire
    sauce
1 teaspoon dry mustard
1 teaspoon salt
1 teaspoon paprika
¼ teaspoon black pepper

Wipe spareribs with a damp cloth and arrange in a single layer in the bottom of a shallow baking pan. Place under broiler to brown, turning once. Skim off fat. Meanwhile, combine onions, water, chili sauce, vinegar, brown sugar, Worcestershire sauce and seasonings. Simmer sauce 30 minutes, then pour over browned ribs. Place in moderate oven, 350° F., and bake for 1½ to 2 hours, or until meat is tender. Spoon sauce over spareribs several times during baking. Cut into sections for serving.

GO WITHS: Scalloped potatoes, corn on the cob, green salad.

WINE: California Burgundy.

△

SPARERIBS SOYA   *Six to Eight* SERVINGS

This is a very, very delicious treat for 6 big appetites.

5 pounds spareribs, cut in 2-rib portions
¼ cup flour
1 teaspoon salt
1 tablespoon ground ginger
2 cloves garlic, mashed
½ cup soy sauce
2 tablespoons lemon juice

Roll ribs in flour mixed with salt. Brown well in 1 tablespoon fat in a heavy pan. Combine ginger, garlic, soy sauce, and lemon juice and pour over ribs. Cover and bake at 325° F. for 2 hours, basting frequently with the sauce. Uncover and bake or broil a few minutes longer to crisp the ribs. Ribs may be soaked in soy sauce before browning to intensify flavor.

GO WITHS: French fries, green beans.

WINE: California Burgundy.

■

HAWAIIAN GLAZED RIBS   *Two* SERVINGS

Pre-cooking the ribs makes the browning and glazing very simple.

2 pounds lean spareribs
1 medium onion, quartered
1 teaspoon cornstarch
1 can (6 ozs.) frozen pineapple
  orange juice, thawed

⅓ cup barbecue sauce
⅓ cup packed brown sugar
1 tablespoon oil
1 teaspoon salt
1 teaspoon instant onion

Simmer ribs with onion in water to cover for an hour. Blend cornstarch and fruit juices in a small saucepan over low heat. Add barbecue sauce, brown sugar, oil, salt, onion flakes. Simmer sauce 5 minutes. Drain ribs, cut in serving-size portions and place on grill over well-burned-down coals. Turn and baste until ribs are well browned and glazed, about 15 minutes. Serve with the rest of the sauce. Glazing may be done under broiler or in a 375° F. oven.

NOTE: To double the amount of ribs, keep the same sauce ingredients, but double the sauce for more than 4 pounds of ribs.

GO WITHS: Fluffy hot rice, Chinese Bean Salad (page 222).

WINE: New York State claret or Burgundy.

TENDERLOIN TOWERS *Four* SERVINGS

You'll think of all kinds of variations for these savory sky-scrapers. They're great party food.

4 pork tenderloin patties
  Soy sauce, prepared mustard, or barbecue sauce
4 slices Spanish onion
4 slices tomato
  Salt, pepper, salad herbs
4 slices Cheddar or Swiss cheese
4 slices bacon, cut in half

Brush patties on both sides with soy sauce, mustard, or barbecue sauce and place in baking dish. Top each with a slice of onion, then a slice of tomato, sprinkling each layer lightly with salt, pepper, and salad herbs. Add a slice of cheese to each stack, then criss-cross bacon pieces on top. Skewer each stack to hold it together. Cover and bake at 350° F. for 45 to 50 minutes. Uncover and bake 15 minutes more.

Go WITHS: Baked sweet potatoes, bran muffins.

WINE: California Burgundy.

◆

◇ ✗ ◇ ✗ ◇ ✗ ◇

POULTRY

AMERICANS ARE eating five times as much chicken as they did twenty years ago, and there's a reason: Chickens have improved in quality, and they are invariably tender. They are also economical and easy to use. You can get just the pieces you want if you don't care for the whole bird.

Versatility counts. We could serve chicken 365 days a year, a completely different dish appearing each meal. None of us wants to do that, of course, but chicken comes to the table at least once a week in most homes.

Most, if not all, of the recipes calling for cooked chicken may be used for turkey. Not many palates can tell the difference, but turkey is sometimes a better choice simply because it has more meat in proportion to bone.

By far the most popular chicken is the broiler-fryer, a more or less standardized bird that comes to market at about nine weeks, weighing on the average 2½ to 3 pounds. It may be split, quartered, or cut in pieces for cooking.

The stewing chicken weighs 4½ to 5 pounds and is the choice for soup, stews, chicken salads, and the many wonderful chicken dishes which require 1 cup, 2 cups, or more of cooked chicken meat. Keep in mind that a stewing chicken

179

of 4½ pounds yields about 4 cups diced cooked chicken and a quart of stock or broth for sauces and soup.

The broiler-fryer may be simmered, and a 3-pound bird gives about 2½ cups diced chicken and 2 to 2½ cups broth. I prefer the larger bird which is fatter for stewing. There is much flavor in chicken fat and in the bones, too. The longer cooking needed for the stewing chicken brings out that flavor. Chicken fat is excellent for cooking purposes.

There are two other kinds of chicken: the Rock Cornish game hen, a little-bitty bird usually served one to a person, and the big roaster which may weigh 5 pounds, or 7 pounds if it is a capon (de-sexed chicken).

Modern, meaty, tender chickens have made Mom's recipes and Grandmom's out of date. Chicken takes about 40 minutes to fry, or even to stew or simmer (a better word), if you're cooking the broiler-fryer. A stewing chicken takes 2 hours instead of the 4 hours once required for a barnyard fowl. Today's hen doesn't have to scratch for a living, so her meat is more tender—and she goes to market at a more succulent-fleshed age.

STORING AND FREEZING
CHICKEN AND OTHER POULTRY

Unless it is frozen, chicken should be cooked within a day of purchase. Leftover chicken should be refrigerated promptly; the same goes for all cooked birds including turkey.

Don't refreeze thawed birds. Once thawed, cook them, after which, if necessary, you may freeze them—properly cooked and wrapped, of course.

In summer do not let cooked poultry sit around before or after a picnic or a family meal. Many an epidemic of food poisoning has been traced to improperly cared-for poultry. If you haven't facilities for keeping fried chicken or roast turkey cold until it is eaten, choose some other, less perishable food for the feast.

HOW TO STEW OR SIMMER A CHICKEN

This recipe will make about 4 cups diced chicken or 3 to 4 cups stock or broth.

1 stewing hen, about 4½ pounds
1 quart water
1 onion
1 stalk celery, with tops
1 tablespoon salt
1 teaspoon whole black pepper or ½ teaspoon ground pepper
1 bay leaf
1 slice lemon
  A few sprigs parsley

Put everything into a big kettle, cover, bring to a boil, then reduce heat to a simmer and cook until chicken is tender, about 2 hours. Cool in broth, then remove chicken, take the meat from the bones, and dice or slice it for use. Chicken skin, which contains much flavor, may be ground or whirled in the blender and returned to stock, unless you have a nice cat that would like it.

Strain and chill stock, remove the fat from the surface, and use for sauces and gravies.

BASIC CHICKEN STOCK SAUCE   *One* CUP

2 tablespoons chicken fat or butter
2 tablespoons flour
  Salt, pepper as needed
1 cup chicken broth

Melt fat in saucepan, stir in flour, and add broth. Cook and stir over moderate heat until sauce is smooth and thickened. Taste and add seasoning if needed. Double or triple the recipe as necessary for the amount of sauce you need.

For gravy, make the sauce in the roasting pan or skillet and include all the cooked-in bits of chicken. (See Turkey Gravy, page 214).

MUSHROOM SAUCE. Sauté ¼-pound sliced mushrooms 5 minutes in the butter before adding the flour in the foregoing recipe.

DELICIOUS FRIED CHICKEN   *Four* SERVINGS

Everybody's favorite chicken dish offers many variations in flavor, depending upon the seasonings you choose.

1 broiler-fryer chicken, cut up, or 2½-3 pounds chicken
    parts
Seasoned flour (see below)
Shortening or salad oil

Shake pieces of chicken in a bag with seasoned flour, a few at a time. Heat shortening or oil to fill skillet to ½ inch. Place meatiest pieces in skillet first, skin side down. Cook uncovered, 15 to 25 minutes on each side, turning only once. Drain crisply browned chicken on paper toweling. Remove excess fat from skillet, leaving 2 tablespoons for every cup of gravy you want. Stir in 2 tablespoons flour per cup, then add 1 cup milk or chicken bouillon or broth and cook and stir to smooth texture.

A gravy differs from a sauce in that it contains all the good bits of meat and scrapings from the skillet.

SEASONED FLOUR: Combine ½ cup flour, 1 teaspoon salt, 1 teaspoon paprika, ¼ teaspoon pepper. If you wish, add ½ teaspoon poultry seasoning, savory or thyme, or 1 teaspoon mixed dried salad herbs. For curry fried chicken, add 1 teaspoon curry powder and ¼ teaspoon ginger.

Oven-Fried Chicken. Follow basic directions for fried chicken, but place chicken pieces in a baking pan without crowding, instead of in a skillet. Turn once and bake at 400° F. about 40 minutes. Half butter may be used.

BAKED CHICKEN WITH CHEESE   *Eight* SERVINGS

An unusual and delicious crumb coating makes this dish.

¼ cup grated Parmesan cheese	2 cups fine fresh bread crumbs
¼ cup grated Romano cheese	(2 slices bread crumbled
2 teaspoons salt	into electric blender)
¼ cup minced parsley	2 frying chickens, cut up
½ teaspoon garlic powder	½ pound butter, melted

Combine cheeses, salt, parsley, garlic powder, and bread crumbs. Dip chicken in butter and coat with crumbs. Place in shallow baking pan and bake at 350° F. for 1 hour or until tender.

GO WITHS: Creamed new potatoes, corn on the cob, or zucchini. Maybe baking powder biscuits, too, and a jellied fruit salad.

WINE: California Pinot Chardonnay.

BAKED HERBED BROILER   *Two* SERVINGS

No French chef ever made a small bird look prettier or more inviting!

    1 broiler, split
    ½ cup chopped fresh or frozen parsley
    2 teaspoons chopped fresh or frozen chives
    4 minced green onions, with tops
    ½ cup finely chopped watercress
        Salt, pepper, soft butter
        Melted butter for basting

With a small, sharp-tipped knife, work skin loose from breast of each half of the chicken, starting at cut edge and working toward the wing and leg. Don't loosen all the way to the back!

Mix herbs, ½ teaspoon salt, and about ¼ teaspoon coarse black pepper and blend with 2 tablespoons soft butter. Work this mixture under the loosened skin as evenly as possible. Pin skin to meat at loosened edges with tiny skewers. Rub chicken all over with butter and place bone side up in a roasting pan. Bake 20 minutes at 400° F., basting occasionally with butter. Turn and bake 20 to 30 minutes more, or until tender, basting occasionally with butter. The green herbs show through the skin most attractively and flavor the meat.

GO WITHS: A spiced peach, a mound or bed of fluffy wild rice, and broccoli or asparagus hollandaise will do justice to this handsome bird. Salad might be halved cherry tomatoes in a crisp head of bibb lettuce. With the coffee, a sherbet.

WINE: California Gamay or Rosé.

BAKED CHICKEN, TAVERN STYLE

Eight SERVINGS

The yellow of turmeric is a little surprising, and the blend of flavors is very good.

1 stewing chicken, cooked (page 181), in fairly large pieces
2 cans (3 ozs. each) broiled mushrooms, sliced; or ½
      pound fresh mushrooms, sliced and sautéed in butter.
½ cup chicken fat and butter
½ cup flour
    Salt, pepper
3 cups chicken broth and milk or cream (include liquid from canned mushrooms)
½ teaspoon turmeric
½ teaspoon oregano
½ cup grated sharp Cheddar cheese
3 cups cooked rice

Melt chicken fat and butter; stir in flour, salt, pepper, and turmeric. (Start with 1 teaspoon salt, keep tasting and add more later, if you need to). Stir in broth and milk and cook and stir over low heat until thickened and smooth. Add oregano and half the cheese; stir until cheese melts. Spread rice in buttered shallow baking dish, top with chicken and mushrooms, and pour sauce over them. Sprinkle with rest of cheese. Bake at 350° F. for half an hour.

GO WITHS: Canned creole tomatoes, Boston lettuce salad with pine-apple ring, and creamy fruit salad dressing.

WINE: California Emerald Dry Riesling.

BROILED CHICKEN WITH SOUR CREAM AND WINE SAUCE

Four SERVINGS

Here's what gourmets dream about!

2 broilers (1½ pounds each) split
   Melted butter

Salt
Pepper

SAUCE

  1 small onion, chopped fine
  3 tablespoons butter
  1 clove garlic, mashed with 1 teaspoon salt
 ¼ teaspoon pepper
  2 cups chopped peeled tomatoes
  3 tablespoons flour
 ¼ cup dry white wine
  1 cup sour cream
 ½ cup slivered toasted almonds
  2 tablespoons minced parsley

Brush chicken halves with melted butter. Place skin side down on greased preheated broiler rack, 6 inches from heat. Broil 15 to 20 minutes, season with salt and pepper, turn and broil 10 to 15 minutes longer. Sauté onion in butter for 5 minutes, add garlic, pepper, and tomatoes. Cook slowly for 10 minutes. Stir in flour and blend. Add wine, then cream, a small amount at a time. Add chicken drippings, almonds, and parsley, and heat through. Serve chicken on warm chop plate, sauce in gravy boat.

GO WITHS: Parsley potatoes, artichoke hearts, greens with Roquefort dressing.

WINE: Same one used in sauce, possibly a New York State Rhine wine.

LEMON BARBECUED CHICKEN   *Four* SERVINGS

Pleasingly tart in flavor; delicious!

1 broiler, quartered
Salt, pepper

¼ pound (1 stick) butter

LEMON SAUCE

1 small clove garlic, mashed
½ teaspoon salt
¼ cup salad oil
½ cup lemon juice

2 tablespoons grated onion
½ teaspoon black pepper
½ teaspoon dried thyme

Season chicken with salt and pepper. Melt butter in heavy skillet and brown chicken, skin side down. Turn and brown. Pour combined ingredients for Lemon Sauce over chicken quarters. Cover and cook slowly until tender, about 30 to 40 minutes.

GO WITHS: Boiled new potatoes sprinkled with minced parsley, zucchini squash, a mixed green salad.

WINE: New York State Rhine wine.

CASSEROLED CHICKEN WITH SOUR CREAM   *Four* SERVINGS

This is the kind of recipe everyone demands after tasting the dish!

1 frying chicken, cut up
¼ cup (½ stick) butter
1 teaspoon salt
¼ teaspoon pepper
1 cup sherry or Marsala
1 cup sour cream
1 cup sliced ripe olives

186

Brown chicken all around in butter, season with salt and pepper, and place in a casserole. Add wine to drippings in skillet and mix well. Stir in cream. Pour over chicken, cover with foil, and bake 45 minutes at 350° F. Add olives and bake 15 minutes more.

GO WITHS: Hominy, green beans with water chestnuts, baking powder biscuits.

WINE: California Chablis or Rosé.

△

CHICKEN AND WILD RICE CASSEROLE
Four SERVINGS

Count this among your recipe treasures.

    2 cups cooked wild rice (½ cup raw)
    2 cups cooked sliced or diced light and dark meat of
        chicken
    ½ pound fresh mushrooms, washed and sliced
    ½ green pepper, chopped
    ½ small onion, chopped
    ¼ cup butter
    3 tablespoons flour
    1½ cups stock or milk
    ¼ cup white wine (or more stock)
        Salt, pepper

Divide wild rice among four individual casseroles and cover with the chicken. Sauté mushrooms, green pepper, and onion in butter until soft, add flour, then stir in stock or milk and cook to smooth sauce, stirring constantly. Add wine and salt and pepper to taste. Pour over rice and chicken and place casseroles in a 375° F. oven 15 to 20 minutes, or under the broiler until the sauce bubbles.

GO WITHS: Crumbed broiled tomato halves, hot biscuits, a tray of crisp celery, radishes and olives.

WINE: Lake Erie Islands Rhine wine, or an Ohio Rosé.

CAN-OPENER CASSEROLE   *Eight* SERVINGS

"This is right down my alley!" says a "bride" who has spent thirty-five years looking for shortcuts. "I like to cook by just opening cans."

   3 jars (1 lb. each) chicken or turkey with noodles
   2 cans (6 ozs. each) boned chicken or turkey
   1 small can peas (8½ ozs.) drained
   1 can drained whole kernel corn
   1 can (4 ozs.) mushroom stems and pieces, drained
   1 can (4 ozs.) pimientos, chopped
   1 can (8 ozs.) tomato sauce
1½ cups grated Cheddar cheese
   2 tablespoons chopped onion
   2 tablespoons chopped green pepper
     Salt, pepper

Save out ½ cup cheese and put everything else into a 9x12-inch baking dish. Sprinkle with remaining cheese and bake for an hour at 350° F.

GO WITHS: Perfection Salad (page 224), warm sourdough bread, or French bread.

WINE: With this good "peasant fare," any ordinary California red, white, or rosé wine would be good, possibly a Chablis or Sauterne.

CHICKEN AND VEGETABLE LOAF   *Four to Five* SERVINGS

Delicious and really chickeny in flavor.

2 cups diced cooked chicken
2 cups cooked peas, or peas and carrots
1 cup soft bread crumbs
¼ cup chopped celery
1 cup chicken stock or milk

2 eggs, beaten
1½ teaspoons salt
1 tablespoon minced onion
1 tablespoon minced pimiento
Chicken gravy or mushroom sauce

Combine ingredients, pack lightly into small greased loaf pan (8½x 4¾ inches), and bake at 350° F. for 40 minutes. Turn out on serving platter and serve with chicken gravy made with chicken fat and broth (page 181) or canned chicken gravy.

Make mushroom sauce by adding drained canned sliced mushrooms to gravy or by diluting 1 can mushroom soup with ½ cup milk.

GO WITHS: Potatoes au gratin and a sliced orange and avocado salad.

WINE: California Rosé.

CHICKEN BISCUIT ROLL   *Six* SERVINGS

With a salad, you have a meal!

1¼ cups diced cooked chicken
⅓ cup minced ripe olives
1 teaspoon minced onion
1 tablespoon chopped pimiento
¼ teaspoon paprika

BISCUIT DOUGH

2 cups flour
¾ teaspoon salt
3 teaspoons baking powder

⅓ cup shortening
¾ cup milk

SAUCE: 1 can cream of mushroom soup, ½ cup milk

Mix chicken, olives, onion, pimiento, and paprika together. Sift flour, salt, and baking powder together. Rub in shortening with finger tips, making coarse crumbs, and add milk, stirring quickly until a soft dough is formed. Turn out on a lightly floured board and roll into a rectangle about 8x12 inches. Spread filling over dough evenly. Roll as for jelly roll. Place in a shallow greased pan. Bake at 450° F., for 20 minutes. Heat mushroom soup and milk and pour over roll on a hot platter. Slice to serve.

GO WITHS: Coleslaw with Buttermilk Dressing (page 229), for lunch, or a green vegetable such as green beans, and slaw.

WINE: A California Rosé.

SHORT-CUT CHICKEN CACCIATORE
Four SERVINGS

*Canned spaghetti sauce works as well as the packaged mix,
if you'd rather try that. Then you won't need the tomatoes.*

2 pounds chicken legs or thighs
1 teaspoon seasoned salt
¼ cup oil
1 package spaghetti sauce mix

1 can (3½ cups) Italian tomatoes
¼ cup dry white wine

Sprinkle chicken with seasoned salt and brown well in oil. Remove
from skillet and drain off fat. Blend spaghetti sauce mix and tomatoes
in skillet, add chicken, cover and simmer gently until chicken is tender.
Add wine and cook 15 minutes more. Total time: about 45 minutes of
cooking after the browning.

GO WITHS: Cooked rice or spaghetti and a big tossed greens salad.
Plus crusty rolls or bread.

WINE: Same wine used in recipe, possibly a California dry Semillon.

CHICKEN CALIFORNIA
Six SERVINGS

This dish is made to order for a party.

3 avocados
   Lemon juice, salt
2 tablespoons butter
   or margarine
2 tablespoons flour
1 cup milk

1 cup diced cooked
   or canned chicken
1 cup cooked peas
2 tablespoons minced parsley
   Pepper
   Toasted buttered bread crumbs

Cut each avocado into halves lengthwise and remove seed. Sprinkle with
salt and lemon juice. Melt butter and blend in flour. Add milk and cook

and stir until thickened. Stir in chicken, peas, and parsley. Taste and add extra salt and pepper if needed. Place half shells in shallow pan containing ¼-inch warm water. Fill avocado halves with hot chicken mixture and sprinkle tops with crumbs. Bake in moderately slow oven, 325° F., for 15 minutes. Serve immediately. Don't overheat avocados as this harms their flavor.

Serve with instant mashed potato puffs and Caesar Salad (page 219).

WINE: California Dry Semillon or Sauterne.

X

CHICKEN COUNTRY CAPTAIN   *Four* SERVINGS

The recipe for this popular curried dish is easily doubled, tripled, or even multiplied by four.

1 broiler-fryer chicken, cut up
1 teaspoon salt
¼ teaspoon pepper
¼ cup butter
1 medium onion, chopped
1 small green pepper, chopped
1 clove garlic, crushed
2 teaspoons curry powder

½ teaspoon leaf thyme
1 can (1 lb.) seasoned stewed
   tomatoes
¼ cup currants or seedless raisins
2 cups hot cooked rice
Toasted blanched almonds
Chutney

Sprinkle chicken with salt and pepper and brown well in butter. Remove from skillet and add onion, green pepper, garlic, curry, and thyme to skillet. Cook until onion is tender; don't allow it to brown. Add tomatoes, currants, and chicken. Cook covered 20 to 30 minutes, until chicken is tender. Serve over rice with almonds and chutney.

GO WITHS: Broccoli or whole green beans, a fresh fruit salad, or one of mixed greens with cucumber, radishes, and avocado. And your own homemade bread, from Chapter 3.

WINE: California Zinfandel.

CHICKEN CHOW MEIN   *Four to Five* SERVINGS

This is a very satisfactory dish, you'll find.

1 stewing chicken, cooked (page 181)
½ cup diced green peppers
2 large onions, diced
1 cup diced celery
1 cup sliced mushrooms

½ cup butter or margarine or cooking oil
1 tablespoon cornstarch
5 tablespoons soy sauce
2 hard-cooked eggs
Fried noodles

Cook vegetables in the butter or oil until tender-crisp; do not allow them to brown. Add cornstarch mixed to a paste with a small amount of water. Add soy sauce and about ½ cup of the chicken broth. Cook until smooth and thickened. Add diced chicken (save ½ breast meat for garnish), heat, and serve over fried noodles with narrow strips of chicken breast meat and sliced hard-cooked eggs as garnish.

GO WITHS: Cinnamon Apple Salad (page 230).

WINE: New York, Ohio, or California Rosé.

CHICKEN CREAM HASH   *Six* SERVINGS

You couldn't choose better than this for a Sunday brunch!

2 cups finely diced cooked chicken
1 cup finely diced cooked potatoes
1 tablespoon each: minced onion, minced green pepper, minced parsley
Salt, celery salt, pepper to taste
1 cup whipping cream
¼ cup grated Parmesan cheese

Combine ingredients except cheese, turn into a buttered casserole and top with cheese. Bake at 350° F. for 20 minutes.

GO WITHS: Bacon strips, cantaloupe or honeydew salad, Blueberry Muffins (page 54).

WINE: For a brunch, California or New York State champagne.

CHICKEN DIVAN
Six SERVINGS

*This classical favorite is a delight in most of its many varia-
tions, several of which are suggested here. Of course this is a
perfect combination for turkey, too.*

2½ to 3 pounds chicken breasts, fresh or frozen, cooked;
     or 1 stewing chicken, cooked (page 181), sliced
½ cup diced celery
½ cup butter
½ cup flour
3 cups chicken stock and milk or cream
   Salt, pepper
1 bunch broccoli or 2 packages frozen broccoli spears,
   cooked
   Paprika

Sauté celery in half the butter; set aside. Melt rest of butter, stir in
flour, then add milk and chicken stock gradually, stirring to keep sauce
smooth. Add cooked celery with salt and pepper as needed (depends
upon saltiness of stock). In cooking broccoli, keep it at the tender-crisp,
bright green point. Drain and place it in baking dish with sliced chicken
on top. Pour sauce over combination and sprinkle with paprika. Bake
25 minutes at 375° F.

VARIATIONS

1. Use ¼ cup dry white wine as part of the liquid.
2. Top with 1 cup Buttered Crumbs (page 255), or ½ cup slivered
   toasted almonds.
3. Fold ½ cup mayonnaise and 1 tablespoon lemon juice into sauce;
   add also 1 teaspoon curry powder.
4. Alternate slices of chicken and slices of really smoky ham in the
   casserole.
5. Top with ½ cup or more sharp grated cheese before baking.

GO WITHS: Frozen potato puffs, molded Cranberry and Orange Salad
(page 232), homemade Whole Wheat Bread (page 47).

WINE: California Grey Riesling.

CHICKEN PIE   Six SERVINGS

Here's an old-fashioned treat in a new-fashioned version.

1 stewing chicken, cooked (page 181), diced
2 cups chicken sauce or gravy (page 181)
  Dash of mace
1 package (10 ozs.) frozen peas
1 cup sliced carrots, cooked barely tender
  Salt, pepper as needed
  Pie crust mix for 1 crust

Heat together the chicken, sauce, seasonings, and vegetables. Place in glass casserole or baking dish and top with rolled pastry cut to fit. Gash pastry for escape of steam. Bake at 450° F. for 20 minutes or until crust is browned and filling bubbly.

GO WITHS: Fresh pear salad or molded fruit salad.

WINE: California Sylvaner or Riesling.

X

CHICKEN KIEV   Six SERVINGS

This classic dish is not too difficult, but you must be careful that the packages of chicken don't leak any of their butter.

3 large chicken breasts, boned
  Salt, pepper
1 stick butter
1 tablespoon chopped chives
1 tablespoon lemon juice
½ teaspoon rosemary
  Flour
2 eggs, slightly beaten
2 tablespoons water
1 cup fine dry bread crumbs

194

Pound chicken between pieces of wax paper until as thin as possible. Avoid breaking skin or flesh. Split each breast lengthwise. Season with salt and pepper.

Cream the butter and work in chives, lemon juice, and rosemary. Shape into six rolls and place on foil in the freezer to firm. Lay one on each chicken portion and fold outer edges in over butter. Then roll tightly crosswise. Dredge in flour. Dip in egg, then in crumbs; repeat the egg and crumbs and chill 1 hour. Fry in deep fat heated to 350° F. for 10 minutes. Serve at once.

Go WITHS: Au gratin potatoes, peas or green beans, tossed salad.

WINE: California Pinot Chardonnay.

CHICKEN SHORTCAKE   *Four* SERVINGS

Cooked chicken giblets are good fixed this way.

- ¼ cup chopped celery
- ¼ cup chopped green pepper
- 1 tablespoon chopped onion
- 2 tablespoons butter
- 1 can condensed cream of chicken or cream of mushroom soup
- ⅓ cup milk
- ¼ cup chopped pimiento
- 1 cup cooked diced chicken or turkey
- 4 large baking powder biscuits or cornbread squares, split and buttered

Sauté the celery, green pepper, and onion in butter until soft. Add soup and milk. Heat and stir to blend. Add chicken and pimiento. Simmer 10 minutes and serve between and over tops of biscuits.

Go WITHS: Fresh, frozen, or canned asparagus spears; sliced orange and sweet red onion salad.

WINE: California Chablis.

CHICKEN-RICE LOAF   *Twelve* SERVINGS

There's lots of chicken flavor in this custardy loaf.

1 stewing chicken (page 181), diced fine
2 cups fresh soft bread crumbs
1 cup cooked rice

1½ teaspoons salt
3 cups milk and broth
4 eggs, well beaten

Mix chicken with crumbs, rice, salt, and milk. Fold in eggs and pour into a well-greased large loaf pan (about 9x5 inches). Bake at 350° F. for 1 hour and 15 minutes. Unmold on a hot platter (let loaf stand 10 minutes in pan first), and serve with chicken gravy or mushroom sauce.
    Loaf may be baked in a 9x12-inch pan and cut in squares.

GO WITHS: French Beets (page 261), minted peas and a sliced cucumber and tomato salad.

WINE: California Johannisberg Riesling.

CHICKEN ROSÉ WITH HERBS   *Four* SERVINGS

It's delicious, and couldn't be easier!

4 meaty breast pieces of chicken (2 split breasts)
¼ teaspoon garlic salt
¼ teaspoon paprika
1 tablespoon flour
3 tablespoons butter and oil

¼ teaspoon dried rosemary
¼ teaspoon dried basil
1 tablespoon instant onion
½ cup California Rosé wine
½ cup sour cream

Dredge chicken with salt, paprika, and flour, and brown on both sides in hot butter and oil. Sprinkle with herbs, add wine and onion, cover and cook slowly until tender, about 25 minutes. Skim any excess fat from pan liquid and thicken if you like with 1½ teaspoons cornstarch mixed with 1 tablespoon water. Stir in sour cream.

GO WITHS: Glazed young carrots, French Peas (page 270), bakery hard rolls.

WINE: More of the same Rosé.

CHICKEN SUPERBA WITH PINEAPPLE

Six SERVINGS

An old favorite is modernized in this handsome platter.

6 half-breasts chicken or 6 portions chicken parts
Seasoned flour (page 182)
1 onion, chopped
¼ cup oil
6 slices canned pineapple
Juice from pineapple
1 can chicken gravy or 1 packet prepared as directed
1½ cups finely cut or chopped cooked ham
2 tablespoons butter
4 cups cooked rice
1 avocado, sliced, for garnish

Shake chicken pieces in a bag with seasoned flour. Sauté onion until transparent in oil, then skim from pan and brown chicken in oil. Return onion, add ½ cup pineapple juice, cover and simmer until chicken is tender, about 30 minutes. Remove from pan and keep warm. Add the chicken gravy to the pan, and a little more of the pineapple juice, if you wish.

Sauté ham in butter and add to hot rice. Sauté pineapple rings in same butter. Place ham-rice in center of a hot platter and surround with pineapple slices topped with chicken. Garnish with avocado and serve with the hot chicken gravy.

Go WITHS: Tray of crisp relishes, basket of warm rolls.

WINE: New York State Delaware or Niagara.

CHICKEN SPAGHETTI
Eight SERVINGS

Looking for an easy casserole for company?

    1 stewing chicken, cooked (page 181), diced
    2 tablespoons chicken fat or butter
    2 tablespoons flour
    2 cups chicken broth
    1 teaspoon poultry seasoning
    ½ pound Cheddar cheese, grated
    1 pound fresh mushrooms, sliced and sautéed in ¼ cup
        butter
    1 package (8 ozs.) spaghetti, cooked

Melt chicken fat or butter, add flour and blend, then add broth and seasoning (taste and add salt and pepper if you need it). Cook to a smooth, thin sauce. Add cheese, mushrooms, spaghetti and chicken, mix well, place in buttered casserole, and bake at 350° F. for 30 minutes. If you like, reserve half the cheese for the top of the dish.

GO WITHS: Asparagus with Sour Cream (page 257), cherry tomatoes served in a bowl with ripe olives and green onions.

WINE: California Gamay or Gamay Rosé.

CHICKEN TAMALE LOAF
Eight to Ten SERVINGS

This is a perfect dish for an informal party.

    1 4-to-5-pound stewing chicken,
        simmered tender (page
        181)
    1 cup chopped onion
    1 minced clove garlic
    ½ cup butter or margarine
    3½ cups canned tomatoes
        (No. 2½ can)
    1 can (2 cups) whole kernel
        corn

    1½ teaspoons salt
    1 teaspoon black pepper
        Dash cayenne pepper
    1 cup ripe olives
    3 eggs
    1¾ cups yellow corn meal
    1 cup milk
    1 cup grated American cheese

Remove skin and bones of chicken, leaving meat in large pieces. Sauté onion and garlic in butter 5 minutes. Add tomatoes, corn, salt, pepper, cayenne, and 1 cup broth from chicken, and simmer 20 to 30 minutes. Cut olives from pits in large pieces. Beat eggs lightly and blend in corn meal and milk. Stir olives, chicken, and corn meal mixture into vegetable mixture. Turn into large baking dish. Bake at 325° F. 1 hour, sprinkling top with cheese at the halfway point.

GO WITHS: A big crisp salad of mixed greens with onion, avocado, and orange and grapefruit sections.

WINE: California Gamay or Rosé.

CHINESE CHICKEN   *Six* SERVINGS

You might put soy sauce on the table for those who want to add a dash.

1 can (9 ozs.) pineapple tidbits drained	2 cups cooked chicken or turkey diced
3 tablespoons butter	½ cup chopped celery
¼ cup flour	½ cup chopped green pepper
1 teaspoon salt	3 cups cooked rice
1½ cups clear chicken broth	¼ cup slivered toasted almonds Stuffed olives

Sauté pineapple in butter for 5 minutes. Add flour and salt and blend. Add chicken broth and cook, stirring constantly, until thick and smooth. Add chicken, celery, and green pepper; cook slowly for 10 minutes. Spoon around a mound of fluffy rice and sprinkle almonds over the dish. Garnish with sliced olives.

GO WITHS: Cantaloupe and honeydew slices on leaf lettuce with a fruit salad dressing (bottled) and a sprinkle of diced candied ginger; refrigerated buttermilk biscuits.

WINE: California Riesling.

CREAMED CHICKEN AND HAM   *Six* SERVINGS

A ladies' luncheon favorite, this could also be a family treat.

4 tablespoons butter or
    margarine
5 tablespoons flour
1½ cups hot chicken stock
1 cup cream
2 hard-cooked egg yolks, mashed
1 cup diced cooked ham

1½ cups cubed cooked chicken
⅓ cup sliced stuffed olives
¼ teaspoon Worcestershire
    sauce
1 teaspoon salt
¼ teaspoon paprika

Melt butter in a saucepan, add flour, and stir until smooth. Add hot chicken stock mixed with cream and cook, stirring constantly, until smooth. Add remaining ingredients and heat through. Serve on toast, hot biscuits, waffles, or in patty shells.

GO WITHS: Watermelon pickles, broccoli, more of the bread it's served on.

WINE: California Chenin Blanc or Pinot Blanc.

CRISP-CRUSTED CHICKEN WINGS   *Three* SERVINGS

We forget how good and how meaty wings can be!

1 pound chicken wings, fresh or frozen
1 egg
½ cup flour
1 teaspoon salt
⅛ teaspoon pepper
⅓ cup milk
1 cup fine bread crumbs
    Vegetable shortening for frying

Beat together egg, flour, salt, pepper, and milk. Dip chicken in batter and roll in crumbs. Brown in deep fat at 350° F. for 2 minutes. Place chicken in shallow pan and bake in moderately slow oven, 325° F., for 25 minutes or until tender.

GO WITHS: Scalloped Potatoes, (page 274), frozen baby peas in butter sauce, mixed greens salad.

WINE: California Johannisberg Riesling.

◼

OVEN-FRIED DRUMSTICKS   *Four* SERVINGS

This is an excellent method for any of the chicken parts; drumsticks are more fun for the younger crowd.

  8 chicken drumsticks or drumsticks and thighs
½ cup pancake mix
  1 teaspoon salt
¼ teaspoon pepper
  1 stick butter, melted in pan
  2 cups milk for gravy

Shake pieces of chicken in a paper bag with pancake mix, salt and pepper. Melt butter in pan about 9x13 inches and place chicken pieces in pan, turning each over to coat it with butter. Bake at 375° F. for 45 minutes or until tender and brown.

To make gravy, remove chicken to a hot platter, add any flour mixture left in the bag to the pan, stir smooth and add milk gradually. Cook and stir until gravy is thickened. Add more salt and pepper if you need it.

Chicken cooked this way may be sprinkled with herbs or basted with barbecue sauce as variations.

GO WITHS: Mashed or baked potatoes, succotash, sliced tomato and cucumber salad.

WINE: California mountain white.

HUNGARIAN CHICKEN PAPRIKA

Four or Five SERVINGS

Don't worry about the large amount of paprika. It's necessary!

1 fryer, about 3½ pounds, cut up
2 large onions, diced
2 tablespoons oil
2 tablespoons paprika
2 green peppers, cut up
6 medium fresh tomatoes, skinned and cut up
1 clove garlic, minced
  Salt
1 cup sour cream

Cook onions gently in oil until yellow, add paprika and stir well. Add green pepper and tomatoes. Place chicken on vegetables, season with salt, cover pot, and cook over low heat 1½ hours. Stir in sour cream and heat thoroughly.

Go WITHS: Mashed potatoes (instant?), Stir-and-Roll Biscuits (page 53), stuffed prune salad.

WINE: New York State Rosé.

CRUSTY DEVILED CHICKEN

Six or Eight SERVINGS

Poultry seasoning is for the chicken as well as its stuffing.

2 frying chickens, cut up
2 teaspoons poultry seasoning
½ cup butter or margarine
2 teaspoons prepared mustard
1 teaspoon salt

Dash of pepper
2 teaspoons vinegar
1 teaspoon paprika
1 cup fine bread crumbs
2 tablespoons butter

Place chicken in shallow baking pan, sprinkle with poultry seasoning, and set under broiler as far from heat as possible for 10 minutes. Cream the ½-cup butter with the mustard, salt, pepper, vinegar, and paprika. Rub this mixture over the chicken. Melt the 2 tablespoons butter and mix with the cup of crumbs; sprinkle over chicken. Bake for 1 hour in 350° F. oven, basting often with the butter that melts and runs off. Crumbs should be browned and chicken tender.

GO WITHS: Potatoes hashed in cream, glazed carrots, applesauce.

WINE: New York State Delaware or Niagara.

△

CHICKEN LIVERS, CHINESE STYLE

Four SERVINGS

Here's an attractive and interesting dish, but don't overcook the livers!

2 medium green peppers, cut in sixths
4 slices canned or fresh pine-apple, in chunks
2 tablespoons oil or drippings
1 pound chicken livers
½ teaspoon salt

Dash of pepper
1 cup chicken broth or bouillon
2 tablespoons cornstarch
2 teaspoons soy sauce
½ cup wine vinegar
½ cup sugar

Sauté green peppers and pineapple in oil until peppers are slightly soft, but still a little crunchy. Don't allow them to brown. Remove from pan and add livers, with salt and pepper. Add a little more oil if necessary. When livers are lightly browned and tender, remove to hot platter. Mix cornstarch to a paste with a little of the broth, add remaining broth, soy sauce, vinegar, and sugar, and add to skillet in which livers were browned. Cook and stir until sauce thickens and is clear. Add peppers and pineapple. Heat thoroughly and pour over livers. Serve with steamed rice or spaghetti or noodles.

GO WITHS: Wheat germ muffins, Chinese Bean Salad (page 222).

WINE: California Grenache Rosé.

CHICKEN LIVERS EN BROCHETTE

Four SERVINGS

So easy, so good!

1 dozen chicken livers
1 dozen caps from large mushrooms
¼ cup melted butter
   Sherry or a dry red wine
   Fine chopped parsley
   Salt, pepper

Wash livers and drain dry. Cut in half and thread onto skewers (small ones), alternately with mushroom caps. Brush with the melted butter and sprinkle with the wine and parsley. Broil until tender, turning several times. This takes only about 15 minutes. As soon as they are heated through, both livers and mushrooms have cooked sufficiently. Sprinkle with salt and pepper and serve.

LILY GILDING: String green pepper squares or pineapple chunks or small onions or half-cooked bacon on the skewers with the livers.

GO WITHS: When these aren't cocktail party fare, put them on rice or wild rice and garnish the plates with broiled tomato halves.

WINE: California Claret.

CHICKEN ONIONDINE

Four to Six SERVINGS

Onion soup mix is probably the most versatile of the shortcut seasoners. This dish is a fine example of the magic it works.

2 pounds chicken parts, fresh or frozen and thawed
2 tablespoons oil
1 can or packet onion dry soup mix
3 tablespoons flour
1½ cups water
½ cup sour cream

Brown chicken in skillet in oil and pour off oil. Add soup mix and flour; gradually stir in water. Cover and cook gently over low heat until chicken is tender, stirring now and then. Blend in sour cream and heat gently. Add a little more water if needed.

GO WITHS: Parsleyed noodles, baked acorn squash, Mint Julep Salad (page 234).

WINE: A New York State or California claret.

TROPICAL CHICKEN IN PINEAPPLE SHELLS

Six SERVINGS

This dish is a beauty!

    2 cups cubed white meat (or white and dark) of chicken
    2 cups Medium White Sauce (page 254)
    ½ cup chopped canned or cooked mushrooms
    ¼ cup chopped green pepper
    ¼ cup chopped almonds
    1 teaspoon Worcestershire sauce
      Dash each: black pepper, nutmeg
    ½ cup finely chopped fresh pineapple
      Parmesan cheese
      Paprika
      Sliced avocado
    3 medium pineapples, halved lengthwise

Combine chicken and sauce in saucepan. Add mushrooms, green pepper, almonds. Add seasonings. Stir and simmer over low heat for 15 minutes. If mixture becomes too stiff, add a little chicken stock. With grapefruit knife, cut out centers of pineapples. Save fruit not used for fruit salad or dessert. Leave stems on pineapple, and about ½ inch of shell. Fill with chicken and pineapple mixture, sprinkle with cheese, then paprika, and place in broiler as far as possible from heat. Broil about 10 minutes with a piece of aluminum foil over pineapple stems to keep them from browning. Garnish with sliced avocado sprinkled with paprika, and serve.

GO WITHS: Noodles, asparagus.

WINE: New York State Pink champagne.

PAELLA WITH FROZEN FOODS

Ten to Twelve SERVINGS

This party dish would take so much time as to be a nuisance, if it weren't for having the ingredients on hand in the freezer. It's a Spanish classic, or rather an American version of one. See page 92 for another Paella.

1 package (1 lb.) frozen chicken drumsticks
1 package (1 lb.) frozen chicken thighs
1 teaspoon salt
1/4 teaspoon pepper
1/2 teaspoon oregano
1/4 cup olive oil
1/2 cup chopped onion
1/2 cup chopped green pepper
1 clove garlic, minced
1 jar (4 ozs.) pimiento, cut in strips

2 cups uncooked rice
1 can (1 lb. 4 ozs.) tomatoes
1/4 teaspoon ground saffron
1 can (8 ozs.) clam broth
2 cups chicken broth or bouillon
1/2 cup (3 ozs.) thinly sliced chorizos (Spanish sausage) or other peppery sausage
1 package (1 lb.) frozen shelled jumbo shrimps
1 package (10 ozs.) frozen peas

Thaw chicken, season with salt, pepper, and oregano and brown in hot olive oil in heatproof casserole with cover. Remove chicken. Add onion, green pepper, garlic, and pimiento. Cook until onion is soft. Add rice, stirring to coat evenly with oil. Add tomatoes, saffron, clam broth, chicken broth, then chicken and sausage. Bring mixture to boil, cover, lower heat, and cook 15 minutes. Meanwhile, cook shrimps according to package directions and add with frozen peas to casserole. Mix lightly and cook 10 minutes.

The list of ingredients is long, but the method is easy. Don't be discouraged by the look of the recipe—the dish is delish!

GO WITHS: Crusty bread and a green salad are all you need.

WINE: California Pinot Noir.

△

LITTLE CHICKEN AND OYSTER PIES

Six SERVINGS

Here's a recipe for a very tasty supper dish, and it divides neatly if there are only three of you.

½ cup flour
2 cans cream of chicken soup
2 cups chicken stock and oyster liquor
2 cups sliced cooked or canned chicken or turkey
2 cups oysters (pick them over for bits of shell)
1 tablespoon minced parsley
  Pie crust mix

Blend flour with soup; add stock, chicken, oysters, and parsley. Heat to bubbling and place in individual casseroles. Top with rounds of pastry gashed to let out steam. Bake at 450° F. for 20 minutes.

GO WITHS: Green beans or corn on the cob, and a pickled peach for each.

WINE: California Chablis.

QUICK CHICKEN FOR LUNCH

Four SERVINGS

If your pantry shelf is stocked with the essentials, you're all set, any time!

1 can cream of chicken soup
1 can chicken rice soup
1 can (6 ozs.) evaporated milk
1 can (4 ozs.) Chinese noodles
1 jar (5½ ozs.) chicken, diced
½ cup crumbled potato chips

Don't dilute the soups or milk. Put everything together into a buttered casserole, excepting the chips, which go on top. Bake at 350° F. for 30 minutes.

GO WITHS: Leaf lettuce and whole wheat bread sandwiches, and milk. Carrot sticks, too. Dessert? How about baked apples?

WINE: Any Rosé.

SESAME SEED CHICKEN   *Four or Five* SERVINGS

*The little bit of crunch is interesting, and so is the subtle
wine flavor.*

    1 fryer (3–3½ lbs.) in serving pieces
      Flour coating (see below)
  ¼ cup oil
    1 tablespoon instant onion
  ½ cup dry white wine
    1 tablespoon sesame seeds

Put ⅓ cup flour, 1 teaspoon salt, 1 teaspoon paprika, and ¼ teaspoon
pepper into a bag and shake chicken pieces in it to coat well. Brown in
oil; add onion and wine and sprinkle with sesame seeds. Cover and bake
at 350° F. about 30 minutes.

GO WITHS: Baked or candied sweet potatoes, baby lima beans, Waldorf
Salad (page 239).

WINE: Grenache Rosé (use it for chicken also).

SKILLET CHICKEN WITH   *Four* SERVINGS
GREEN BEANS

Everything but the salad is in the skillet!

    8 pieces chicken, or a cut-up broiler-fryer
  ¼ cup butter or margarine or bacon drippings
    1 large sliced onion
    1 can condensed cream of celery soup
  ¼ cup water, broth, or white table wine
    1 cup diced potatoes
  ½ teaspoon salt
      Dash pepper, dash poultry seasoning
    1 package frozen cut green beans, thawed

Brown the chicken in the butter; add onion and brown lightly. Add soup, water, potatoes, seasonings. Cover and cook over low heat 20 minutes; stir occasionally. Add green beans and cook 20 minutes more or until chicken is tender.

Of course you might use cream of chicken or cream of mushroom soup for this.

Go withs: Sliced tomatoes on head lettuce, and Casserole Bread (page 48).

Wine: California Gewürztraminer.

ROCK CORNISH HENS WITH RED CURRANT GLAZE (Rotisserie Roasted)

Four SERVINGS

If you'd rather, bake them in a 400° F. oven for 40 minutes or so.

4 Rock Cornish hens, about 1 pound each
Salt, pepper, butter

Red Currant Glaze:
½ cup red currant jelly

2 tablespoons lemon juice
1 tablespoon cornstarch
¼ cup red wine vinegar
1 teaspoon salt
3 whole cloves

Rinse birds (thaw first, if frozen) and season inside with salt and pepper. Place on spit of rotisserie. Tie wing tips and legs if necessary. Brush with melted butter. Cook over well-burned-down coals or in electric rotisserie at even heat of about 375°–400° F. for 30 minutes. Brush with glaze and let turn for 15 minutes more, or until tender. Brush several times with the glaze.

To make glaze, melt 1 tablespoon butter, add jelly and lemon juice and heat. Make paste of cornstarch and vinegar. Add with salt and cloves. Cook and stir for 5 minutes.

Go withs: Wild rice or brown rice, Brussels sprouts, sliced ripe tomatoes.

Wine: California Rosé or Cabernet Sauvignon.

ROCK CORNISH HENS WITH WILD RICE AND SOUR CREAM MUSHROOM SAUCE

Eight SERVINGS

For a very special occasion, here is a very special bird.

8 frozen rock cornish hens, thawed
Melted butter for basting birds

STUFFING:

8 green onions with tops, sliced thin
1½ pounds fresh mushrooms, coarsely chopped
6 tablespoons butter (¾ stick)
1 teaspoon sage
¼ cup minced parsley
1½ cups wild rice or wild and brown rice
4 cups chicken broth

½ cup dry white wine
1½ teaspoons salt
¼ teaspoon pepper

SAUCE:

⅓ cup butter
⅓ cup flour
1½ teaspoons paprika
1 cup dry white wine
1¼ cups chicken broth
1½ cups sour cream

Remove giblets from birds. Wash and dry hens; chop giblets. To prepare stuffing, cook onions and mushrooms 5 minutes in butter, remove from pan and add sage, parsley, rice, broth, wine, salt, pepper, chopped giblets and necks to pan. Simmer 45 minutes; discard necks. Add half the mushrooms and onions to the rice mixture and stuff birds. Truss and place in shallow pan. Roast at 375° F. for 1 hour, basting several times with melted butter.

To prepare sauce, melt butter, blend in flour, paprika, wine, broth, and remaining mushrooms and onions. Cook and stir until thickened and smooth. Stir in sour cream and heat through. Season if necessary.

GO WITHS: Fresh asparagus, green salad.

WINE: California Pinot Chardonnay.

DUCK HAWAIIAN STYLE   *Four* SERVINGS

Tantalizing flavor!

1 4-pound duck, quartered
¼ cup salad oil
1 tablespoon cornstarch
½ teaspoon salt
1 teaspoon soy sauce
½ teaspoon ginger
½ teaspoon onion salt
1½ teaspoons curry powder

1 cup chicken broth
1 cup pineapple juice
⅔ cup water
1 cup pineapple cubes or wedges
1 bunch green onions cut in 1-inch pieces (tops, too)

Brown duck in oil. Place in greased baking pan or casserole. Mix cornstarch and seasonings and make into a paste with a little chicken broth. Add remaining ingredients except onions. Pour over duck. Cover and bake 1½ to 2 hours at 325° F. Ten minutes before duck is done, sprinkle onions on top.

GO WITHS: Rice, Asparagus Salad (page 220).

WINE: California Pinot Noir.

DUCK WITH ORANGE SAUCE   *Four* SERVINGS

This duck is almost as "gourmet" as anything served in Paris!

4 to 5 pound duckling, ready to cook
Salt, pepper
½ cup sugar
1 tablespoon lemon juice
1 cup orange juice
¼ cup orange liqueur (Cointreau or Grand Marnier)
⅓ cup finely shredded orange peel (outer part only)

Salt and pepper the duckling inside and out and roast uncovered at 325° F. for about 2 hours. Remove to a hot platter. Pour fat from roasting pan. Combine sugar and lemon juice in a heavy pan and let sugar melt and just start to caramelize. You should be stirring all this time. Add orange juice, liqueur, and rind. Blend. Add to juices in roasting pan and bring to a boil. Stir well and pour over duck.

Duck may be stuffed with orange slices for roasting. Sauce may be thickened by stirring in 1 tablespoon cornstarch blended with 2 tablespoons orange juice or cold water, and simmering for 5 minutes.

GO WITHS: Wild rice cooked in stock made from giblets and neck, Brussels Sprouts with Grapes (page 262), endive salad, warm rolls.

WINE: California Pinot Noir.

PREPARING A FROZEN TURKEY

Frozen birds need time to thaw, and should be thawed in the refrigerator. If you are caught on a holiday with a bird only partly thawed, there's nothing to do but start the cooking and let it proceed to the point where you can get the neck and giblets out of the bird's interior and replace them with stuffing. The bigger the turkey, the longer the time needed for thawing. Sometimes it takes several days.

If you buy a frozen stuffed turkey, follow directions which come with the bird. These turkeys are cooked from the frozen state and usually are cooked in a covered roaster. That was Grandma's method. (By the way, don't listen to Grandma if she insists you need all day to cook turkey. Modern birds are much more tender than the kind she cooked for so many years!)

If you start the cooking with a very cold bird, you'll need more time than the schedule allows. Here you'll have to use some judgment.

There are differences in breed of turkey and in thickness of meat which cause some variations. It is better to allow a little leeway when you set the time of a Thanksgiving dinner.

A "setting" period of 20 minutes after roasting helps the meat to become firmer and easier to carve. Ask your carver to slice the meat very thin, for it will be more tasty and tender sliced thin than thick.

HOW TO ROAST A TURKEY

There's nothing to it. Preheat your oven to 325° F. Rinse turkey with cold water, drain and pat dry. Sprinkle inside with salt. Stuff neck and body cavities with your own or a prepared stuffing. Fasten neck skin to back with a steel skewer, and push drumsticks under the band of skin at the tail to hold stuffing in and make a compact bird. If there's no skin band, tie the legs together and then to the tail.

Place the turkey on a rack in a shallow roasting pan, breast side up. Brush with butter or oil. Insert roast meat thermometer in the inside thigh muscle or the thickest part of the breast meat. (Some modern turkeys come with their own built-in plastic thermometers; a red tip pops out to indicate when the turkey is done.) The thermometer shouldn't touch bone or you won't get an accurate reading. Roast to 185° F., or 165° F. if you've lodged the thermometer in the center of the stuffing, which is permissible.

Roast the turkey, brushing with butter or pan drippings occasionally, according to the following schedule:

6– 8 pound turkey	2–2½ hours
8–12 pound turkey	2½–3 hours
12–16 pound turkey	3–3¾ hours
16–20 pound turkey	3¾–4½ hours
20–24 pound turkey	4½–5 hours

Put a loose tent of foil over the bird when two-thirds cooked to prevent overbrowning. Press the thickest part of the drumstick with mitted hands to double check for doneness. The meat should feel soft.

Turkey and stuffing should be refrigerated promptly after the meal is over, and it is better to remove the stuffing from the body cavity, the better to cool it promptly. Stuffing is the greatest little culture center for spoilage bacteria you ever saw!

If you are going to freeze turkey leftovers, cool them, wrap well in meal-size packages and freeze promptly. Don't wait for two days and THEN decide to freeze the meat.

At the end of five days, you've had that turkey long enough. Don't push your luck!

TURKEY BONE SOUP

When you take the meat from the bones to chill or freeze it, break up the bones and simmer them in a couple of quarts of water, with the scraps of meat and skin, a stalk or two of celery, some salt, pepper, a bay leaf, and an onion or two. You'll have stock for sauces for leftover turkey dishes, and the base for a fine soup, after you've discarded the bones and strained the broth. You can strengthen the flavor of the soup by boiling it down to concentrate it, or by adding some chicken stock base, or bouillon cubes. Then you can cook all kinds of cut-up vegetables and rice and barley in the soup; delicious!

GOOD TURKEY GRAVY   *One* QUART

*The principles are the same as for any good gravy—get all
the rich brown flavor that clings to the roasting pan, and use
the basic Medium White Sauce formula: 2 tablespoons fat, 2
tablespoons flour to 1 cup of liquid—in this case, broth.*

    ½ cup fat drippings from roast turkey
    ½ cup flour
    4 cups turkey stock (from cooking giblets and neck), or
        water
    Salt, pepper

When your turkey is roasted and has been transferred to the hot platter
to await the carver, pour off the fat from the roasting pan, leaving all
the good brown goo in the bottom. Measure back into the pan your ½
cup fat, add the flour, and stir to blend. Let the flour brown a little over
low heat. Then add the stock or water. Stir constantly over moderate
heat until uniformly thickened and smooth. Season to taste with salt
and pepper. If the gravy lacks flavor, add a teaspoonful of chicken base,
or a bouillon cube or two. Chopped or ground giblets can be added to
the gravy. Also a tablespoon or two of wine, if you like wine-flavored
gravy. Any good dry red or white table wine will do.

If you like thinner gravy, just add a little more broth.

Turkey cream gravy is made with milk instead of stock or water.

QUICK MODERN TURKEY STUFFING

This amount will stuff an 18- to 20-pound bird.

    3 packages (8 ozs. each) herb stuffing
    3 cups water or lightly seasoned stock
    ½ pound (2 sticks) butter, melted
    1 can (8 ozs.) sliced mushrooms
    1½ cups chopped walnuts
    2 cups chopped celery

Mix stuffing in large bowl with water and remaining ingredients. Toss
lightly to mix well.

214

WILD AND WHITE RICE STUFFING

A combination of the two kinds of rice is less expensive than wild rice alone, and many persons prefer it. This amount will stuff a ten- to twelve-pound turkey.

3 cups cooked wild rice (1 cup raw)
2 cups cooked white rice (½ cup raw)
2 cups chopped celery with tops
½ cup chopped onion
½ pound fresh mushrooms, sliced

½ cup butter
2 teaspoons sage
1 teaspoon salt
1 teaspoon poultry seasoning
1 tablespoon grated lemon peel
2 eggs, beaten

Combine rices in large bowl. Sauté vegetables in butter until tender but browned. Add to rice with seasonings. Stir in eggs. Toss to mix well.

TURKEY AND NOODLES CASSEROLE   *Six to Eight* SERVINGS

Just two cups of the frozen diced leftover turkey will do it!

1 package (7 or 8 ozs.) egg noodles
1 onion, chopped
¼ green pepper, chopped
½ pound fresh mushrooms, sliced (or use 1 cup canned or reconstituted freeze-dried)
3 tablespoons butter
1 can condensed tomato soup
1 teaspoon salt
1 tall can (12 ozs.) evaporated milk
2 cups cooked diced turkey or chicken

Cook noodles in 2 quarts boiling salted water with 1 tablespoon salt until tender; drain. Sauté onion, green pepper, and mushrooms in the butter until tender but not brown. Add soup, salt, evaporated milk. Arrange alternate layers of noodles and turkey in a casserole and pour soup mixture over it. Bake an hour at 350° F.

LILY-GILDING: Top with ½ cup grated Parmesan or Cheddar cheese before baking.

GO WITHS: A big mixed salad with radishes, cucumbers, green beans, grated carrot, two or three leafy greens, Italian dressing. Crusty rolls.

WINE: California or New York State Rosé.

ROTISSERIE BARBECUED TURKEY ROLL

This is a handsome, easy-to-cook roast, better than the whole bird for spit-cooking, and easier to slice. You can figure on three to four servings per pound.

3 to 9 pound boneless turkey roll
  Salt, pepper, if needed
  Butter
  Bottled barbecue sauce

Thaw turkey roll in its wrapper. It may take a day or two in the refrigerator. If you have to hurry it, thaw under cool running water. Remove wrapper and leave string in place. If roast is not pre-seasoned, rub with salt and pepper. Insert the spit rod through the center of the roll and secure the skewers firmly in the ends. Fasten tightly and test the balance. Place spit on rotisserie, brush roll with butter and barbecue sauce, and when your fire is right, start the motor. A charcoal fire should be started 45 minutes before you begin to cook in order for the coals to burn down to a gray-ashed exterior.

Baste occasionally with barbecue sauce during cooking. A 3-to-5-pound roll takes about 2 hours or a little over; a 5-to-7-pound roll takes 2 to 3 hours; and a 7-to-9-pound roll requires up to 3½ hours.

WINE: California Claret or mountain red.

△

SALADS

THE MORE kinds the better when you tuck greens into the salad bowl. Lettuce isn't just lettuce any more. We have head lettuce, leaf lettuce, Boston lettuce with its very tender, soft leaves, romaine and others, including the very popular Bibb or limestone lettuce, which makes the finest salads in many of our expensive restaurants. This little beauty is green-green, grows in succulent flower-like heads, and is crisp yet very tender. It makes a beautiful salad all by itself. The leaves are so small that they needn't be broken up—they shouldn't be broken up, as a matter of fact, for this kind of lettuce wilts quickly when torn.

Chicory, often called curly endive, is a popular salad green because of its attractive ruffly edges and its bitter taste, so good in a mixture of greens. The tenderest leaves are at the heart of the cluster, the pale yellow ones. But the greener, coarser leaves are more laden with vitamins. Use both in a salad when you can, cutting the green chicory into bite-size or fork-size pieces.

Escarole is one of the coarser salad greens, good as a cooked vegetable as well as for salads. Break or cut it fairly small for the bowl of greenery.

Many other greens are delightful in mixtures. Watercress has deep color, crispness, and peppery flavor, but add it last, as its leaves shrivel quickly under dressing.

Chinese cabbage, ordinary green and red cabbage, celery tops, mustard greens, parsley, and dandelion all have a place in salads, and we mustn't forget spinach, which may be broken or shredded into the bowl, and makes an excellent wilted salad with Hot Bacon Dressing (page 252) poured over it.

SALAD DRESSINGS

The packet and bottle dressings now available for use on salads are so various and so good that few modern cooks make anything more than a basic French dressing any more; many never make a dressing. One of the best dressings of all is the oil, vinegar, and herb mixture known as "Italian" dressing, although it is as French as Italian. (A French friend complains that she must always ask for Italian dressing in a restaurant to avoid getting a "thick red sauce" unknown in France that often masquerades as French in the United States.) If one asks for an oil and vinegar dressing, this problem can usually be avoided.

The oil and vinegar dressing or basic French dressing is the most satisfactory one for general use. And there are many variations. One may add Roquefort or blue cheese, or garlic or chili sauce to vary it. The other basic dressing is a good mayonnaise, readily available in the jar under several well-known commercial labels. There is also "salad dressing," which is more or less the equivalent of the old-fashioned cooked dressing. It is not a true mayonnaise, mayonnaise being an emulsion of oil with vinegar or lemon juice, but it is less expensive, and in mixed salads such as potato, meat, fish or chicken, sometimes serves almost as well. For your very best salads, however, I would recommend mayonnaise rather than "salad dressing."

SEASONINGS

Greens for salad should be crisp and dry, and I suggest drying them on paper towels or tea towels after washing. If the leaves are wet, dressing does not adhere properly, and becomes diluted. I would recommend that you keep on hand an herb mixture known as "salad herbs," frozen or freeze-dried chives, parsley and green pepper, as well as onion and garlic salt or powder, and instant onion. These handy salad seasoners can usually benefit a bowl of greens. Another good salad helper is the can of Parmesan cheese. Shake it over a mixture of greens after adding the dressing, now and then.

And we must not forget pepper. Coarse black pepper, the coarser the better, is a necessity for good salads. Grind it from the pepper-mill which you keep handy on the counter. Be generous.

▼

EASY CAESAR SALAD   *Six* SERVINGS

This famous West-Coast original is made with many a flourish in fine restaurants. There's many a flourish in this short-cut Caesar salad, too, but you can make it at the table in half the usual time!

Salad bowl of romaine in bite-size pieces

¼ cup Italian style salad dressing

Juice of 1 lemon (3 tablespoons)

2 teaspoons Worcestershire sauce

¼ cup grated Parmesan cheese

¼ cup olive oil

1 garlic clove

1 cup packaged croutons

1 egg, simmered 1 minute

Salt, freshly ground pepper

Carry bowl of crisp romaine to table on a tray with little dishes to hold other ingredients, five in all. Mix Italian dressing, lemon juice, and Worcestershire and place in one dish; in the next place the cheese. Let crushed garlic stand in oil an hour or so; strain out and place the oil in a third dish. In the fourth, the croutons; in the fifth, the egg, out of its shell.

Now, pour on dressing, toss salad. Add cheese, toss again. Add egg and toss very well. Pour garlic oil over croutons, add to salad with salt and pepper to taste, toss again, and serve at once.

A PRETTY GREEN SALAD   *Eight* SERVINGS

The light and dark greens are pretty together and there's tomato red for contrast.

1 small bunch watercress
½ head curly endive, tender inside leaves
2 small heads Boston lettuce
2 cups spinach, cut in shreds

6 to 8 sliced green onions with tops
1 cucumber, sliced
2 dozen cherry tomatoes
French or Italian dressing
2 grated hard-cooked egg yolks

Wash and dry greens and combine in salad bowl, adding onions. Circle the bowl with cucumber slices and tomatoes. Chill well. At the table add the dressing, sprinkle with egg and toss well.

This kind of salad could function as an appetizer course, preceding a roast meat or turkey dinner.

ASPARAGUS SALAD   *Six* SERVINGS

Don't overcook the asparagus. It should be firm, not limp.

1½ pounds fresh asparagus, cooked, chilled
Bottled Italian dressing
Romaine or Boston lettuce

Lay the asparagus stalks on crisp greens on salad plates and cover with dressing. Canned or cooked frozen asparagus stalks may be used. A can or a package will usually make 4 salads.

Asparagus-Tomato Salad. Use ½ as much asparagus and lay the stalks on sliced ripe tomatoes.

EASY ASPIC   *Four* SERVINGS

You couldn't ask for anything simpler!

1 tablespoon (envelope) unflavored gelatin
2 cups canned vegetable juice cocktail

Soften gelatin in ½ cup of the vegetable juice; heat the rest and dissolve the softened gelatin. Turn into individual molds and chill until firm. Unmold on crisp greens and serve with mayonnaise. Double the recipe for a ring mold. Unmold ring and fill with salmon or seafood salad or chicken salad.

Nice variation: Make the aspic and chill until mixture is the consistency of unbeaten egg white. Fold in 1 cup diced or shredded shrimp or crab-meat, plus ½ cup diced celery. Cooked dressing, commercial salad dressing, or mayonnaise is suitable.

BRIDGE PARTY MOLDS *Four* SERVINGS

A welcome luncheon on a warm summer day.

    1 tablespoon (envelope) plain gelatin
  ¼ cup cold water
  ½ cup chili sauce
    1 cup cottage cheese
  ½ cup fine-cut celery
  ½ cup mayonnaise
  ¼ cup sliced stuffed olives
  ½ cup sweet pickle relish
  ¼ teaspoon salt
    4 tomato slices, size of top of molds
       Lettuce, watercress

Soften gelatin in cold water. Heat chili sauce to boiling point and dis-solve gelatin in it. Cool until sirupy. Combine cottage cheese, celery, mayonnaise, olives, relish, and salt and add to gelatin mixture. Fill four molds rinsed with cold water and chill until firm. Turn out each mold onto a slice of tomato on a leaf of lettuce. Garnish with sliced olives and watercress, and serve with more mayonnaise.

BROCCOLI BAVARIAN SALAD   *Six* SERVINGS

*Don't overcook that broccoli! It should be green and fairly
firm in texture.*

1 tablespoon plain gelatin	⅛ teaspoon pepper
¼ cup cold water	2 cups cooked broccoli, chopped
1 cup hot consommé or bouillon	2 hard-cooked eggs, chopped
¾ cup mayonnaise	Greens
¼ teaspoon salt	2 hard-cooked eggs, sliced

Soften gelatin in cold water for 5 minutes. Dissolve in very hot
consommé. Chill until slightly thickened. Fold in mayonnaise and seasonings, mixing until well blended. Fold in broccoli and chopped eggs.
Fill 1-quart mold rinsed in cold water. Chill until firm. Unmold on
large platter; garnish with greens and egg slices. Serve with mayonnaise.

CHINESE BEAN SALAD   *Six to Eight* SERVINGS

*Bean salads are always popular, especially for buffet serving.
This one is a little unusual, adding water chestnuts and soy
sauce to the more prosaic ingredients.*

1 can (1 lb.) diagonal-cut green beans, drained
1 can (1 lb.) diagonal-cut wax beans, drained
1 can (5 ozs.) water chestnuts, drained, sliced
½ sweet red onion, sliced thin and separated in rings
⅓ cup vinegar
⅓ cup sugar
2 tablespoons salad oil
2 tablespoons soy sauce
½ teaspoon celery salt

Combine beans, water chestnuts, and onion rings in a large bowl. Put
the other ingredients into a covered jar and shake. Pour over beans.
Chill several hours or overnight, stirring occasionally.

CARROT SALAD   *Four* SERVINGS

Chill this salad several hours for a good blend of flavor.

8 medium carrots, cooked, cut in thin strips
1 clove garlic, minced
  French Dressing (page 250) or a commercial one
  Shredded lettuce or other greens

Combine carrots, garlic, about ⅓ cup dressing, chill, and serve on greens.

CELERY ROOT SALAD   *Four* SERVINGS

Here's an unusual and very flavorsome salad.

1 medium celery root (about ½ pound)
2 tablespoons lemon juice
2 tablespoons salad oil
½ teaspoon salt
2 tablespoons minced onion
2 or 3 tablespoons chopped parsley
  Pimiento for garnish

Peel root, quarter it, and boil in salted water about 15 minutes. Drain, chill, and slice, not too thin. Make dressing of remaining ingredients, pour over sliced root, toss lightly, and serve on crisp greens. Garnish with pimiento.

KIDNEY BEAN AND EGG SALAD   *Four* SERVINGS

Garnish with tomatoes and eat with rye bread!

1 can (1 lb.) kidney beans, drained
3 hard-cooked eggs, chopped
1 cup chopped celery
2 tablespoons minced onion
½ cup chopped sweet or dill pickles
½ cup mayonnaise
1 teaspoon salt

Combine ingredients, tossing lightly to blend well. Chill. Serve in crisp lettuce cups.

MOLDED VEGETABLE SALAD   Six SERVINGS

Vary the vegetables, if you wish—the recipe is adaptable.

1½ tablespoons plain gelatin
½ cup cold water
 3 cups chicken broth (page
    181) or canned
½ teaspoon salt, or to taste
¾ cup diced cooked carrots
¾ cup diced cooked green beans
¾ cup cooked peas

¾ cup whole kernel corn
1 cup diced celery
1 teaspoon grated onion or 2
    tablespoons minced green
    onions
Thousand Island Dressing
    (page 251)

Soften gelatin in cold water. Heat broth, add gelatin and stir to dissolve.
Season and add vegetables. Pour into oiled ring mold and chill. Serve
with Thousand Island Dressing.

Ⅹ

PERFECTION SALAD   *Eight* SERVINGS

*This salad has been around for many years. Perhaps the
name explains why.*

2 tablespoons unflavored gelatin
½ cup cold water
½ cup sugar
1 teaspoon salt
2 cups boiling water
½ cup tarragon vinegar

¼ cup lemon juice
1½ cups finely shredded cabbage
 2 cups finely chopped celery
 1 jar (2 ozs.) pimiento, chopped
 2 carrots, grated
½ cup chopped green pepper

Soften gelatin in cold water. Add sugar, salt, and boiling water. Stir
until granules are dissolved. Add vinegar and lemon juice. Chill mixture
until it is partially thickened. Fold in remaining ingredients. Turn salad
into individual molds or into a large mold and chill until firm. Serve on
platter garnished with lettuce and tomato wedges.

TOP—*Rock Cornish Hens with Wild Rice, page*
BOTTOM—*Oven-fried Chicken, page 182; Au Gr*
Potatoes, page 274

CHEESE SALAD
Six to Eight SERVINGS

A bowl of tomato soup and some crackers are all you need now.

2 cups diced Cheddar cheese
2 cups celery, cut in pieces
3 sweet pickles, cut up
2 pimientos cut in strips
¼ cup broken pecans
½ teaspoon salt
¼ teaspoon pepper
   Mayonnaise to moisten
3 hard-cooked eggs, diced or sliced

Toss everything together lightly but eggs. Add them last, and stir just enough to mix without mashing the yolks. Serve in lettuce cups with additional mayonnaise.

DELMONICO SALAD
Six SERVINGS

A sprinkle of dried basil and tarragon adds savor.

1 cup fresh cooked peas
1 cup diced celery
¼ cup finely chopped sweet pickles
½ cup diced Swiss or Cheddar cheese
½ cup diced cucumber
1 tomato, diced
   French dressing, mayonnaise, lettuce

Combine salad ingredients with a mixture of French dressing and mayonnaise and serve in a bowl of lettuce. Garnish with ripe olives. Or add pitted ripe olives to the salad.

Roast Turkey, page 212

MACEDOINE SALAD   *Four* SERVINGS

Of course you could mix the vegetables but aren't they attractive on their own?

1 cup drained cooked green beans (whole preferably)
1 cup drained cooked small lima beans
1 cup sliced cooked carrots
1 cup diced cooked beets
  Bottled Italian dressing
  Crisp lettuce leaves
4 radish roses

Moisten each vegetable separately with French dressing and chill. Arrange 4 small lettuce leaves on each of 4 salad plates, spoon string beans in one leaf, lima beans in another, carrots in the third, beets in the fourth. Garnish with a radish rose. Serve with mayonnaise.

POTATO SALAD   *Six* SERVINGS

Freshly cooked potatoes make better salads.

6 cups diced, cooked potatoes
2 cups chopped celery
¼ cup chopped green onions and tops
¼ cup minced parsley
½ cup chopped cucumber, optional
2 hard-cooked eggs, sliced

½ cup French dressing
½ cup mayonnaise
½ cup cooked salad dressing
½ cup sour cream
¼ cup tarragon vinegar
2 teaspoons salt (more if needed)
¼ teaspoon pepper

Place diced, cooked potatoes, celery, green onions, parsley, cucumber, and one of the sliced eggs in a large bowl. Add the French dressing and mix lightly. Cover and chill for several hours. Blend the remaining ingredients and add to the potatoes. Toss lightly and chill before serving. Garnish with remaining sliced egg.

POTATO AND ONION SALAD   *Four* SERVINGS

Don't be fooled by the simplicity of this one—it's very good!

    4 medium potatoes, cooked in skins
    1 large mild onion, thinly sliced
      Salt, pepper
    ¼ cup French dressing
      Mayonnaise
      Minced parsley

Skin and slice potatoes while warm, add onion and sprinkle with salt and pepper. Pour French dressing over combination and let stand until cool. Combine with enough mayonnaise to moisten well. Garnish with parsley.

▼

HOT POTATO SALAD   *Six* SERVINGS

Leftover salad may be warmed over hot water.

    6 strips bacon, chopped
    1 tablespoon flour
    ½ cup chopped green onions
      and tops
    ¼ cup vinegar
    1½ teaspoons salt
    ½ teaspoon pepper

    1 tablespoon sugar
    ½ cup water
    1 quart hot cooked, sliced
      potatoes
    1 teaspoon celery seed
    2 hard-cooked eggs, sliced
    6 frankfurters cooked (optional)

Fry chopped bacon until crisp; blend in flour until smooth. Add onion, vinegar, salt, pepper, sugar and water; cook for 5 minutes. Pour over hot potatoes, add celery seed, and mix lightly. Serve immediately, while still warm. Garnish with slices of hard-cooked egg and frankfurters.

POTATO SALAD ITALIAN STYLE   *Six* SERVINGS

This is a pleasant change from the usual mayonnaised po-tato mixtures.

8 medium potatoes, cooked, diced
6 green onions and tops, sliced
3 medium tomatoes, cut in chunks
½ green pepper, diced

1 teaspoon sweet basil or oregano
¼ cup olive oil
1 teaspoon salt (or more)
¼ teaspoon freshly ground pepper
3 tablespoons red wine vinegar

Mix ingredients lightly and chill.

SALADE NICOISE   *Six or Eight* SERVINGS

Nice is the home of this newly popular Mediterranean salad; however, I first ate it in Tangier.

3 cups cold lightly cooked green beans
3 or 4 tomatoes, quartered
1 cup herb French dressing or Italian dressing
1 head Boston lettuce, washed, dried
3 cups cold potato salad
1 can (6½–7 ozs.) tuna, drained, broken in chunks
½ cup pitted black olives (Greek style)
2 to 3 hard-cooked eggs, peeled, quartered
6 to 12 anchovy fillets, drained
   Minced fresh chives or salad herbs
   Thin slices Spanish onion

Chill beans in a little of the dressing and add some to tomatoes shortly before serving. Arrange lettuce around salad bowl and put potato salad in the middle. Arrange beans, tomatoes, tuna, olives, eggs, and anchovies in an attractive pattern around potato salad. Scatter herbs and onion rings over salad and pour remaining dressing over combination.

When serving this salad, be sure everyone gets a bite or two of each salad ingredient, plus a little scoop of the potato salad.

COLESLAW WITH BUTTERMILK DRESSING

A tangy slaw is always better!

    4 cups finely shredded cabbage
 1/2 cup chopped green pepper
 1/2 cup chopped pared cucumber
    1 jar or can (2 ozs.) pimiento, diced
      Buttermilk Dressing (see below)

Mix vegetables with chilled dressing and serve.

BUTTERMILK DRESSING: In the top of a double boiler mix 2 tablespoons flour, 1 teaspoon mustard, 1 1/2 teaspoons salt, 1/8 teaspoon paprika, 1/2 teaspoon celery seed, and 2 tablespoons sugar. Add 1/3 cup vinegar and 1 cup buttermilk. Cook and stir until thickened and smooth. Chill.

AMBROSIA SALAD

Peaches and pineapple may be added for a bigger or more luxurious salad. Or add marshmallows and turn it into dessert!

    2 bananas, sliced
    1 cup diced orange or mandarin orange slices
 1/2 cup grapes, halved and seeded
 1/4 cup chopped dates or diced prepared dates
    1 fresh pear, diced
      Juice of 1 lemon or 3 tablespoons lemon juice
      Whipped cream mayonnaise (equal parts)
 1/4 cup flake coconut

Combine fruits, sprinkle with lemon juice, and chill. Add dressing and mix lightly. Serve on crisp lettuce with sprinkle of coconut.

CINNAMON-APPLE SALAD   *Six* SERVINGS

Fresh pears make an equally attractive salad.

6 small apples, pared, cored
1 cup sugar
1 cup water
6 tablespoons red cinnamon candies (or 2 little packages)
    About 3 ounces nippy process cheese or cream cheese
2 tablespoons cream

Cook sugar, water, candies until candies dissolve. (Add a few drops red coloring if sirup is not red enough.) Add apples and simmer gently until tender, turning occasionally for even coloring. Do not overcook. Remove from sirup and chill. Fill centers with mixture of cheese and cream. Place on lettuce and serve with whipped cream mayonnaise.

Leftover sirup may be covered and refrigerated until the next batch, or used as a pudding sauce.

Minted Apple Salad. Omit the red candies and cook a handful of fresh mint leaves with the sirup. Strain and add a few drops of green food coloring. Or flavor the sirup with a few drops of oil of peppermint. Proceed as directed for cinnamon apples.

P.S. The apples minus lettuce, dressing, and cheese are an excellent garnish for baked ham. Use both red and green ones at Christmas, alternating them on the platter around the meat.

AVOCADO GARNET SALAD   *Six* SERVINGS

Jewel colors and contrasting sharp and bland flavors—interesting!

1 package lime-flavored gelatin
1 cup boiling water
¾ cup cold water
1 cup diced avocado

3 tablespoons lemon juice
½ teaspoon salt
1 tablespoon minced onion
⅓ cup diced pickled beets

Dissolve gelatin in boiling water, add cold water and chill until slightly thickened. Add remaining ingredients and chill in loaf pan until firm. Unmold on greens and serve with mayonnaise.

AVOCADO BUTTERMILK RING   *Six* SERVINGS

Fill the ring with shrimp, chicken, or crabmeat salad for a special occasion—beautiful indeed!

1½ tablespoons (envelopes) unflavored gelatin
½ cup cold water
1½ cups sieved ripe avocado
2 cups buttermilk
½ cup mayonnaise

1½ teaspoons salt
1 teaspoon grated onion
Sprinkle celery salt
Dash Tabasco sauce
Watercress

Soften gelatin in cold water and dissolve over hot water. Add to avocado and combine with remaining ingredients. Pour into an 8-inch ring mold and chill until firm. Turn out and ring with watercress.

BLUE CHEESE MOLD WITH FRUIT   *Eight* PORTIONS

Fresh peaches or melon and strawberries, with creamy-sharp cheese—a summer plate to keep guests talking for weeks!

1 package (3 ozs.) cream cheese
2 ounces blue or Roquefort cheese
2 tablespoons cream
½ teaspoon salt
1 tablespoon (envelope) plain gelatin
¼ cup cold water
½ cup cream, whipped
½ cup chopped toasted pecans
Fresh fruit

Blend cheeses with cream and salt until smooth. Soften gelatin in cold water, dissolve over hot water and add to cheese. Fold in whipped cream and nuts. Pour into small round mold and chill until firm. Unmold and serve in the center of a platter of fresh fruit such as sliced peaches or cantaloupe, pears, cherries, strawberries. Garnish with watercress. Fruit salad dressing may be served separately.

MOLDED CRANBERRY SALAD   *Four* SERVINGS

A meal mate for turkey, chicken, ham, or pork.

2 cups fresh cranberries
1 cup water
1 cup sugar
1 teaspoon plain gelatin

1½ tablespoons cold water
¼ cup chopped celery
½ cup chopped apples
¼ cup chopped nuts

Cook cranberries with 1 cup water until soft. Strain, add sugar, and cook 3 minutes. Add the gelatin which has been softened in 1½ table-spoons water. Stir mixture until gelatin is dissolved, then chill until it begins to thicken. Fold in remaining ingredients, pour into individual molds rinsed in cold water. Chill until firm. Unmold on salad greens and serve with or without dressing.

MOLDED CRANBERRY,   *Eight* SERVINGS
ORANGE, AND PINEAPPLE SALAD

Half a cup of port could replace that much water if you feel festive.

2 packages raspberry gelatin
1 cup boiling water
1½ cups cold water
1 orange
1 can (1 lb.) pineapple chunks, drained
1 can (1 lb.) whole cranberry sauce, slightly beaten
1 cup chopped walnuts
Sour cream or mayonnaise
Greens

Dissolve gelatin in boiling water. Add cold water and chill until partially thickened. Peel orange and cut segments in half. Cut pineapple chunks into thirds. Fold orange, pineapple, cranberry, and nuts into gelatin. Pour into one large mold or individual molds and chill until firm. Turn out on chilled plate and serve with sour cream or mayonnaise garnished with crisp greens.

232

CRANBERRY JEWEL SALAD   *Eight* SERVINGS

Cranberry sauce makes a beautiful holiday salad, one good any time of year.

2 packages raspberry gelatin
3 cups boiling water
2 cans (1 lb. each) jellied or whole cranberry sauce
2 oranges, quartered, seeded, ground

Dissolve gelatin in boiling water and chill until mixture begins to jell. Crush jellied sauce with a fork. Fold cranberries and orange into gelatin. Spoon into a 2-quart mold and chill until firm. Serve on crisp lettuce.

MELON AND SWEET CHERRY   *Four* SERVINGS
SALAD

You might regard this as a pretty, feminine salad, but men like it, too!

1 cantaloupe, honeydew, or Persian melon
1 pound sweet cherries, pitted
1 package (3 ozs.) cream cheese
1 tablespoon cream
¼ cup chopped nuts or 2 tablespoons chopped
      candied ginger
  Greens
  Fruit salad dressing

Cut melon in inch-thick rings or slices, removing seeds and rind. Flute edges of melon. Mix cheese, cream, and nuts or ginger. Stuff cherries. Place melon rings on greens on salad plates and fill centers with cherries. Accompany with a thin Lemony Fruit Salad Dressing (page 252).

MINT JULEP SALAD   *Eight* SERVINGS

There's a tangy flavor present to make this mold "different."

2 packages lemon gelatin
1 cup boiling water
1 can (6 ozs.) frozen lemonade
   mix, undiluted
2 cups ginger ale

⅛ teaspoon mint flavoring
1 cup watermelon balls
1 cup cantaloupe balls
2 bananas, sliced
1 cup seedless grapes

Dissolve gelatin in boiling water and add lemonade mix. Add ginger ale and flavoring. Chill until partly set, then fold in fruits. Chill in a large mold or individual molds until firm. Turn out and serve with whipped cream-mayonnaise.

JELLIED OLIVE AND GRAPEFRUIT SALAD   *Six* SERVINGS

This is a very refreshing combination.

1 package lemon or lime gelatin
1 cup hot water
⅛ teaspoon salt
1 cup grapefruit sections, cut in pieces
1 cup grapefruit juice and water
¼ cup chopped stuffed olives
¾ cup diced celery
   Greens

Dissolve gelatin in hot water and add salt. Drain the canned or fresh grapefruit thoroughly and add water to make 1 cup. Add juice and water to gelatin and chill until slightly thick. Fold in grapefruit, olives, and celery and turn into molds. Chill until firm. Turn out on crisp greens and accompany with mayonnaise.

PEAR BLUSH SALAD   *Four* SERVINGS

This is one of the prettiest and simplest of fruit salads.

8 halves fresh pared or canned Bartlett pears
1 package (3 ozs.) cream cheese
1 tablespoon cream
   Few drops red food coloring
   Sprigs mint or watercress
   Lettuce or curly endive

Put two pear halves together with softened cream cheese blended with cream. Dilute red color with a little water or fruit juice and paint a blush on the side of each pear with your fingertip. Put a sprig of mint or cress in the stem end and serve on greens. Accompany with a fruit salad dressing.

Such a salad is delicious with a roast pork dinner.

ORANGE-GINGER GELATIN SALAD   *Six to Eight* SERVINGS

This is a perfect salad to accompany a chicken dinner.

2 tablespoons (envelopes) plain
   gelatin
¼ cup cold water
1 cup orange juice
½ cup sugar
⅛ teaspoon salt

2 tablespoons lemon juice
1½ cups ginger ale
½ cup pineapple pieces
1 cup orange chunks
2 to 3 tablespoons preserved
   ginger, cut in fine pieces

Soften gelatin in cold water; melt over hot water. Add orange juice, sugar, salt, lemon juice, and ginger ale; mix well. Chill until mixture begins to set; fold in pineapple, orange chunks, and ginger. Chill until firm in an 8-inch square baking dish. Cut in large squares and arrange on crisp salad greens. Garnish with peeled orange wedges. Serve with mayonnaise.

ORANGE AND ONION SALAD   *Four* SERVINGS

Fruit and onions? Yes, if it's this combination, an old timer, still one of the most palatable of salads.

2 large seedless oranges, pared and sliced
½ to 1 large sweet onion, sliced paper thin
   Lettuce
   French dressing

Alternate slices of orange and onion on lettuce-lined plates and top with dressing. A sprig of parsley may garnish each salad. This is an excellent salad for any dinner if there's no other form of onion, and no member of the cabbage family.

⚠

EMERALD CUCUMBER-PINEAPPLE MOLD   *Six* SERVINGS

A pretty luncheon salad garnished with shrimps is a meal in itself.

1 package lime gelatin
¾ teaspoon salt
1 cup hot water
¾ cup cold water
2 tablespoons vinegar
1 teaspoon grated onion
8 thin slices cucumber, scored
   with fork
2 slices canned pineapple,
   quartered

⅓ cup mayonnaise
1 cup diced cucumber
1 cup diced canned pineapple
2 tablespoons pimiento, cut in
   ¼-inch strips
1½ cups cooked shrimp,
   marinated in French
   dressing

Dissolve gelatin and salt in hot water. Add cold water, vinegar, and onion. Pour ¾ cup mixture into 9x5-inch loaf pan. Chill until slightly thickened. On this arrange cucumber slices and quartered pineapple slices. Chill until firm. Chill remaining gelatin until slightly thickened. Place in bowl of ice and water and whip with rotary beater until fluffy and thick. Fold in mayonnaise, then diced cucumber, pineapple, and pimiento. Turn into mold over firm gelatin. Chill until firm. Unmold. Arrange marinated shrimps in crisp lettuce cups around salad.

MOLDED PINEAPPLE-CHEESE SALAD

Eight SERVINGS

Green pepper, pimiento for color, Cheddar cheese for flavor contrast.

    2 tablespoons (envelopes) plain gelatin
    ½ cup cold water
    2 cups crushed pineapple
      Juice of 1 lemon or 3 tablespoons bottled lemon juice
    1 cup sugar
    1 cup grated Cheddar cheese
    1 cup cream, whipped
    2 tablespoons finely chopped green pepper
    2 tablespoons finely chopped pimiento
      Curly endive
      Mayonnaise

Soften gelatin in cold water, 5 minutes. Heat pineapple, lemon juice, and sugar. Stir until sugar is dissolved. Dissolve gelatin in hot mixture. Chill until partially set; fold in remaining ingredients. Pour into a mold and chill firm. Unmold on curly endive and serve with mayonnaise.

FROZEN POMEGRANATE SALAD
Twelve SERVINGS

Extract the pomegranate juice with your orange juicer, then strain out the seeds, for this.

1½ tablespoons (envelopes) plain gelatin
½ cup pineapple juice
1 cup pomegranate juice (or cranberry cocktail)
2 tablespoons sugar
¼ teaspoon salt
1 tablespoon lemon juice
1 cup mayonnaise
1 cup cream, whipped
2 cups mixed fruit, cut fine

Soften gelatin in pineapple juice and dissolve over hot water. Add pomegranate juice with sugar and salt. Add lemon juice. Cool. Beat mayonnaise gradually into the whipped cream and gradually add gelatin mixture. Fold in fruit, freeze in refrigerator trays, or in a melon mold.

SUMMER FRUIT SALAD
Eight SERVINGS

Made to order for the younger members of the family.

2 packages strawberry gelatin
2 cups hot water and juice from canned fruit
2 cups cold water
1 cup chopped pecans
16 marshmallows, cut in quarters
1 small can (1 cup) crushed pineapple, drained
3 bananas, sliced
1 large can mixed fruit salad, chopped, drained
½ cup pitted fresh cherries
Whipped cream mayonnaise, greens

Pour hot water and juices drained from fruit used over gelatin and stir until dissolved. Add cold water. Chill until partially thickened. Mix remaining ingredients, and fold into gelatin mixture. Pour into 1 large mold or individual molds and chill until firm. Serve on crisp salad greens topped with whipped cream mayonnaise.

238

STRAWBERRY ROSÉ MOLD
Ten to Twelve SERVINGS

Serve this lovely ring as salad with a summer buffet supper.

    3 packages strawberry flavor gelatin
1½ cups boiling water
1½ cups rosé wine
    1 quart fresh strawberries
½ cup sugar

Dissolve gelatin in boiling water; stir in wine. Set aside a dozen of the prettiest berries for the top of the mold. Slice the rest and mix with the sugar. Halve and arrange the prettiest berries cut side down in a 6½-cup ring mold; cover with a thin layer of gelatin and chill until firm. Add remaining berries to the rest of the gelatin and pour over first layer. Chill until firm.

To substitute frozen for fresh berries, use 2 packages (16 ozs. each) frozen strawberry halves and omit the sugar.

WALDORF SALAD
Eight SERVINGS

Here is a classic salad calling for juicy, red-skinned apples.

    6 apples
    2 tablespoons lemon juice
1½ cups chopped celery
½ cup chopped walnuts or pecans
¾ cup mayonnaise or cooked salad dressing
½ cup cream, whipped
    Apple slices and whole nuts for garnish
    Lettuce

Wash apples, core, and dice coarsely without peeling. Sprinkle with lemon juice, tossing quickly to prevent discoloration. Add chopped celery and nuts to apples, blending well. Fold mayonnaise or cooked salad dressing into whipped cream. Gently mix dressing with fruit. Place in large salad bowl. Garnish with apple slices and nuts and tuck lettuce around sides of bowl.

THREE-LAYER FRUIT SALAD

Eight to Twelve SERVINGS

Everybody loves this kind of refreshing fruit mold.

LAYER I

    1 package strawberry gelatin
    ¾ cup hot water
    1 package (10 ozs.) frozen strawberries, thawed

LAYER II

    1 package lemon gelatin
    1 cup hot water
    ½ cup mashed banana
    ½ cup sour cream

LAYER III

    1 package lime gelatin
    1 cup hot water
    1 can (9 ozs.) crushed pineapple, drained

Dissolve strawberry gelatin in hot water, chill until rather thick, add strawberries and juice, and turn into a 1½ quart mold. Chill until firm. Dissolve lemon gelatin in water, chill until thick and fold in banana and sour cream. Spread over firm first layer. Dissolve lime gelatin in water, chill until thick, and fold in pineapple. Top second layer and chill overnight. Unmold on a platter for serving.

CHEF'S SALAD

Four to Six SERVINGS

Every restaurant has its own version, but most chef's salads resemble this.

    Wooden bowl of crisp, dry greens (lettuce, plus escarole, watercress, spinach, curly endive or romaine)
    2 or 3 washed tomatoes, cut into eighths
    ½ cucumber, washed, sliced thin
    ½ cup julienne strips of cooked chicken, turkey, ham, or beef
    ¼ cup julienne strips Cheddar or Swiss cheese
    2 hard-cooked eggs, quartered
    Blue cheese or French dressing

This salad is particularly delicious with a blue cheese dressing, but any good French dressing will do. Toss greens, tomatoes, and cucumbers gently with enough dressing to coat well, and garnish the bowl with the strips of chicken or meat and cheese in the center, quartered eggs around the outside. Carry the bowl to table and toss lightly just before serving.

SCANDINAVIAN CHICKEN CURRY SALAD

Eight SERVINGS

Instead of mixing the salad yourself, you might arrange the ingredients prettily on a tray around a bowl of the dressing and let guests do their own mixing.

    3 cups cooked chicken or turkey, cut in strips
    1 cup apples, cut in strips
    1 cup celery, cut in thin strips
    1 cup cucumber, cut in thin strips
    ½ pound fresh raw mushrooms, sliced
      Curry Mayonnaise (see below)
      Garnish of hard-cooked egg, crisp bacon, tomato wedges
      Lettuce to line bowl or plate

CURRY MAYONNAISE: Add to 1 cup mayonnaise 1 tablespoon lemon juice, 1 tablespoon curry powder. Fold in 1 cup whipping cream, whipped.

Toss salad ingredients lightly with mayonnaise to moisten and nest in lettuce with garnish of quartered hard-cooked eggs, crisp quarter-strips of bacon, and tomato wedges.

With warm rolls, this would be an excellent bridge luncheon dish.

CHICKEN AND FRUIT SALAD   *Ten* SERVINGS

This is one of the nicest possible salads for a feminine luncheon.

3 cups diced cooked chicken
1 cup diced celery
1 cucumber, diced
1 tablespoon each, minced onion, parsley
½ cup French dressing
1 large, meaty grapefruit, peeled sections
1 cluster Tokay grapes, halved and seeded
1 can drained pineapple chunks
1 cup salted blanched almonds, halved
Mayonnaise
Greens

Add French dressing to first 5 ingredients. Chill. Drain well, add remaining ingredients, and blend with mayonnaise. Pile into a bowl lined with greens.

CHICKEN AND GRAPE SALAD   *Four* SERVINGS

A few simple ingredients make one of the best chicken salads.

3 cups diced cooked chicken or turkey
1 cup seedless grapes or halved seeded grapes
½ cup whole salted pecans or sliced toasted almonds
Mayonnaise to moisten
Lettuce or other greens

Combine chicken, grapes and nuts and mix with mayonnaise to moisten well. Mound on lettuce or other greens. Garnish with a bouquet of watercress sprigs when you can.

LUNCHEON SALAD: Double the recipe if you need to and serve the salad centered in rings of ripe cantaloupe, garnished with greens. Warm, buttery rolls are all you need with this lovely salad—plus coffee, of course. Very easy entertaining.

ORIENTAL CHICKEN AND RICE SALAD

Six SERVINGS

Discovered in Kansas City once upon a time. It's why I like Kansas City!

1½ cups diced cooked chicken	1 cup chutney
Tart French dressing	Mayonnaise
2 cups cooked rice	Grated coconut

Marinate chicken in French dressing for an hour or so. Combine with rice and chutney, adding enough mayonnaise to moisten. Chill thoroughly. Mound on greens and top with fresh grated coconut.

Much of the flavor of this salad depends upon the kind of chutney you use. Select one that's really fruity, but not oversweet.

COBB SALAD

Eight SERVINGS

Bring this arrangement on for admiration; toss it at the table.

1 quart cut-up lettuce
2 cups cut-up curly endive
½ bunch watercress, cut up
1 large tomato, in chunks
2 chicken breasts, cooked, cubed (about 3 cups chicken)
6 strips bacon, cooked crisp, crumbled
2 avocados, diced
  Juice of ½ lemon (or 1½ tablespoons)
2 tablespoons freeze-dried or fresh-cut chives
1 hard-cooked egg, chopped
3 ounces Roquefort or blue cheese, crumbled (½ cup)
½ cup bottled Italian dressing (or more)

In a large salad bowl toss greens with tomato. Arrange chicken, bacon, avocado sprinkled with lemon juice on top. Sprinkle with chives, egg and cheese. Just before serving, toss with the dressing.

Muffins or crusty rolls and something to drink equal a fine lunch!

"MY" SALAD   *Four* SERVINGS

From the Wrigley Restaurant in Chicago, where you may also order "Your" salad (tuna) this concoction was named by versifier Edgar A. Guest.

1½ cups cooked chicken or turkey, cut in thin strips
3 cups shredded lettuce
1 cup mayonnaise
1 tablespoon each, minced green pepper, pimiento, tarragon vinegar
2 tablespoons chili sauce
6 ounces Roquefort or blue cheese, crumbled
2 hard-cooked eggs, quartered

Combine chicken and lettuce in salad bowl. Add other ingredients except eggs to mayonnaise and mix gently with chicken and lettuce. Garnish with eggs.

⚠

CRAB SALAD IN AVOCADO SHELLS   *Four* SERVINGS

Many a fine restaurant makes a specialty of this salad.

1 can (6½ ozs.) crabmeat
2 hard-cooked eggs
¾ cup minced celery
¼ cup minced green pepper
½ teaspoon salt
¼ teaspoon pepper
½ cup mayonnaise
2 tablespoons lemon juice
2 medium avocados
Leaf lettuce

Flake crab, removing any shell or cartilage. Grate eggs, reserving the grated yolk of 1 egg. Mix remaining eggs, celery, and green pepper with crab. Season. Stir in blended mayonnaise and lemon juice. Chill. When ready to serve, peel and slice avocados in halves, lengthwise. Remove pits and mound crab salad on avocado halves. Sprinkle remaining egg yolk on top for garnish. Serve on leaf lettuce and trim salad plates with thin carrot sticks and radishes.

CRAB LOUIS

One SERVING

You want fresh-cooked crab for this West Coast delicacy, a meal in itself.

    Shredded lettuce or romaine
1 cup fresh cooked crabmeat
    Thousand Island Dressing (page 251)
    Crab legs
1 small tomato, cut in eighths
1 artichoke heart, split (optional)

Heap the chilled crabmeat on the greenery and top with dressing. Garnish with crab legs, tomato, and artichoke. A ripe olive or radish rose on top, if you like.

x

MOLDED CRAB or LOBSTER SALAD

Six SERVINGS

Use a fish mold for this delicacy, if you own one.

1 pound crabmeat, cooked shrimps, or lobster tail meat
1 tablespoon (envelope) plain gelatin
¼ cup cold water
½ cup boiling water
½ cup mayonnaise or salad dressing

¼ cup catsup
2 tablespoons lemon juice
½ cup chopped celery
2 tablespoons each chopped sweet pickle, chopped stuffed olives
¼ teaspoon salt
    Salad greens

Remove any shell or cartilage from crabmeat. Soften gelatin in cold water 5 minutes. Add boiling water and stir until dissolved. Cool. Blend mayonnaise, catsup, and lemon juice. Combine all ingredients except salad greens; mix well. Pour into mold and chill until firm. Unmold on salad greens and garnish with more mayonnaise.

CORAL REEF SALAD   *Four to Six* SERVINGS

Colorful and seasoned perfectly, this mixture has its own dressing.

1 quart coarse-cut lettuce
1 clove garlic
1 cup cleaned cooked shrimps
2 medium tomatoes, diced
1 medium avocado, diced
  Salt, pepper

DRESSING: ⅓ cup mayonnaise, 1 tablespoon each wine vinegar and lemon juice, 2 tablespoons salad oil, 3 tablespoons chili sauce, ½ teaspoon each prepared horseradish and grated onion, ¼ teaspoon Worcestershire sauce, dash Tabasco sauce.

Put lettuce in bowl rubbed with garlic. Add shrimps, tomato, and avocado. Sprinkle with salt and pepper. Blend together dressing ingredients and pour over salad. Toss lightly.

■

SHRIMP AND CAPER SALAD   *Four* SERVINGS

Capers may be sprinkled over the salad rather than mixed with it.

1 pound cooked shrimps, cut in half
1 cup finely sliced celery
1 tablespoon lemon juice
2 tablespoons capers
  Mayonnaise to moisten
  Bibb lettuce or romaine

Combine ingredients lightly and serve well chilled on lettuce. It always helps if seafood chills in its dressing for an hour or so before it is served.
  Multiply the recipe for an excellent buffet salad. It will be popular!

SHRIMP AND GRAPEFRUIT SALAD
Six SERVINGS

*A colorful dressing is appealing with this pleasant com-
bination.*

¾ to 1 pound shrimps, cooked, shelled, de-veined
1 large meaty grapefruit, in sections
   Curly endive or other greens
   Russian dressing or other tomato-flavored dressing.

Place shrimps and grapefruit in alternating rows on greens and streak
the dressing across the assembled salad without being too generous.
   This salad can function as a kind of shrimp cocktail in the menu,
or make a lunch with a cup of vegetable soup.

SALMON AND WALNUT SALAD
Six SERVINGS

*This mixture is a little unusual, and has an excellent balance
of textures.*

2 cans (1 lb. each) top quality red salmon
1 cup finely cut crisp celery
1½ tablespoons lemon juice
1 cup coarsely broken walnuts
1 cup mayonnaise
   Salt, paprika
   Leaf lettuce

Remove skin and bones from salmon and break into chunks. Combine
with rest of ingredients, mix lightly, and serve in lettuce-lined salad
bowl.
   With a cream cheese sandwich or a cup of soup, this salad would
make a very nice lunch.

247

SALMON SALAD   *Six* SERVINGS

Just sharp-flavored enough to pique the appetite.

> 1 pound can salmon or 1 pound fresh or frozen salmon,
>   cooked
> ½ cup chopped sweet pickles
> 2 diced hard-cooked eggs
> 1 tablespoon capers (optional)
> ⅔ cup diced celery
> 2 teaspoons lemon juice
>   Mayonnaise or cooked dressing to moisten
>   Watercress or other greens

Flake salmon, combine with other ingredients, except greens, and chill.
Serve on watercress, very green lettuce, escarole or spinach—any *green*
greens.

EGG AND SEAFOOD SALAD   *Six* SERVINGS

*A good bottled dressing takes all the work out of this kind of
salad.*

> 6 hard-cooked eggs, cut in half lengthwise
> 1 can (6½–7 ozs.) tuna or salmon, drained and flaked or
>   crabmeat or shrimps, shredded or cut up
> 3 green onions, with tops, chopped
> ½ cup chopped celery
> 2 tablespoons sweet pickle relish
> ¼ cup sour cream
>   Lettuce

Combine onions, celery, pickle relish, and sour cream with tuna or seafood. (If you use canned shrimps, run cold water over them to firm the
flesh and remove excess salt; drain well). For each salad, place two
halves of egg on a lettuce leaf or two and spoon the dressing over them.
Garnish with parsley or radish roses or both.

Serve as a first course before meat or poultry, if you wish.

TUNA SALAD IN AVOCADOS   *Six* SERVINGS

Here's one of the most attractive of luncheon salads.

2 cans (7 ozs. each) tuna, broken in small pieces
1 can (8 ozs.) water chestnuts, sliced thin
¼ cup stuffed olives, sliced
2 hard-cooked eggs, chopped fine
1 teaspoon minced onion
2 teaspoons capers
Special dressing (see below)
3 avocados, fully ripe, halved, peeled and seeded
Greens, cherry tomatoes

Mix tuna, water chestnuts, olives, eggs, onion, capers and special dressing. Chill until ready to serve. Scoop into avocado halves and bed on greens. Garnish with the baby tomatoes.

DRESSING: Combine ½ cup mayonnaise, ½ cup sour cream, ¼ cup lemon juice, 1 teaspoon salt, 1 teaspoon curry powder.

MACARONI, HAM, AND CHEESE SUPPER SALAD   *Six to Eight* SERVINGS

Here's an excellent party salad, easy to step-up in quantity.

1 package (7 or 8 ozs.) elbow macaroni, cooked, chilled
1 can (1 lb. 4½ ozs.) pineapple chunks, drained
1 cup diced cooked ham (or chicken or seafood)
1½ cups thinly sliced celery
1 cup sliced stuffed olives
1 cup diced sharp Cheddar cheese
¼ cup sweet pickle relish (drained)
¼ cup chopped green pepper
2 tablespoons chopped pimiento
4–5 sliced green onions with tops
1 cup mayonnaise or salad dressing
Salt, pepper as needed
Lettuce or other greens

Combine ingredients and chill for at least an hour before serving on lettuce.

SALMAGUNDI SALAD   *Six* SERVINGS

A pattern recipe for meat salad which can be adjusted to the contents of your refrigerator.

2 cups cold diced meat (lamb, veal, beef, pork, tongue, or
　　corned beef)
½ cup each cooked potatoes, diced, cooked carrots, diced,
　　green peas, or green beans
½ cup onion French dressing
½ cup chopped sweet pickles
2 hard-cooked eggs, chopped fine
1 cup mayonnaise
　Cold sliced beets
　Lettuce

Combine cold diced meat with vegetables in mixing bowl and marinate in French dressing for about 20 minutes. Then add chopped pickles and hard-cooked eggs. Add mayonnaise and mix lightly. Arrange on crisp lettuce leaves and garnish with cold sliced beets cut in diamond shape.

X

BASIC FRENCH DRESSING   *One* PINT

C'est bon! Oui!

½ cup vinegar
1½ cups salad oil
1½ teaspoons salt
2 teaspoons sugar (optional)
1 teaspoon minced onion (optional)
½ teaspoon paprika
½ teaspoon dry mustard
　Dash pepper

Shake or blend ingredients together and store in covered jar in the refrigerator.

CREAMY GARLIC DRESSING: Follow basic French dressing recipe, substituting 1 small clove garlic for onion. Place ingredients in an electric blender container. Whirl until ingredients are emulsified, ½ minute or so. Store in covered jar in the refrigerator. The final product is creamy in color and almost as thick as thin mayonnaise.

GREEN GODDESS DRESSING   One PINT

Pretty and popular, this dressing. Serve it on greens, seafood.

1 cup mayonnaise
1 clove garlic
4 anchovies
6 green onions with tops, cut
    into pieces
¼ cup parsley, packed

1 tablespoon lemon juice
1 tablespoon tarragon vinegar
½ teaspoon salt
¼ teaspoon coarsely ground
    pepper

Mix all ingredients in blender until anchovies, onions, and parsley are in fine pieces. If you wish, mix ½ cup sour cream or whipped cream with dressing before serving over greens, vegetable salads, or cold fish.

⚠

THOUSAND ISLAND   One and one-half CUPS
DRESSING

This mixture is a favorite for a bowlful of mixed greens.

1 cup mayonnaise
¼ cup chili sauce
¼ cup drained pickle relish
1 hard-cooked egg, chopped
1 tablespoon minced parsley

Combine ingredients. If you are in a hurry, you may leave out the egg. Sometimes minced onion and finely chopped green pepper are added.

HOT BACON DRESSING   *Six* SERVINGS

*Pour this mixture hot over a bowlful of greens, or over warm
sliced potatoes for a hot potato salad.*

    4 slices bacon, fried crisp, crumbled
 1/2 small onion, chopped
 1/4 cup vinegar
    2 teaspoons sugar
    1 teaspoon salt
      Pepper

Add onion to drippings and cook until tender. Add other ingredients.
Heat thoroughly and pour over a bowlful of mixed greens. Toss and
serve at once. Crumbled blue cheese may be added. Tarragon-flavored
vinegar or wine vinegar offers a slight change of flavor, good, I think.

◨

LEMONY FRUIT SALAD   *Two* CUPS
DRESSING

Isn't this a sunny idea? Vitamin C with the salad!

    1 can frozen orange juice, thawed
    1 can frozen lemonade, thawed
    1 cup salad oil
 1/2 teaspoon Worcestershire sauce
      Dash cayenne

Shake ingredients in a tightly covered jar or mix in blender. Keep in
covered container in refrigerator.

△

◎ ▫ ◎ ▫ ◎

VEGETABLES

VEGETABLE cookery has been made so easy with the availability of good-quality canned and frozen prepared products that some families are forgetting what the fresh, nonprocessed vegetable is like! In many instances the frozen product may be of better quality than the fresh. I am thinking especially of peas which lose sweetness and tenderness rapidly in the market, and may have less garden freshness on the table than those packaged, boil-in-the-bag baby peas in butter sauce.

In cooking fresh vegetables, the basic rule is this: To preserve freshness, eating quality, and vitamin values, cook in a small amount of boiling, salted water just to the point of tender-crispness. Overcooking is damaging, particularly to the bright-colored and strong-flavored vegetables.

Vegetables can add a great deal of interest to meals, if they are carefully prepared. Little tricks for adding flavor include these:

Adding chicken stock base or a chicken bouillon cube to cooking water.

Dropping a slice of bacon into green beans or mixtures of greens as they cook.

253

Adding a tablespoon or two of lemon juice to a cooked green vegetable (add it just before serving, as acid tends to fade the color).

Sautéeing sliced or chopped almonds in butter, then pouring almond butter over the vegetable. This is especially good for asparagus, broccoli, and green beans.

Adding a pinch or two of mixed salad herbs to the vegetable as it cooks.

Adding a pinch of dry onion soup mix or dry herb salad dressing mix to the vegetable, during cooking.

Sprinkling a cooked green vegetable with crumbled crisp bacon.

Combinations of vegetables can be more interesting than their separate components, at times.

In choosing vegetables for a meal, think of the color you need on the dinner plate—with fish, for example, you would add great appetite appeal with the green of peas or beans and the red of broiled tomato. Think of textures, also, and size and shape. If everything on the plate is soft-textured and reduced to small pieces, even color won't help the meal much!

WHITE SAUCE OR CREAM SAUCE   *One* CUP

This kind of sauce is so basic to a number of foods in almost all categories that every cook should know how to make it. Medium White Sauce is most commonly used. Thin White Sauce is a base for soups, and Thick White Sauce is the foundation for croquettes and soufflés.

Use this for any creamed dish, and as a base for other sauces.

2 tablespoons butter
2 tablespoons flour
½ teaspoon salt

Few grains pepper
1 cup milk

Melt butter in a saucepan over moderate heat. Blend in flour, salt and pepper. Pour in milk and stir continuously until sauce thickens and becomes smooth.

A good formula for preparing any vegetable in a cream sauce is this: Place the cooked vegetable in a casserole or heat-proof serving dish, pour the hot sauce over it, sprinkle with buttered crumbs, slivered almonds, or grated cheese, if you wish, and bake at 375° F. or broil until just bubbling and lightly browned on top.

Thin White Sauce. Use 1 tablespoon butter and 1 tablespoon flour.

Thick White Sauce. Use 4 tablespoons butter, 4 tablespoons flour.

Cheese Sauce. Melt ¼ to ½ cup shredded sharp Cheddar cheese in the Medium White Sauce.

OTHER VARIATIONS OF WHITE SAUCE

Bouillon, broth, consommé, vegetable cooking liquid, or fish stock may be used to replace part of the milk. Adjust the salt downward when you use a salty replacement.

Minced onion may be sautéed in the butter before the flour is stirred in for an onion-flavored sauce.

For Mushroom Sauce, sauté the mushrooms in the butter (usually adding an extra tablespoon), then add flour and proceed as usual.

Lemon juice, prepared mustard, Worcestershire sauce, chili sauce, or catsup may be added in discreet amounts to sharpen the flavor of white sauce for a particular dish. Herbs, curry, horseradish, sliced stuffed olives, pimiento, and pickle relish are other seasoners which may vary the White Sauce for the food it dresses.

BUTTERED CRUMBS: Buttered crumbs are an excellent topping for vegetables and many casserole dishes. To prepare them, add ¼ cup melted butter to 1 cup soft crumbs. Crumbs may be stirred in the butter over heat to brown them a little. Make the crumbs in your electric blender, if you have one. They should not be too fine.

STUFFED ARTICHOKES, ITALIAN   *Six* SERVINGS

Serve these as the star attraction for lunch.

6 medium artichokes, trimmed*,
    parboiled 10 minutes in
    salted water
1 cup soft bread crumbs
⅓ cup olive oil
1 can (2 ozs.) anchovies, chopped

¼ teaspoon pepper
1 clove garlic, crushed with ¼
    teaspoon salt
1 cup water, stock, or white
    wine

Mix crumbs, oil, anchovies, and seasonings and press with spoon into centers of artichokes and between leaves. Place in casserole with water, stock, or wine and bake 30 minutes at 350° F.

    *To trim, cut off stem at base, cut off upper third of artichoke and remove discolored leaves. Smash top down against counter to open up, then cut out the "fuzz" on the surface of the heart of artichoke.

ASPARAGUS AND PEAS WITH HERBS   *Four* SERVINGS

For your successful dinner party, use fresh vegetables.

2 cups cooked tender asparagus, in short pieces
1 cup cooked peas
1 tablespoon chopped parsley
1 tablespoon chopped fresh or frozen chives
¼ teaspoon chopped fresh tarragon or ⅛ teaspoon dried
2 tablespoons melted butter
    Salt, pepper

Combine freshly cooked vegetables. Heat herbs in butter (don't cook) and pour over peas and asparagus. Season and serve hot.

TOP—*Strawberry Rosé Mold, page 239*
BOTTOM—*Cauliflower and Green Beans, page 26?*
Baked Stuffed Potatoes, page 272

ASPARAGUS WITH ALMOND LEMON BUTTER

Six SERVINGS

Perhaps this is the choicest asparagus of all!

2 pounds fresh asparagus
1/2 cup slivered almonds
1/2 cup butter
1/2 teaspoon salt
4 teaspoons lemon juice

Cook asparagus until tender-crisp in a very small amount of salted water, after snapping off the tough parts of the stems. Sauté almonds in butter over low heat until golden, stirring occasionally. Add salt and lemon juice. Pour over hot asparagus and serve.

◆

ASPARAGUS WITH SOUR CREAM

Four SERVINGS

Irresistible, that's what it is!

1 package frozen asparagus spears
1 cup sour cream
1/4 cup mayonnaise
2 tablespoons lemon juice
1/2 teaspoon salt
1/2 cup Buttered Crumbs (page 255)

Cook asparagus according to package directions, drain and place in heated serving dish. Heat gently cream, mayonnaise, lemon juice, and salt. Pour over asparagus and top with crumbs. Place under the broiler a minute or two until delicately browned and bubbly.

257

tuffed Artichokes, Italian, page 256;
urkish Eggplant, page 268

GREEN BEAN CASSEROLE   *Twelve* SERVINGS

*This dish has been described as a boon to party-giving moth-
ers because it can be made early, baked later.*

2 packages French style frozen green beans, thawed
1 teaspoon salt
1 can (8 ozs.) water chestnuts, drained, sliced
1 can (1 lb. 3 ozs.) bean sprouts, drained well
2 cans cream of mushroom soup
1 can French fried onions, crumbled

Place half the beans in a casserole and sprinkle with ½ teaspoon salt.
Add water chestnuts and bean sprouts. Spread 1 can of soup on top.
Add second package of green beans, rest of salt, and spread with second
can of soup. Bake at 350° F. for 20 minutes; sprinkle with onions and
bake 10 minutes more.

▼

SWISS BEANS   *Four* SERVINGS

*Fix early and bake just before serving, if you need to stream-
line meal preparations.*

1 package French-style frozen   ½ teaspoon salt
    green beans, cooked   ⅛ teaspoon pepper
1 tablespoon butter   1 cup sour cream
1 teaspoon minced onion   3 slices Swiss cheese
1 tablespoon flour   1 teaspoon paprika
½ teaspoon sugar

Place beans in a small shallow baking dish. Sauté onion in butter 3 minutes. Add flour, sugar, salt, and pepper and blend. Stir in cream and
heat through. Pour over beans. Cut cheese into strips and arrange on
cream mixture. Sprinkle with paprika. Bake at 350° F. for 15 minutes.

GREEN BEANS WITH MUSHROOMS AND SOY SAUCE

Four SERVINGS

There's just a bit of mystery in a vegetable thus prepared.

- 1 package frozen French-cut green beans
- 1/4 pound fresh mushrooms, sliced
- 2 tablespoons butter
- 1 tablespoon olive oil
- 1/4 teaspoon garlic powder
- 2 tablespoons chopped onion
- 2 tablespoons soy sauce
- 1 tablespoon wine vinegar

Cook beans according to package directions. Sauté mushrooms in butter for 5 minutes and add to beans with rest of ingredients. Mix well and serve.

X

GREEN BEANS WITH DRESSING

Six SERVINGS

Salad dressings offer limitless variations in flavor for vegetables.

- 1 pound green beans, cut on the diagonal, cooked
- 2 strips bacon, diced, fried crisp
- 1/2 cup good garlic French dressing
- 2 tablespoons minced onion
- 1/2 teaspoon oregano

Cook beans in 1/2 cup water with 1 teaspoon salt for 10 minutes and drain. Add bacon (not the bacon fat), salad dressing, onion, and oregano. Heat through and serve.

CREAMED GREEN BEANS AND ONIONS
Six to Eight SERVINGS

Excellent holiday fare, this combination might go to the table with the turkey or roast beef.

    1 can (1 lb.) blue-lake variety green beans
    1 can (1 lb.) small whole onions
1½ cups Medium White Sauce (page 254)
    Fleck of nutmeg

Drain vegetables well, heat in the white sauce, and sprinkle with nutmeg to serve.

LIMA BEANS WITH GARLIC VINEGAR AND HERBS
Five SERVINGS

Limas need a little vinegar, and garlic seems a natural flavor for them.

1 package frozen lima beans (small size)
1 strip bacon, diced
1 tablespoon garlic wine vinegar
1 teaspoon minced parsley
  Pinch mixed dried herbs
  Salt, pepper

Cook beans according to directions on package, adding diced bacon at beginning of cooking. As soon as beans are tender, add remaining ingredients. Keep covered and hot until served.

ARTHUR GODFREY'S BEANS
Six SERVINGS

"Best beans you ever ate," said this radio and TV star, offering his recipe. Maybe he was right!

2 1-pound cans pork and beans
6 strips bacon

1 cup catsup
1 cup brown sugar

Put beans in a buttered casserole. Top with bacon, then pour on the cat-sup. Scatter sugar over top. Bake at 325° F. for 2 hours.

FRENCH BEETS *Six* SERVINGS

They're nicely seasoned and with a proper amount of tart-ness.

    4 cups diced cooked beets
    3 tablespoons French or Italian-style dressing
    1 small onion, minced
    ¾ teaspoon salt
    ⅛ teaspoon pepper

Combine ingredients and heat thoroughly.

△

BROCCOLI-CHEESE CUSTARD *Six* SERVINGS

Try the same method with other frozen green vegetables.

    1 package frozen chopped broccoli
    ½ cup milk
    1½ tablespoons flour
    1 teaspoon grated onion
    1 can cheese soup
    3 eggs, slightly beaten

Cook broccoli according to package directions and drain. Place in but-tered shallow baking dish. Blend milk and flour until smooth. Add onion, the soup, and eggs and beat with rotary beater until blended. Pour over broccoli; set casserole in a shallow pan of water and bake at 350° F. for 40 minutes or until a knife inserted in the center of the dish comes out clean.

BRUSSELS SPROUTS WITH GRAPES
Four SERVINGS

Grapes are unusual, but very good with this vegetable.

1 pint fresh or 1 box frozen Brussels sprouts
½ teaspoon salt
⅛ teaspoon pepper
1 cup seedless green grapes
2 tablespoons butter

Wash and trim sprouts and steam in one inch water with the salt and pepper for 10 to 12 minutes, until just tender. Frozen sprouts will take less time, never more than 5 minutes after they are thawed. Add grapes, heat through, drain, and add butter.

CABBAGE WITH CARAWAY CHEESE SAUCE
Six SERVINGS

Cooked in this manner, cabbage is an epicure's dish.

1 medium cabbage (about 2 pounds, cooked as described below)
2 tablespoons butter
1 tablespoon caraway seeds
2 tablespoons flour
1½ cups milk
Pepper, salt as needed
1 cup shredded sharp Cheddar cheese

Remove outer leaves from cabbage and cut head into six wedges. Place in a pot with an inch of boiling salted water or beef stock, cover and cook 10 to 15 minutes or until cabbage is tender. Remove cabbage to serving dish. Melt butter in a saucepan, add caraway seeds and flour. Stir in milk gradually and cook to a smooth sauce. Season with salt and pepper. Stir in cheese, allow it to melt; then pour sauce over hot cabbage and serve.

Excellent with a ham or pork chop dinner.

SCALLOPED CABBAGE Six SERVINGS

You can make a luncheon dish of this by tucking in some diced ham or quartered hard-cooked eggs.

1 medium head cabbage, shredded or coarsely chopped
2 cups Medium White Sauce (page 254)
1 cup grated sharp cheese or Buttered Crumbs (page 255)

Cook the cabbage covered for 5 minutes in an inch of boiling water with a teaspoon of salt. Use some of the cooking liquid in the sauce, if you wish. Place cabbage in baking dish and pour sauce over it. Top with cheese or crumbs and bake 20 minutes at 375° F.

◼

SWEET-SOUR RED CABBAGE Six SERVINGS

The old-fashioned recipes required hours of cooking, but who wants to smell up the house? Here's the modern way.

3 slices bacon, diced and fried crisp
6 cups shredded red cabbage
  Salt, pepper
3 whole cloves
2 apples, peeled and sliced
1 cup boiling water
3 tablespoons flour
⅛ teaspoon cinnamon
¼ cup brown sugar
3 tablespoons vinegar

Fry bacon, then remove from skillet and add cabbage to drippings, sprinkling with salt and pepper and adding cloves and apples. Add the hot water (or water and red or white wine, in equal parts). Cover and cook gently 15 minutes. Blend flour, cinnamon, brown sugar, and vinegar. Add to cabbage; heat until thickened, add bacon, and serve hot.

CARROTS WITH MANDARIN ORANGES

Four SERVINGS

If you can find fresh mint, chop some to sprinkle over this glamorous dish.

  2 cups sliced or julienne-cut carrots, cooked
  1 can (11 ozs.) mandarin oranges, drained
  1 tablespoon cornstarch
  ½ teaspoon salt
  1 tablespoon butter

Blend 2 tablespoons juice from oranges with cornstarch and salt. Add rest of juice and cook until thick and clear. Add carrots, oranges, and butter and heat through.

GLORIFIED CARROTS

Six SERVINGS

Whole carrots in a crusty coating.

  2 eggs, slightly beaten
  2 tablespoons milk
 12 medium carrots, cooked whole
  2 cups crushed corn flakes
  ¼ cup butter
  ¼ cup brown sugar
  1 tablespoon lemon juice

Mix eggs and milk together. Dip carrots in mixture and then in corn flakes. Repeat. Brown lightly on all sides in butter in skillet. Sprinkle with brown sugar and lemon juice. Serve hot.

264

CELESTIAL CARROTS

Four to Five SERVINGS

The name describes the flavor!

1 bunch young carrots, cut in
    chunks
1 green pepper, in strips
1 tablespoon oil
3 tablespoons sugar

1 tablespoon cornstarch
1 tablespoon vinegar
½ cup water
Salt

Cook carrots and pepper in oil 10 minutes. Mix sugar, cornstarch; add vinegar, water, and a pinch of salt. Pour over vegetables and simmer 5 minutes longer.

X

CAULIFLOWER AND GREEN BEANS HOLLANDAISE

Eight SERVINGS

A whole head of cauliflower looks beautiful with a wreath of beans.

1 small head cauliflower
2 packages frozen Italian green beans
    Hollandaise, from a jar, or recipe below

Cook washed, trimmed cauliflower covered in 1-inch boiling salted water for 20 to 30 minutes or until tender; drain well and place on platter. Surround with beans cooked according to package directions. Accompany with warm hollandaise, some of which may be spooned over the cauliflower.

To PREPARE HOLLANDAISE: Combine 3 egg yolks and 3 tablespoons cream in a small earthenware bowl. Add 2 tablespoons wine vinegar, ½ teaspoon salt, a speck of cayenne, and ¼ teaspoon dry mustard. Place bowl over hot water and whip with a wire whisk until creamy and thick. Keep water under sauce just below boiling. Beat in ½ stick butter, a piece at a time, until mixture is smooth. Keep warm over hot (not boiling) water, until served.

CAULIFLOWER CUSTARD   *Six* SERVINGS

Try broccoli and cabbage this way, too.

1 cup sieved cooked cauliflower
2 tablespoons butter or margarine, melted
2 eggs, separated
1/4 cup grated cheese
2 tablespoons sour cream
1/2 cup bread crumbs softened in milk
1/2 teaspoon salt
1/4 teaspoon pepper

Combine ingredients, folding in the stiffly-beaten egg whites last. Bake in a greased dish set in a pan of hot water at 350° F. for 30 minutes, or until inserted knife comes out clean. Serve with tomato sauce and more grated cheese.

FRESH CREAM-STYLE CORN   *Three* SERVINGS
IN CREAM

As delicious as corn-on-the-cob, and easier to eat!

2 cups corn cut from cob
2 tablespoons butter
1/2 cup cream
1/2 teaspoon salt
1/2 teaspoon sugar
Dash of pepper

Scrape cobs to obtain the milky residue after cutting kernels—and use that too. Add other ingredients and simmer 5 minutes.

CURRIED CORN AND PEAS   *Six* SERVINGS

The dish is simple, but a little out of the ordinary.

1 package (2 cups) frozen peas,
    cooked
1 package frozen whole kernel
    corn, cooked

3 tablespoons butter
$\frac{1}{2}$ teaspoon curry powder
Salt, pepper

Combine peas and corn. Melt butter; add curry powder; blend. Pour over vegetables. Add salt and pepper as needed.

QUICK CORN PUDDING   *Four to Five* SERVINGS

For an accompaniment to chicken, you couldn't do better.

3 eggs
1 cup cream-style corn
    Dash pepper
1 can cream of mushroom soup

Break the eggs into a 1-quart casserole; beat well. Add other ingredients, mix, and bake in a shallow pan of water at 325° F. for 1¼ hours or until a silver knife inserted in the center comes out clean.

FRENCH-FRIED EGGPLANT   *Four* SERVINGS

These are delicious as a vegetable or as an appetizer.

1 small eggplant, sliced $\frac{1}{2}$ inch thick, then cut in strips
    $\frac{1}{2}$–1 inch wide
    Flour, salt, pepper, onion salt

Pare the eggplant or not, as you wish. Dip in seasoned flour and fry in hot oil, 365° F., for 1 minute or until browned. Drain on rack or paper toweling and serve hot.

Eggplant slices or strips may be fried in butter, or brushed with butter and broiled for 2 to 3 minutes. Sprinkle with oregano or Parmesan cheese, if you wish.

TURKISH EGGPLANT   *Six* SERVINGS

Authentically it is served with boiled cracked wheat, but rice is good too.

    1 medium eggplant, pared, sliced
    ¼ cup oil
    ¾ pound minced beef or lamb
    1 clove garlic, minced
    ¼ cup chopped green pepper
    2 large tomatoes, fresh or canned
    2 large onions, chopped
    1 teaspoon salt
      Pepper

Quarter eggplant slices and brown pieces carefully on both sides in oil. Remove from skillet, and brown meat in same oil. Add garlic, green pepper, chopped tomatoes, onion, and eggplant. Season to taste, cover and simmer gently for 45 minutes. If necessary, a little water may be added.

◻

SAUTÉED ESCAROLE   *Six* SERVINGS

The greens are prepared with olive oil and garlic, in the Italian manner.

      About 2 pounds escarole
    1 clove garlic
    ¼ cup olive oil
      Salt and pepper
      Juice of ½ lemon

Wash escarole well, removing tough or faded leaves. Drain thoroughly and break leaves in half. Brown garlic in olive oil; remove, add escarole, cover, and cook over medium heat until tender, about 20 minutes. Season to taste with lemon juice, salt, and pepper.

BAKED STUFFED ONIONS
Four SERVINGS

The bigger the onion, the better!

4 large Bermuda onions, boiled 15 minutes
1/4 cup butter or drippings
1 cup coarse dry bread crumbs
1 tablespoon minced celery tops
1/4 cup grated cheese
1/2 teaspoon salt
1/4 teaspoon pepper

Drain onions, cut off tops and scoop out centers. Chop centers fine and sauté in butter. Add crumbs, celery, cheese, and seasonings and stuff onions. Bake in greased pan with 1/2-inch water in it at 350° F. for about 30 minutes or until tender.

PIQUANT ONIONS
Five SERVINGS

A quick-and-easy, with canned onions.

1 can (16 ozs.) whole onions
2 tablespoons butter or margarine
2 tablespoons chopped parsley
1 teaspoon Worcestershire sauce
1/4 teaspoon celery salt
1/8 teaspoon pepper
1 cup grated sharp cheese

Drain onions and place in buttered baking dish. Melt butter, add parsley and seasonings. Pour over onions. Sprinkle cheese over the top. Bake at 350° F. for about 15 minutes, or until cheese is melted. You might add 1/4 cup chopped walnuts.

FRENCH PEAS
Four SERVINGS

A few pea pods in the pan will also add extra γavor.

2 pounds fresh peas, shelled, or 1 package frozen peas
2 tablespoons butter
3–4 wet outer leaves of lettuce
Salt, pepper, pinch of sugar

Add peas to melted butter in saucepan, cover with lettuce, cover pan tightly and steam about 10 minutes (5 minutes for frozen peas). Add seasonings.

PEPPERS STUFFED WITH CORN PUDDING
Four SERVINGS

For a roast of pork or veal, here's a perfect accompaniment.

4 medium green peppers
1 egg
1 cup evaporated milk
1 cup whole-kernel corn

2 tablespoons minced onion
1 teaspoon salt
Few grains black pepper

Wash peppers, cut a slice from the stem end of each, and remove seeds. Mince pepper tops to add to the filling. Beat egg with a fork, add milk, corn, onion, seasonings, and green pepper. Blend and pour into pepper cups. Place in small deep baking dish with 1/2-inch water in bottom. Cover and bake at 350° F. until pudding is set, about 35 minutes.

FRIED PEPPERS
Six SERVINGS

If you can't find both green and red peppers, use one kind alone for an unusual vegetable dish.

6 green peppers, stemmed, seeded, sliced in rings
6 red peppers, stemmed, seeded, sliced in rings
1/4 cup (1/2 stick) butter
Salt, pepper

Sauté the pepper rings (cut about ¼-inch thick) in butter until just tender, about 5 minutes, turning only once. Season to taste with salt and pepper.

CREAMED NEW POTATOES   *Four* SERVINGS

New potatoes have wonderful flavor; don't overcook them!

>   8–12 small new potatoes, cooked in jackets, then skinned
>   1½–2 cups Medium White Sauce (page 254)
>   1 tablespoon minced parsley or chives or green onion
>   tops

Heat potatoes in well-seasoned sauce, turn into hot serving dish and sprinkle with the greens.

VARIATIONS: Two tablespoons or more of chopped pimiento add both color and flavor.

One cup of fresh-cooked or frozen peas may be added. Prepare frozen peas as directed on package.

POTATOES IN SOUR CREAM   *Six* SERVINGS

So good! You might like a teaspoonful of caraway or dill seeds, too.

>   6 medium cooked potatoes
>   2 cups sour cream
>   3 tablespoons finely chopped onion
>   Salt, pepper, parsley

Cook potatoes in jackets until tender, cool, remove skins, and cut into pieces. Pour sour cream in skillet. Add potatoes and onion. Heat slowly until cream bubbles over potatoes. Season with salt and pepper. Serve at once with a garnish of parsley.

BAKED STUFFED POTATOES   *One* DOZEN

*These are great to have on hand in the freezer; do the work
on an easy day—you'll be glad you did!*

12 large Idaho potatoes, baked
1½–2 cups milk or half-and-half
1 stick butter
2 teaspoons salt
¼ teaspoon pepper
1 tablespoon grated onion

1 egg
1 jar (2 ozs.) pimiento,
   drained, chopped
1 cup grated sharp Cheddar
   cheese

Cut lengthwise slice from each hot potato (baked at 425° F. for 1 hour
or until tender). Scoop out potato pulp with spoon, leaving shells intact.
Mash potatoes with electric mixer, gradually adding hot milk, butter,
and seasonings. Add egg and whip until fluffy. Fold in pimiento and
cheese. Fill shells with potato mixture, using spoon or pastry tube.
Freeze individually in foil. Allow 1 hour and 15 minutes for the foil-
wrapped frozen potatoes to bake at 350° F. Enough for one meal may
be refrigerated instead of frozen, and will take 30 to 40 minutes at
350° F. to make them table-ready.

BARBECUED POTATOES   *Six to Eight* SERVINGS
WITH CHEESE

Cook them on the outdoor grill, if you wish.

4 large potatoes, pared and
   sliced (about 1 quart,
   prepared)
½ cup chopped onion
1½ cups milk
¼ cup catsup (hickory flavor is
   good)
½ teaspoon Worcestershire
   sauce

Dash Tabasco sauce
2 tablespoons chopped fresh
   parsley, or 1 tablespoon
   dried
1 teaspoon salt
¼ teaspoon pepper
1 cup diced process Cheddar
   cheese

Combine all ingredients in a buttered Dutch oven or heavy skillet with a cover. Cover and cook over very low heat until potatoes are tender, about 1 hour. Stir from bottom once or twice with a spatula.

DELMONICO POTATOES   *Six* SERVINGS

Cook potatoes fresh for this dish. It is not for leftovers.

6 boiled potatoes, cut in large cubes
1/4 cup chopped onion
3 tablespoons butter
1 1/2 cups cream
1 tablespoon chopped parsley
1/2 teaspoon paprika
1/8 teaspoon pepper
1/4 teaspoon salt (more if potatoes weren't salted in cooking)
1/4 cup Buttered Crumbs (page 255)

Sauté onion in butter. Add remaining ingredients except bread crumbs. Place in greased casserole, sprinkle with crumbs, and bake at 350° F. for 30 minutes.

A variation of this replaces cream with a can of cream of tomato soup plus 1/2 cup water. It isn't authentic, but it's good.

O'BRIEN POTATOES   *Six* SERVINGS

This is a good leftover dish, but it's better with freshly cooked potatoes.

6 cooked potatoes, cubed
1 medium green pepper, chopped
1 medium onion, chopped
1/2 cup grated sharp cheese
Salt, pepper to taste
1 tablespoon flour
1 cup milk
1/2 cup fine Buttered Crumbs (page 255)

Place potatoes, pepper, onion, and cheese in buttered baking dish. Add seasonings and a sprinkling of flour. Pour the milk over them and top with buttered crumbs. Bake at 350° F. for 25 to 30 minutes.

SCALLOPED POTATOES   *Eight* SERVINGS

Thin, even slices are characteristic of scalloped potatoes.

6 medium potatoes, pared and
    sliced thin
⅓ cup butter
⅓ cup flour
1 teaspoon salt
¼ teaspoon pepper

3 cups milk, scalded
1 jar (2 ozs.) pimiento, chopped,
    optional
4 green onions and tops, sliced
    thin

Place potatoes, ½ cup water, and 1 teaspoon salt in a pan. Cover, cook to boiling. Lower heat and cook for 10 minutes. Drain. Melt butter, blend in flour, 1 teaspoon salt, and the pepper. Add milk and cook, stirring constantly, until thick and smooth. Stir in pimiento and onions. Turn mixture into a casserole and bake at 350° F. for 30 minutes.

Au Gratin Potatoes. Add ½ pound diced sharp Cheddar cheese to potatoes and top with 1 cup Buttered Crumbs (page 255).

POTATOES PARISIENNE   *Four to Five* SERVINGS

Try this when you know your mashed potatoes must wait a while.

3 cups mashed, seasoned potatoes, instant or freshly cooked
2 tablespoons chopped chives
2 tablespoons pimiento
    Melted butter or grated cheese

Mix chives and pimiento with potatoes. Pile potatoes into buttered baking dish, brush with butter or sprinkle with cheese, and brown lightly at 375° F.

Duchess Potatoes. Whip an egg into the potatoes. Omit chives and pimiento; otherwise proceed in the same way.

274

POTATO PUFFS   *Six* SERVINGS

Here's an excellent way to use leftover mashed potatoes.

3 eggs, well beaten
2 cups mashed potatoes
¼ cup grated sharp process cheese
1 cup flour
2 teaspoons baking powder
1 teaspoon salt

Mix ingredients thoroughly. Drop by tablespoonfuls into hot fat, 375° F. Fry to a golden brown. Drain on soft paper. Puffs may be sautéed in butter instead of deep-fat fried.

CANDIED SWEET POTATOES   *Six* SERVINGS
WITH PINEAPPLE

Serve them with ham, roast pork, or roast turkey.

½ cup brown sugar
½ teaspoon salt
1 tablespoon cornstarch
1 can (9 ozs.) crushed pineapple, not drained

1 cup orange juice
¼ cup butter
6 to 8 cooked sweet potatoes
½ cup salted pecans

Mix sugar, salt, and cornstarch in heavy pan. Add pineapple, orange juice, and butter. Cook, stirring constantly, until sauce is thick and clear. Peel potatoes and cut them into halves. Place in a casserole and cover with sauce. Bake at 350° F. for 20 minutes. Top with nuts and serve.

If the potatoes are hot, there's no need to bake the preparation. Simply mix hot potatoes with sauce and serve. If you're entertaining, the potatoes and other ingredients may be prepared early in the day and baked just before serving.

SWEET POTATO CASHEW RING

Six to Eight SERVINGS

Pecans, peanuts, or walnuts may be used if you prefer them.

¾ cup chopped salted cashews
3 cups mashed sweet potatoes
½ cup sugar
1 teaspoon cinnamon
¼ cup pineapple or orange juice

Coat a 1-quart ring mold thickly with soft butter or margarine, dust with flour, then sprinkle cashews over the bottom. Mix together the sweet potatoes, sugar, cinnamon, and fruit juice. Press mixture carefully into mold. Bake 1 hour at 350° F. Remove from oven, let stand 15 minutes, unmold, and fill center with a cooked vegetable such as peas.

X

SPINACH WITH ROSEMARY

Six SERVINGS

In my opinion, this is spinach at its very best.

2 or 3 strips bacon or small slices ham, with drippings
2 thin-sliced onions
2 pounds washed spinach
1 cup loosely packed parsley, chopped coarse
½ teaspoon dried rosemary
1 teaspoon salt
¼ teaspoon pepper
2 tablespoons vinegar or lemon juice

Cook bacon or ham and chop fine. Add onions, spinach, and parsley to the meat and drippings. Add seasonings and cover pan. Cook until wilted, stirring occasionally. This takes but a few minutes. Add vinegar and serve. Good reheated, too.

TROPICAL SQUASH *Six* SERVINGS

This mixture usually starts pleasant conversation.

>   3 cups cooked Hubbard squash or 2 packages
>   (12-ozs. each) frozen squash
>   6 tablespoons butter or margarine
>   1 can (9 ozs.) crushed pineapple
> 1½ teaspoons salt
>   ¼ teaspoon pepper
>   Dash nutmeg or mace (optional)

Heat fresh mashed squash or thaw frozen squash according to directions, in saucepan. When hot, add butter or margarine, drained pineapple, seasonings. Beat hard until well mixed. Beat in enough of the pineapple sirup to make the mixture light and fluffy. Serve hot.

ZUCCHINI WITH CHEESE *Four* SERVINGS

*Use Cheddar, Swiss, or Parmesan cheese—they're all good
on this harmony of flavors.*

>   4 large zucchini, sliced thin, crosswise
>   1 onion, sliced thin
>   1 tomato, cut fine
>   1 green pepper, seeded and minced
>   Salt, pepper, butter
> ½ cup grated cheese

Place a thick layer of squash in buttered casserole. Sprinkle with salt and pepper, then cover with a layer of onion, tomato, and green pepper. Season that layer and repeat the performance. Then dot with butter and sprinkle with cheese. Cover and bake at 375° F. for 45 minutes.

ZUCCHINI AND TOMATOES   *Six* SERVINGS

6 medium zucchini
¼ cup butter
½ small clove garlic mashed with
    1 teaspoon salt
¼ teaspoon sweet basil

¼ teaspoon oregano
¼ teaspoon freshly ground
    black pepper
3 medium tomatoes, peeled and
    cut into eighths

Wash zucchini and cut into half-inch rounds. In the ¼ cup butter, cook the slices with garlic and seasonings, turning them frequently until they are golden brown. Cover pan and let simmer 20 minutes. Add tomatoes and simmer 5 to 10 minutes more.

VEGETABLE MEDLEY   *Four* SERVINGS

Savor and flavor are the double benefit to the menu.

1 green pepper, sliced
3 tablespoons butter
6 medium tomatoes, skinned, cut in wedges
2 cups fresh or canned whole kernel corn
1 tablespoon sugar
1 teaspoon salt

Sauté green pepper in the butter for 5 minutes. Do not brown. Add tomatoes, corn, and seasonings and cook all together for 10 minutes.

■

▲ ▲ ▲ ▲
▽ ▽ ▽ ▽
COOKIES

THERE REALLY aren't any problems in cooky making except for the time it takes to make, shape, and bake some of the more elaborate kinds. But I have left out the elaborate cookies in this collection. There are plenty of munchy, crunchy cookies, and plenty of rich and buttery ones. There are oatmeal and chocolate and peanut butter and all of the other favorite kinds, but I think you will find all of the recipes easy to use. Most of the doughs may be made ahead, mixed one day and baked the next. All of the cookies except the kisses and meringue types freeze very well.

Cookies may be kept frozen in good condition for up to three months. Doughs will keep that long, too, and the molasses and fruited doughs and batters may keep several weeks in the refrigerator, until you find the time to bake them.

Margarine may be used in place of butter—but never make the mistake of using either in the whipped form. The shortening effect is reduced, and you will be disappointed in the cookies.

COOKY BAKING PRECAUTIONS

Always preheat your oven to the required temperature. Allow 10 minutes. This is very important for good results.

Use aluminum baking sheets, with teflon coating, if you wish. Most cookies do not stick to the pan, greased or ungreased, so the teflon is not too important. Don't use cooky sheets too large for your oven—air should circulate all around the pan. And don't crowd the oven.

Cool baked cookies on racks, or on paper toweling which is a handy help when you are baking a great many cookies.

Many of the cookies in this collection are the kind that you mix, spread in a pan, or drop from a spoon and bake with no fuss or bother. The kind that need shaping may be mixed one day, baked another, to make it less work.

Keep crisp cookies in a tightly covered canister. If the moist drop cookies should dry out too much, put a slice of apple into the cooky jar with them.

SENDING COOKIES AWAY TO SCHOOL?

To keep your cookies whole instead of having them arrive in crumbs, choose the moist, fruited, chewy kinds rather than the crisp ones for mailing. Wrap each individually in plastic wrap, or pack them in layers with wrap crumpled between them, so that they won't shake against each other in transit. Pack them in a strong metal or cardboard box and place that box in a larger one with crushed paper around it for pillows.

Have fun, making cookies!

◆

CHOCOLATE PINWHEEL COOKIES
Seven or Eight DOZEN

You can freeze these buttery brown and white whirls before or ater baking.

1 cup (2 sticks) butter	1 teaspoon vanilla
2 cups sugar	4 cups flour
½ cup brown sugar, firmly packed	3 teaspoons baking powder
	¼ teaspoon salt
2 eggs, well beaten	2 ounces unsweetened chocolate, melted
1 cup chopped nuts	

Cream butter until soft; add sugars, mixing until light. Beat in eggs, then nuts and vanilla. Combine flour, baking powder, and salt. Add flour mixture gradually, mixing well. Divide dough into 2 parts. Add melted chocolate to one part, leaving other plain. Chill until firm. Roll out on floured waxed paper into equal rectangular sheets ⅛-inch thick. Turn chocolate dough over plain dough and remove waxed paper. Roll the two doughs carefully like jelly roll. Slice thin and bake on ungreased cooky sheets at 375° F. for 10 minutes.

You can make up these rolls, wrap them in foil and freeze, then slice and bake weeks later for a special occasion.

VARIATIONS

Ribbon and checkerboard cookies may also be made from this dark and light dough. Divide each batch of dough in two parts. Line a straight-sided loaf pan or freezing tray with waxed paper and pack half of the chocolate dough over the bottom, as evenly as possible. Pack half the light dough over that in an even layer. Then add the rest of the chocolate dough, packing smoothly, and top with the rest of the light dough. You should now have four layers of dark and light dough. Cover with waxed paper and chill.

Ribbon Cookies. Cut the chilled dough lengthwise into two bars, and slice off the ribbons. Bake as for the pinwheel cookies.

Checkerboard Cookies. Slice the ribbon dough ¼-inch thick and stack the slices in groups of four, turning the second and fourth slices so that you have the chocolate part of one over the light part of the next one. Chill these little loaves, then slice ¼-inch thick and you have a pretty checked pattern of light and dark doughs.

281

ANISE CHRISTMAS COOKIES — *Four* DOZEN

Hang these on your tree; they'll look ever so pretty! Make dough one day. Bake and decorate another.

½ cup butter
½ cup sugar
1 egg, beaten
1 tablespoon cream
1¾ cups sifted flour (a little more, if needed)
1 teaspoon baking powder
⅛ teaspoon salt
1 tablespoon aniseed
Lemon Glaze, Decorating Icing (see below)

Cream butter and sugar; beat in egg and cream. Stir in the sifted dry ingredients and aniseed. Cut dough into quarters; roll out each piece in turn on lightly floured board and cut with floured cooky cutters. With pointed end of skewer make a hole ½-inch from top of each cooky. Bake on ungreased cooky sheets at 425° F. about 8 minutes. Cool, frost, and decorate. Slip a piece of fine string through the hole in each cooky and tie in a loop.

HOW TO DECORATE COOKIES

Tint portions of the icing in different colors. Dip each cooky quickly into the glaze, then lay on cooky sheets to dry. To decorate the cookies, use the decorating icing and pipe through the fine stem of a decorating tube; or sprinkle the freshly iced cookies with colored sugar, confetti candies, or silver balls. Make eyes on animals with a toothpick dipped in melted chocolate, or use currants for eyes, applying them before frosting has set.

ICING OR GLAZE: Mix 2 cups confectioners' sugar with a few grains of salt, 2 teaspoons light corn sirup, ¼ teaspoon lemon extract, and 4½ to 5 tablespoons boiling water. This glaze must be thin enough to pour but thick enough to mask tops of cookies completely. If it thickens too much, add a few drops of hot water.

DECORATING ICING: Mix 1 cup confectioners' sugar with 2 tablespoons hot water, ¼ teaspoon butter, ½ teaspoon light corn sirup, and a few drops of vanilla.

AFRICAINES

Five to Six DOZEN

Use your cooky press for these deep chocolate cookies.

½ cup (1 stick) butter
1 cup brown sugar, firmly packed
1 egg
1 teaspoon vanilla
3 ounces unsweetened chocolate, melted

2½ cups flour
1 teaspoon baking powder
¼ teaspoon soda
½ teaspoon salt
½ cup evaporated milk

Cream shortening and sugar, add egg and flavoring, and beat well. Add cooled, melted chocolate. Sift dry ingredients together and add alternately with milk to make a rather stiff dough. Press dough through pastry bag or cooky press to make small cookies. Bake 12 to 15 minutes at 375° F.

▼

AMARETTI (ITALIAN MACAROONS)

Three DOZEN

These dainty morsels are professional looking, but very easy. Serve them with fruit as dessert, or with an afternoon glass of sweet wine.

½ pound blanched almonds, ground or chopped very fine
1 cup sugar
¼ teaspoon salt
2 egg whites, beaten stiff
½ teaspoon almond extract

Almonds should be reduced to a powder, easy enough to do in an electric blender. Add sugar and salt and mix well. Fold almonds and sugar into egg whites. Add almond extract and blend. Drop by teaspoons on buttered, floured cooky sheet and sprinkle with confectioners sugar. Let stand 2 hours before baking. Bake at 300° F. about 25 minutes, or until light golden.

AMISH CHRISTMAS COOKIES   *Four* DOZEN

Long on flavor, these buttery brown sugar bars are spiced just right.

1 cup (2 sticks) butter
1 cup brown sugar, packed
1 egg yolk, beaten
2 cups cake flour
1½ teaspoons cinnamon

¼ teaspoon salt
1 egg white for topping
½ cup coarsely chopped pecans
3 tablespoons confectioners' sugar

Cream butter and brown sugar until light, add egg yolk and mix well. Add sifted flour, cinnamon, and salt. Mix and spread in greased 9x13-inch pan. Beat egg white slightly with a fork and spread over the top. Pat mixture of nuts and sugar into surface of cookies and bake 40 minutes at 350° F. Cut into squares and remove from pan while warm.

APRICOT BARS   *Three* DOZEN

Serve them in squares with ice cream on top for dessert, or pack them in lunch boxes. They go to picnics happily, too.

1 package (10 ozs.) dried apricots
1¾ cups sugar
¼ cup apricot juice
¾ cup butter

2 cups flour
1 teaspoon salt
½ teaspoon soda
½ cup chopped nuts
1½ cups flake coconut

Cook apricots according to package directions without sugar. Drain. Add ¾ cup sugar and the ¼ cup juice, simmer 5 minutes and cool. Cream butter with the rest of the sugar until fluffy, add sifted dry ingredients and mix well. Add nuts and coconut, stir well, and press three-fourths of the mixture into a 13x9-inch pan. Bake at 350° F. for 10 minutes. Spread apricot mixture on top. Crumble the rest of the butter, blend over the top, and bake at 350° F. for 20 minutes more.

BUTTERSCOTCH BLONDIES

Twelve to Eighteen BARS

The no-chocolate version of brownies is good, too!

¼ cup (½ stick) butter
½ cup evaporated milk
2 cups packed brown sugar
2 eggs
½ teaspoon salt

1½ cups flour
2 teaspoons baking powder
1 teaspoon vanilla
1 cup chopped pecans

Melt butter in medium-size saucepan over low heat. Remove from heat and add evaporated milk, sugar, eggs, and salt. Beat until well blended. Sift flour with baking powder. Stir into egg mixture to blend; add vanilla and nuts. Turn into well-greased pan about 7x11 inches, and bake at 350° F. for about 45 minutes. Test with a cake tester or wooden pick for doneness. Mixture should not stick to tester. Cool in pan on a cake rack, then cut into bars.

x

CHEWY CHOCOLATE BROWNIES

Twenty-four BARS

Butterless brownies are the chewy ones, and these are delectable.

2 eggs, well beaten
1¼ cups packed brown sugar
1 teaspoon vanilla
2 ounces unsweetened chocolate, melted
½ cup flour
1 cup broken pecans

When eggs are light, add sugar, vanilla, and melted chocolate. Stir in flour and ¾-cup nuts. Spread in a greased 8-inch square pan and sprinkle the remaining nuts over the batter. Bake at 325° F. for 20 to 25 minutes. Cut into bars while warm and roll in confectioners' sugar, if you like.

DOUBLE-DECK BROWNIES   *Eighteen* COOKIES

*You'll spend more time than usual making these good cookies,
but they are definitely worth it!*

BOTTOM LAYER

½ cup flour
¼ teaspoon soda
¼ teaspoon salt

1 cup rolled oats
½ cup dark brown sugar, packed
½ cup butter (1 stick), melted

TOP LAYER

1 ounce unsweetened chocolate, melted
¼ cup (½ stick) butter, melted
¾ cup sugar
1 egg
⅔ cup flour

¼ teaspoon baking powder
¼ teaspoon salt
¼ cup milk
½ teaspoon vanilla
½ cup chopped nuts

FROSTING: 1 package (6 ozs.) chocolate pieces.

For bottom deck, sift flour, soda and salt, add oats and sugar, and
mix in butter. Pat into pan about 7 x 11 inches and bake at 350° F. 10
minutes.

For top deck, combine chocolate, butter, and sugar; add egg and
beat well. Sift dry ingredients together and add alternately with milk
and vanilla to chocolate mixture. Fold in nuts. Spread batter over baked
bottom layer and return to oven for 25 minutes. Cool and frost with
melted chocolate pieces. Cut into squares.

BRANDY SNAPS   *Three to Four* DOZEN

*The brandy's to sip with them, possibly. There's none in the
cookies, but the name is traditional.*

¾ cup butter (1½ sticks)
¾ cup sugar
½ cup molasses
2 teaspoons ginger
1½ cups flour

Heat together butter, sugar, molasses, ginger. Add flour and beat until smooth. Drop from a teaspoon onto a greased baking sheet, allowing 2 inches between cookies. Bake about 15 minutes at 300° F. Cool about a minute, remove cookies with a spatula, and quickly roll each one over the handle of a wooden spoon, top side out. Or shape into cones. If cookies cool too rapidly to shape, return pan to oven a few seconds and they will soften.

BUTTER BALLS — Eighty SMALL BALLS

Such tender morsels! They melt in your mouth!

¾ cup butter (1½ sticks)
1 cup brown sugar
1 egg
1 teaspoon vanilla
2 cups flour

½ teaspoon salt
2 teaspoons baking powder
¼ cup sugar
½ cup chopped nuts

Cream butter and sugar. Add beaten egg and vanilla. Sift flour, salt, and baking powder together, and add. Chill the dough. Roll into balls the size of marbles. Mix sugar and nuts and roll the balls in the mixture. Bake on a greased cooky sheet at 400° F., for 10 minutes. The cookies will flatten during the baking.

BROWN SUGAR COOKIES — Four DOZEN

These may be dusted with confectioners' sugar, if you like.

4 eggs, well beaten
1 pound (2¼ cups) light brown sugar

2 cups flour
1 teaspoon baking powder
1 cup chopped nuts

Mix eggs and sugar in a double boiler. Cook, stirring frequently, over hot water, for 20 minutes. Add sifted flour and baking powder, and the nuts. Mix well and spread in buttered jelly roll pan, 10½x15½ inches. Bake at 375° F. for 10 to 15 minutes, or until delicately browned. Cut into squares while warm.

BORRACHITOS (LITTLE DRUNKARDS)

Seven or Eight DOZEN

The name may be the most intriguing thing about these little Mexican dainties, but they do have lots of flavor, and are fun to make and eat.

1 cup (2 sticks) butter
⅔ cup sugar
¼ teaspon salt
2 egg yolks
3 cups flour
¼ cup sweet red wine
   Cinnamon-sugar

Cream butter and sugar, add salt and egg yolks, and mix well. Add flour alternately with wine. Shape into small balls between the palms, roll in cinnamon and sugar (heavy on the cinnamon!), and flatten with the bottom of a glass on cooky sheets. Bake at 375° F. about 10 minutes and sprinkle while hot with more of the cinnamon-sugar.

BUTTERSCOTCH COOKIES

Six DOZEN

Crisp, buttery drops to accompany iced tea, perhaps.

½ cup (1 stick) butter, melted
2 cups brown sugar, packed
2 eggs, well beaten
1½ cups flour
1½ teaspoons baking powder
½ teaspoon salt
1½ cups chopped walnuts

Mix butter and brown sugar. Stir in eggs. Add remaining ingredients and mix thoroughly. Drop from a teaspoon several inches apart on greased baking sheets. Bake at 375° F. for about 20 minutes or until brown. Remove from pans while warm.

CANDIED DREAMS   *Three and a half* DOZEN

By all means include these in your holiday assortment!

1 cup flour	1/4 cup milk
1/3 cup confectioners' sugar	3/4 cup rolled oats
1/2 teaspoon salt	1 cup chopped pecans
1/2 teaspoon grated orange rind	42 candied cherries (about 1 cup)
1/2 cup (1 stick) soft butter	

Sift flour, sugar, and salt; add orange rind. Mix in butter and milk. Add oats and pecans, mixing until well combined. Form a small piece of dough, about a teaspoonful, with your fingers to a flat round. Place one candied cherry on the dough and pinch dough together around cherry. Smooth with the fingers and place on greased baking sheets. Bake at 375° F. for 10 to 12 minutes. Dip into thin confectioners' sugar frosting; drain. (To make frosting, just mix to thin consistency confectioners' sugar and warm milk. Flavor with a few drops of vanilla or orange extract.)

CHINESE ALMOND COOKIES

They are crisp, tender, and genuinely Chinese.

2 1/2 cups flour
3/4 teaspoon baking powder
1 cup lard or other shortening
1 1/2 cups sugar
1/2 teaspoon almond extract
1 egg
1 tablespoon water

Cut fat into flour and baking powder and add sugar, extract, egg, and water. Mix well. Shape into small balls 1 inch in diameter and press down in a cooky sheet to form cookies 1/2-inch thick. Press an unblanched almond into the top of each. Bake at 350° F. about 15 minutes.

Use some butter with the lard for flavor, if you prefer. It is not typical.

CREAM CHEESE COOKIES   *Sixty* COOKIES

No Christmas cooky assortment should be without a batch of these easily made delicacies which can be very pretty.

½ pound (2 sticks) butter
2 packages (3 ozs. each) cream cheese
2 cups flour
2 tablespoons sugar
　　Thick strawberry, raspberry, or other red preserves
　　　or jam
　　Confectioners' sugar

Cream butter and cheese until light and fluffy and mix in the flour and sugar. Roll dough about ⅓-inch thick on a floured surface and cut round cookies about 1½-inches across. Make a slight depression in the center of each with your thumb and place ½ teaspoon preserves or jam in it. Bake at 375° F. about 15 minutes. Cool and sift confectioners' sugar over the cookies.

For especially pretty cookies, brush with slightly beaten egg white around the filling and sprinkle with finely chopped pistachios before baking.

CREAM CHEESE NUGGETS   *Three* DOZEN

They're orange flavored and nutty, ever so good.

¼ cup (½ stick) butter
1 3-ounce package cream cheese
1 cup sugar
1 teaspoon grated orange rind
1 cup flour
¼ teaspoon salt
½ cup chopped nuts

Cream butter and cheese until fluffy. Add all but 2 tablespoons sugar, and cream until smooth. Mix in orange rind, sifted dry ingredients, and nuts. Chill dough for several hours. Form into balls about 1 inch in diameter. Roll balls in remaining 2 tablespoons sugar. Place on an ungreased cooky sheet and bake in a moderately hot oven, 400° F., for 10 to 12 minutes, or until delicately browned.

CREAM CHEESE DATE BARS

Twenty-eight COOKIES

This is a sandwich-type cooky, delicate and delicious.

1 cup dates, chopped	½ cup shortening
½ cup sugar	1 package (3 ozs.) cream cheese
½ cup hot water	½ teaspoon salt
2 tablespoons lemon juice	2 cups flour
2 tablespoons chopped nuts	

Combine dates, sugar, and water and cook for 8 minutes. Cool. Add lemon juice and nuts. Cream shortening and cheese. Add flour and salt gradually and mix until crumbly. Press half the dough in a 7x11-inch pan and spread on date filling. Press remaining dough on top. Bake at 400° F. for 12 to 15 minutes. Cut into bars.

GREEK CHOCOLATE BALLS

Three DOZEN

You'll find rose water at the drug store for these unusual delicacies.

½ pound walnuts, ground
½ pound sweet chocolate, ground
9 pieces zwieback, ground or crushed
½ teaspoon cinnamon
1½ tablespoons sugar
2 tablespoons rose water

Mix ingredients and form into balls about 1 inch in diameter. Sprinkle with sugar. No baking.

CHOCOLATE ACORNS   *Eighty* COOKIES

They're attractive with one end coated in chocolate and pistachio nuts.

½ pound almonds, ground fine (use electric blender if possible)
½ pound unsweetened chocolate
1 tablespon flour
3 egg whites
¼ teaspoon salt

1 tablespoon vinegar
1 tablespoon vanilla
1 cup sugar
½ pound sweet chocolate (2 bars, usually)
1 cup chopped pistachio nuts or pecans

Mix nuts and chocolate with flour. Beat egg whites, salt, vinegar, and vanilla together until egg whites are stiff. Fold in sugar gradually, about 2 tablespoons at a time, beating constantly. Fold in almonds, chocolate, and flour mixture. Chill until firm enough to handle. Form into ovals about 1 inch long and ½-inch wide. Bake on ungreased cooky sheets at 300° F. for 40 minutes. Place on cake coolers. Melt sweet chocolate in a double boiler. Dip one end of each cooky in melted chocolate and then in nuts. Chill until chocolate is firm.

x

CHOCOLATE POPPY SEED COOKIES   *Four* DOZEN

They'll keep crisp for several weeks.

½ cup (1 stick) butter
½ cup sugar
2 ounces sweet chocolate, melted
½ teaspoon cinnamon
¼ teaspoon cloves
1 cup currants

1 cup poppy seed soaked in ½ cup hot milk
1¼ cups flour
1 teaspoon baking powder
¼ teaspoon salt

Cream butter and sugar; add chocolate, spices, currants, and poppy seed with milk. Mix in sifted flour, baking powder, salt. Drop from a teaspoon onto greased cooky sheets and bake at 350° F. for 15 minutes.

COCONUT KISSES *Two* DOZEN

Little coconut macaroons with a brown sugar flavor may be made in just a few minutes.

1 cup brown sugar
1 egg, slightly beaten
1 cup shredded coconut
3 tablespoons flour
1/4 teaspoon salt

Mix sugar and egg well. Add remaining ingredients and blend. Drop from a teaspoon onto a buttered cooky sheet. Bake in a moderate oven, 350° F., for about 8 to 10 minutes or until delicately browned. Remove from sheet immediately.

COCONUT RINGS *Two to Three* DOZEN

These are crisp and attractive cookies for a holiday collection.

1/2 cup butter
1 cup sugar
1 egg, beaten
2 1/2 tablespoons milk
1 teaspoon vanilla
2 1/2 cups flour (approximately)

1/2 teaspoon salt
1 1/2 teaspoons baking powder
1 egg white
Sugar, cinnamon, shredded coconut

Cream the butter and sugar. Add the egg, milk, and vanilla. Mix in flour sifted with the salt and baking powder. Roll dough on a floured board 1/4-inch thick, cut with a doughnut cutter, and transfer to a greased baking sheet. Brush each ring with slightly beaten egg white and sprinkle with cinnamon and sugar, then with coconut. Bake at 375° F. about 10 minutes or until pale brown.

COFFEE-FILBERT SANDIES   *Three* DOZEN

Substitute other nuts if you wish in these quickly made crisps.

1¼ cups flour
½ cup sugar
¼ teaspoon salt
 1 tablespoon instant coffee
¾ cup butter (1½ sticks)
¾ cup chopped toasted filberts

Mix flour, sugar, salt, and coffee. Cut in the butter until mixture is the size of small peas. Press dough together. Shape into small balls, roll in nuts, and place on ungreased baking sheets about 2 inches apart. Flatten with the bottom of a glass dipped in sugar. Bake at 300° F. for 20 minutes, or until very lightly browned. Cool slightly before removing from baking sheets. Cool on racks. Store in loosely covered container.

△

COFFEE BARS   *Three* DOZEN

Really coffee-flavored; a nice big batch.

1 cup shortening
2 cups brown sugar, packed
2 eggs, beaten
3 cups flour
1 teaspoon baking powder
1 teaspoon soda

1 teaspoon each cinnamon and
 nutmeg
1 cup strong coffee, brewed or
 instant
1 cup chopped nuts
1 cup raisins
 Coffee Icing (see next page)

Cream sugar and shortening, add eggs and mix well. Add sifted dry ingredients alternately with coffee; stir in nuts and raisins. Spread in greased jelly roll pan (15½x10½ inches) and bake at 350° F. about 25 minutes.

Frost while warm with Coffee Icing: Mix 1 tablespoon soft butter, 1 cup confectioners' sugar, about 2 tablespoons strong hot coffee, or enough to make spreadable.

SUCH GOOD DATE BARS   *Four* DOZEN

Larger squares of these oatmeal cookies may be served as dessert. This is a bar that packs well for sending to college or an army base.

FILLING

    1 pound dates, cut up (usually 2 packages)
    1 cup water
    1 cup sugar
    ½ teaspoon vanilla

COOKIES

1½ cups flour
  ½ teaspoon soda
  ½ teaspoon salt
  1 cup brown sugar

1½ cups rolled oats
  1 cup butter, melted (2 sticks)
  1 cup chopped nuts

Cook and stir dates, water, and sugar over low heat until thickened and smooth. Cool and add vanilla (You may use orange juice instead of water and flavor with a tablespoon of grated rind, if you'd rather). Set aside.

    Sift flour, soda, and salt. Add sugar, oats, butter, and nuts and mix until crumbly. Press half the mixture in a 9x13-inch pan, spread with dates, and top with rest of crumb mixture. Bake at 325° F. for 35 minutes. Cut into squares.

DATE SWIRLS

Five DOZEN

One of the prettiest as well as most delicious of cookies, you'll discover!

FILLING

¾ pound (1½ packages) pitted dates, sliced
2 tablespoons grated orange peel
⅓ cup sugar
⅓ cup water
½ cup finely chopped nuts

COOKIES

½ cup soft shortening
1 cup packed brown sugar
1 egg
½ teaspoon vanilla

2 cups flour
½ teaspoon soda
⅛ teaspoon salt

Make filling first by cooking everything but the nuts together, stirring constantly, until thickened and smooth. Add nuts and cool.

Cream shortening and sugar well, add egg, vanilla, and mix well. Add sifted dry ingredients and stir well. Divide dough into two parts. Roll each on waxed paper into a rectangle about 7x11 inches. Spread with filling. Roll tightly, beginning at wide side by lifting the paper. Chill rolls until firm. Slice ¼-inch thick and bake on lightly greased baking sheet at 400° F. about 10 minutes.

DATE DROPS

Seven DOZEN

Dates are cooked as for filling for these good lunchbox-type cookies.

2 cups chopped dates
½ cup sugar
½ cup water
1 cup (2 sticks) butter
1 cup granulated sugar
1 cup packed brown sugar

3 eggs
1 teaspoon vanilla
4 cups flour
1 teaspoon soda
½ teaspoon salt
1 cup chopped nuts

Cook dates, first measure of sugar, and water in heavy saucepan, stirring until thickened. Cool. Cream butter and remaining sugar until fluffy. Add eggs and vanilla and beat very well. Add sifted dry ingredients and mix. Stir in date paste and nuts. Drop batter from a teaspoon onto buttered cooky sheets and bake at 375° F. for 12 to 15 minutes or until delicately browned.

FRUITED HOLIDAY COOKIES   *Four* DOZEN

Flavorsome drops with raisins and cherries.

½ cup shortening
1¼ cups brown sugar, packed
1 egg
2 cups flour
2 teaspoons baking powder
½ teaspoon salt
½ teaspoon cinnamon
⅓ cup milk
1 teaspoon vanilla
1 cup raisins
½ cup chopped candied cherries
½ cup chopped nuts

Cream shortening and sugar until fluffy. Add egg, mixing well. Sift flour, baking powder, salt, and cinnamon together. Add alternately with milk to creamed mixture. Add flavoring, fruits, and nuts, and blend. Drop by teaspoonfuls on greased cooky sheet and bake at 350° F. 12 to 15 minutes.

DOUBLE DEVIL DROPS *Five* DOZEN

*You can make Triple Devil Drops of these by adding a choc-
olate icing and putting a nut on top of each cooky.*

½ cup butter (1 stick)
1 cup sugar
1 egg
1 teaspoon vanilla
1¾ cups flour

½ teaspoon salt
½ teaspoon soda
½ cup cocoa
¾ cup buttermilk
1 cup semi-sweet chocolate pieces

Cream butter and sugar until light, add egg and vanilla and beat well.
Add sifted dry ingredients alternately with milk, beating until smooth
after each addition. Stir in chocolate pieces. Drop from a teaspoon onto
buttered cooky sheets. Bake at 400° F. for about 8 to 10 minutes.

EGGNOG COOKIES *Six* DOZEN

*Eggnog flavors them, and they're delicious served with more
eggnog.*

1 cup butter (2 sticks)
2 cups sugar
1 cup eggnog
½ teaspoon nutmeg
1 teaspoon soda
5½ cups sifted flour (about)

Cream butter and sugar until light and fluffy. Add eggnog, nutmeg, and
soda; mix well. Add enough flour to make a stiff dough. Chill. Roll out
thin on a lightly floured surface and cut with Christmas cutters. Brush
with slightly beaten egg white and decorate with candied fruits or colored sugar. Bake at 375° F. for 8 to 10 minutes, or until delicately
browned.

FRYING PAN COOKIES

Five DOZEN

Or call them "skillet cookies"—they have many names and many variations. They are moist and quick, need no baking.

1½ cups chopped dates
  1 cup sugar
  2 eggs, well beaten
 ½ cup chopped nuts
  1 teaspoon rum flavoring
  1 teaspoon vanilla
 ½ teaspoon salt
2½ cups crisp breakfast cereal (cornflakes or rice or other)
1½ cups flake coconut

Mix dates, sugar and eggs, place in heavy frying pan and stir over low heat until dates are soft and mixture is thick and smooth, about 10 minutes. Add nuts, flavorings, salt, and cereal. Mix well. Cool and shape into balls, then roll in coconut.

GINGER CREAMS

Five DOZEN

A spiced refrigerator cooky; the dough keeps well chilled or frozen.

1 cup shortening
1 cup sugar
2 beaten eggs
½ cup molasses
4½ cups flour

1½ teaspoons ginger
1 teaspoon cinnamon
½ teaspoon cloves
1 teaspoon soda
1 teaspoon salt

Cream shortening and sugar, add beaten eggs and molasses. Add sifted dry ingredients gradually, mixing well. Shape the dough into rolls, wrap in waxed paper, and chill, or freeze. Slice thin and bake at 350° F. about 12 minutes.

FUDGE FANCIES   *Seven* DOZEN

*Dough for these beautiful cookies will keep in the refriger-
ator for two to three weeks if you don't want to bake it all
at one time. Warm to room temperature before using.*

    1 cup sugar
    ¾ teaspoon salt
    ½ teaspoon soda
    1 cup shortening (¾ vegetable shortening, ¼ butter)
    1 teaspoon vanilla
    1 egg
    2¾ cups unsifted cake flour
    1 cup chopped nuts
      Fudge Topping (see below)

Mix sugar, salt, and soda with shortening and vanilla. Mix well, but do
not cream together. Add egg and mix slightly. Add flour and mix enough
to blend. Divide dough into 4 equal parts and shape each part into a
roll an inch in diameter and about 14 inches long, rolling on a lightly
floured board. Spread ¼ cup chopped nuts on board and roll dough into
nuts. Repeat process with each roll. Cut into ½-inch slices and place
about 2 inches apart on slightly greased cooky sheet. Dent center of each
with finger. Bake at 375° F. for 10 minutes. Do not let cookies brown.

TOPPING: Blend 3 cups confectioners' sugar, 1 tablespoon butter, 1
tablespoon honey, 2 ounces unsweetened chocolate, melted, pinch of salt,
¼ cup hot water, until creamy. After cookies have cooled about 10
minutes, dot each one with about ½ teaspoon of fudge topping. Topping
may be warmed over hot water before using, if it has been refrigerated.

HONEY-FIG BARS Six DOZEN

Extraordinarily delicious and very good keepers, these cookies pack well for sending off to someone you love.

FILLING

2 cups ground figs
1/2 cup honey
2 tablespoons water
Juice of 1 lemon (about 3 tablespoons)

COOKIES

1/2 cup honey
1/2 cup (1 stick) butter
1/2 cup sugar
1 egg
Grated rind of 1 lemon
Juice of 1/2 lemon (about 1 1/2 tablespoons)
3 1/4 cups flour
1 teaspoon baking powder
1/2 teaspoon soda
1/2 teaspoon salt

For filling, cook honey, water, lemon juice, and figs 5 to 8 minutes, stirring constantly until thickened and smooth. Cool.

Cream honey, butter, and sugar until light; add egg, lemon rind, and juice and mix well. Sift dry ingredients together and add, mixing well. Chill dough and roll about 1/4-inch thick. Cut strips about 6 inches by 3. Place filling down center of strip and lap sides over. Place lapped side down on greased baking sheets and bake 15 to 18 minutes at 400° F. Cool and cut crosswise.

HOBNAILS
Three DOZEN

The small hand in the cooky jar will love clutching these!

    1 cup currants
    ¼ cup sweet wine or Concord grape juice
    ½ cup (1 stick) butter
    1 cup brown sugar, packed
    1 egg
    1½ cups flour
    ½ teaspoon soda
    ¼ teaspoon salt

Soak currants in wine for half an hour. Cream butter and sugar until light and fluffy, add egg and beat well. Add sifted dry ingredients alternately with wine and currants and mix well. Drop from a teaspoon onto oiled cooky sheets and bake at 375° F. for 8 to 10 minutes or until delicately browned.

JAM BARS
Two DOZEN

"Absolutely marvelous, crispy and delicious," is the notation on the file card for this recipe. See what you think!

    1½ cups flour
    1 teaspoon baking powder
    ½ teaspoon salt
    1 cup brown sugar, packed
    1½ cups rolled oats
    ¾ cup (1½ sticks) butter
    1 cup thick jam

Sift flour, baking powder, and salt. Mix with sugar and oats. Cut in the butter with finger tips or pastry blender, as for pie crust. Press ⅔ mixture into a 7x11-inch pan and spread with jam. Top with remaining mixture. Bake at 350° F. for 25 minutes.

JAM-FILLED COOKIES *Three* DOZEN

They are toothsome, rich little morsels!

½ pound (2 sticks) butter	2 cups flour
⅓ cup sugar	1 teaspoon baking powder
2 eggs, slightly beaten	⅓ cup jam or marmalade

Cream butter and sugar; add eggs. Gradually add sifted flour and baking powder; chill. Roll dough ⅛-inch thick on a well-floured pastry cloth and cut with a 2½-inch round cutter. Place a half teaspoon of jam in center of cooky and fold; press edges together with a fork. Dip cookies in a shallow dish of sugar and place on a cooky sheet. Bake in a hot oven, 400° F., about 10 minutes or until delicately browned.

△

LEMON-COCONUT BARS *Eighteen* BARS

Pudding and pie filling is part of the flavor secret. Use nuts instead of coconut if you prefer.

½ cup butter (1 stick)
¼ cup confectioners' sugar
1 cup flour
2 eggs
½ cup sugar
1 package lemon pudding and pie filling
½ teaspoon baking powder
1 cup chopped dates
1 cup grated or flake coconut

Cream butter and confectioners' sugar until light and blend in flour. Press evenly into an 8- or 9-inch square pan. Bake at 350° F. for 18 to 20 minutes, or until lightly browned. Meanwhile, beat eggs until thick and lemon colored; gradually beat in granulated sugar. Add pudding and baking powder, then dates and coconut. Spread on hot crust. Return to oven; bake for 25 to 30 minutes, until puffed and browned. Cool; cut into bars. Store in a tightly covered container.

LEMONADE DROPS   *Eight* DOZEN

*Make these cookies tiny; they have a cakey texture and lots
of flavor.*

1 cup butter
1 cup sugar
2 eggs
3 cups flour
1 teaspoon soda
1 can (6 ozs.) frozen lemonade mix, thawed
  Sugar

Cream butter and sugar until light. Add eggs and beat well. Add sifted
flour and soda alternately with half of the lemonade concentrate. Mix
well. Drop from a teaspoon about 2 inches apart on greased cooky sheets.
Bake at 400° F. about 8 minutes or until delicately browned. Brush hot
cookies with remaining lemonade mix and sprinkle thickly with sugar.
Cool on racks or on paper toweling. These keep quite well in a cooky jar,
and freeze beautifully.

△

LEMON WAFERS   *Eight* DOZEN

The distinct lemon flavor is pleasing.

1 cup shortening
1½ cups sugar
3 eggs, well beaten
2 tablespoons lemon juice
1 tablespoon grated lemon rind
4½ cups flour
½ teaspoon salt

Cream shortening and sugar, add eggs, lemon juice, and rind, then flour
and salt. Shape into long rolls and wrap in waxed paper. Chill or freeze.
Slice thin and bake on greased cooky sheets at 400° F. about 12 minutes.

LEMON TEA CAKES   *Four* DOZEN

A thin, lemon-flavored confectioners' sugar icing may be dribbled over the baked cookies if you want them festive.

⅓ cup butter
1 package (3 ozs.) cream cheese
¾ cup sugar
1 egg
3 tablespoons lemon juice
  Grated rind of ½ lemon
1¾ cups flour
1½ teaspoons baking powder
¼ teaspoon salt

Cream butter, cheese, and sugar until light. Add egg, lemon juice, and rind and beat well. Add sifted dry ingredients and mix well. Drop from a teaspoon onto ungreased cooky sheets and bake at 400° F. for 12 to 15 minutes or until cookies are delicately browned.

TOFFEE SQUARES   *Four* DOZEN

Everywhere they appear these are a terrifically popular cooky.

1 cup (2 sticks) butter
1 cup brown sugar, firmly packed
1 egg yolk
2 cups flour

1 teaspoon vanilla
1 8-ounce bar milk chocolate
1 cup chopped nuts

Cream butter and sugar until light. Beat in egg, add vanilla and sifted flour. Spread thinly on ungreased cooky sheet or in a jelly-roll pan, 10½x15½ inches. Bake at 350° F. for 20 minutes. Melt chocolate bar and spread on cooky surface while warm. Sprinkle with nuts and cut into bars while warm.

LIZZIES *Six* DOZEN

For years these fruit and nut drops have been a holiday favorite with members of the Mary Meade staff. They are wonderful for serving with the New Year's eggnog.

½ cup brown sugar
¼ cup butter
2 eggs
1½ cups flour
1½ teaspoons soda
1 teaspoon cinnamon
¼ teaspoon nutmeg
¼ teaspoon cloves

1½ tablespoons milk
⅓ cup bourbon or orange juice
1 pound seeded raisins, washed,
    dried
1 pound small pecan halves
½ pound citron, chopped
1 pound candied cherries, whole
    or halves

Cream sugar and butter, add eggs and beat until light and fluffy. Sift
together ½ cup flour, soda and spices, and add to egg mixture. Coat
raisins well with remaining flour. Add milk and bourbon, mixing well.
Add raisins, nuts, citron, and cherries. Drop onto greased cooky sheet and
bake at 325° F. for 25 minutes.

Note that *seeded* raisins, not seedless, are used. These fat raisins
have much more flavor, but are not always available except around holiday time. They are worth searching for.

MARMALADE PILLOWS *Thirty-two* COOKIES

*They are dainty and delicious, and look exceptionally pretty
if you cut the squares with a pastry jagger.*

2 cups flour
2 teaspoons baking powder
½ teaspoon salt
¾ cup sugar
½ cup melted shortening

2 eggs
½ teaspoon orange extract
1 tablespoon shredded
    orange rind
¾ cup orange marmalade

Sift flour, baking powder, and salt. Add sugar to melted shortening and
mix well. Add eggs, beating until mixture is smooth and well blended.

Stir in extract and orange rind. Gradually add flour mixture, stirring until smooth. Cover and chill for several hours. Divide dough in half, returning one half to refrigerator. Roll the other into a 12-inch square and cut into 16 3-inch squares. Place 1 teaspoon marmalade in the center of each square and bring corners together over filling, sealing edges. Place on baking sheet and bake at 375° F. for 12 to 15 minutes. Roll and prepare remainder of dough in the same way. Bake it at a later time, if you wish. If you hold it, wrap it in foil.

MANDARIN MACAROONS   Six DOZEN

Everyone's crazy about these unusual, crunchy cookies, the recipe for which came from a good cook with the lovely name of Lotus Quon.

⅔ cup confectioners' sugar	½ teaspoon almond extract
⅔ cup granulated sugar	⅔ cup ground almonds
3 tablespoons cake flour	1 cup flake coconut
5 egg whites	1 cup crushed Chinese noodles

Sift sugars and flour. Beat egg whites and flavoring until stiff but not dry. Beat in sugar, 2 tablespoons at a time. Fold in almonds, coconut, and noodles. Drop from a teaspoon onto brown paper on a cooky sheet and bake at 325° F. for 20 to 25 minutes, or until delicately browned.

MARGUERITES   Two DOZEN

Here's an old-fashioned after-school snack, as good now as ever.

1 egg white, beaten stiff	½ teaspoon vinegar
1½ cups confectioners' sugar	¼ cup chopped nuts
¼ teaspoon vanilla	24 crackers

Mix ingredients in order given, except crackers. Spread on crackers and Bake at 350° F. for about 15 minutes, or until delicately browned.

OATMEAL CRISPIES   *Eight* DOZEN

They're an easily made, economical, and delicious cooky.

   ¾ cup shortening or butter
   1 cup brown sugar, packed
   ½ cup granulated sugar
   2 eggs beaten
   1 teaspoon vanilla
   1½ cups flour
   1 teaspoon salt
   1 teaspoon soda
   3 cups quick-cooking rolled oats
   ½ cup chopped nuts

Cream fat and sugar, add eggs and vanilla. Beat well. Add sifted dry ingredients and mix well. Mix in rolled oats and nuts. Form into rolls 1½ inches in diameter. Wrap in waxed paper. Chill. Cut in ¼-inch slices. Bake on ungreased baking sheet at 350° F. for 10 minutes.

◘

OATMEAL DROP COOKIES   *Eight* DOZEN

Molasses and spice and everything nice!

4 cups flour	2 cups rolled oats
1 teaspoon salt	1⅓ cups chopped walnuts
1 teaspoon soda	1⅓ cups shortening
2 teaspoons baking powder	1½ cups brown sugar
1 teaspoon cinnamon	4 eggs
½ teaspoon each, cloves, and	½ cup dark molasses
nutmeg	¼ cup hot water

Sift dry ingredients; add oats and nuts. Cream shortening and sugar, beat in eggs, one at a time. Add molasses, hot water; mix in dry ingredients. Drop from a teaspoon on greased baking sheets. Bake at 400° F. about 10 minutes.

OATMEAL COOKIES WITH VARIATIONS

Four DOZEN

These are done by the quick-mix method used for many cakes.

1 cup flour
1 teaspoon baking powder
½ teaspoon salt
¾ cup soft shortening (not butter or margarine)
1 cup brown sugar, packed
2 eggs
1 teaspoon vanilla
⅓ cup milk
3 cups rolled oats

Sift together flour, baking powder, and salt into bowl. Add shortening, sugar, eggs, vanilla, and half the milk. Beat until smooth, about 2 minutes. On an electric mixer use medium speed. Fold in remaining milk and rolled oats. Drop from a teaspoon onto greased baking sheet; bake at 375° F. for 12 to 15 minutes.

VARIATIONS

Chocolate Chip. Add 1 package chocolate pieces when folding in the remaining milk and rolled oats.

Date or Prune. Add 1 cup chopped dates or prunes.

Coconut. Add 1 cup shredded coconut.

Raisin Spice. Sift 1 teaspoon cinnamon and ¼ teaspoon nutmeg with the dry ingredients. Add 1 cup raisins.

Fruited Nut Drops. Add ½ cup chopped nuts and ½ cup chopped candied cherries.

OLD-FASHIONED SUGAR COOKIES FROM A CAKE MIX

Four DOZEN

Got some raisins in the cupboard?

1 package white cake mix
1/3 cup water
1/2 cup raisins

Empty mix into bowl, add water, and beat vigorously until smooth and creamy. Fold in raisins. Roll out on lightly floured board to 1/8 inch in thickness. Sprinkle with sugar. Cut with floured cutter and bake on greased baking sheet at 375° F. for 8 to 10 minutes.

ROLLED SUGAR COOKIES

Five to Six DOZEN

A pie-crust method of mixing succeeds here.

4 cups flour	2 eggs, beaten
1 teaspoon soda	1 1/4 cups sugar
1 teaspoon baking powder	1/3 cup milk
1/2 teaspoon salt	1 teaspoon vanilla
1 cup (2 sticks) butter	

Sift flour, soda, baking powder, and salt. Cut in butter or margarine as for pie crust. Beat eggs, add sugar, milk, and vanilla. Pour sugar mixture into flour mixture and mix smooth. Roll out on floured and sugared board, cut in desired shapes, and cover with granulated sugar. Bake in a moderately hot oven, 375° F., about 10 minutes.

VARIATIONS

1. Add a square of chocolate, melted, to part of dough before rolling. These cookies are good with icing.

2. Make filled cookies by putting two together with this filling: Cook 1 cup chopped dates, 1/2 cup sugar, 1/2 cup chopped nuts, and 1/4 cup water together over direct heat until thickened, stirring constantly. Cool. Prick top of each cooky sandwich with a fork. Bake about 15 minutes.

ORANGE-GINGER COOKIES   *Five* DOZEN

They're so thin, crisp, and spicy!

3 cups flour	1 egg
2 teaspoons cinnamon	2 tablespoons dark corn sirup
2 teaspoons ginger	2 teaspoons soda
1/2 teaspoon cloves	1 tablespoon warm water
1 cup (2 sticks) butter	Grated rind of 1 large orange
1 1/2 cups sugar	

Sift dry ingredients together. Cream butter and sugar until light. Stir in egg and sirup. Add soda which has been dissolved in warm water and blend well. Add orange rind. Add dry ingredients and mix thoroughly. Chill. Roll very thin on a lightly floured pastry cloth and cut into desired shape. Place half a blanched almond in the center of each cooky. Bake on ungreased cooky sheets at 400° F., 5 to 10 minutes.

ORANGE-OATMEAL   *Three* DOZEN
REFRIGERATOR COOKIES

I always double the recipe for these crisp cookies, because they go fast.

3/4 cup flour
1/4 teaspoon salt
1 1/2 teaspoons baking powder
1 cup rolled oats
1/2 cup brown sugar
1/2 cup (1 stick) butter, melted
3 tablespoons water
1 tablespoon grated orange rind

Sift flour, salt, and baking powder; add oats and sugar. Stir in butter, water, and orange rind. Mix well. Chill for several hours. Form into a roll about 1 1/2 inches in diameter, wrap in waxed paper or plastic wrap, and chill overnight. Slice about 1/4-inch thick. Bake on ungreased cooky sheets at 350° F. 12 to 15 minutes or until delicately browned.

GLAZED ORANGE WAFERS   *Seven* DOZEN

They're very attractive, very munchable.

¾ cup (1½ sticks) butter
1 cup sugar
2 eggs
3 cups flour

½ teaspoon baking powder
¼ teaspoon salt
2 teaspoons grated orange rind

GLAZE: ¼ cup butter, ½ cup honey, 2 tablespoons orange juice, ½ cup finely chopped nuts.

Cream butter and sugar until light, add eggs and mix well. Stir in sifted dry ingredients and rind and mix thoroughly. Chill dough for several hours or overnight. Roll very thin, about 1/16 of an inch, on a floured pastry cloth. Cut into desired shapes. Bake on ungreased cooky sheets at 425° F., for 5 to 7 minutes, or until delicately browned. Cool. Mix ingredients for glaze together and heat through. Brush glaze on cookies with a pastry brush. Sprinkle with nuts.

△

ORANGE-PECAN   *Six* DOZEN
REFRIGERATOR COOKIES

Brown sugar and pecans together with orange juice and rind
—how can they miss!

1 cup shortening
½ cup brown sugar, packed
½ cup white sugar
1 egg, beaten
1 tablespoon grated orange rind

2 tablespoons orange juice
2¾ cups flour
¼ teaspoon soda
¼ teaspoon salt
½ cup chopped pecans

Cream shortening and brown and white sugar. Add beaten egg, orange rind, and orange juice. Add dry ingredients, sifted together, and chopped pecans. Shape into roll 2 inches in diameter, wrap in waxed paper, chill several hours or overnight. Slice thin; bake on ungreased cooky sheet at 400° F. for 10 minutes, or until lightly browned. You can put the dough through your cooky press if the nuts are fine.

312

PEANUT BUTTER REFRIGERATOR COOKIES

Six to Seven DOZEN

These are a good plain cooky, crisp and really tasting of peanut butter.

¾ cup shortening
¾ cup peanut butter
¾ cup brown sugar, firmly packed
¼ cup granulated sugar
2 eggs

1 teaspoon vanilla
2 cups flour
2 teaspoons baking powder
½ teaspoon salt

Cream shortening, peanut butter, and sugars together until light and fluffy. Add eggs and vanilla, beating well. Add sifted flour, baking powder, and salt, and mix until well blended. Shape dough into rolls 1½ inches in diameter; wrap in waxed paper. Chill or freeze. Slice thin and bake on ungreased baking sheets at 375° F., 10 to 12 minutes.

◘

PECAN DREAMS

Two DOZEN

Here are buttery, nutty bars baked in two layers—and so delicious!

½ cup (1 stick) butter
¼ cup confectioners' sugar
1 cup flour
2 eggs
1½ cups brown sugar
½ teaspoon baking powder
½ cup shredded coconut
1 cup chopped pecans

Blend the butter, confectioners' sugar, and flour and spread evenly over the bottom of a 7x11-inch baking pan. Beat the eggs, add brown sugar, baking powder, coconut, and pecans. Mix thoroughly and pour over the first mixture. Bake at 350° F. for 30 minutes. Cool and cut into squares.

313

PECAN MERINGUE DROPS   *Two* DOZEN

Serve these confections with a pretty sherbet for dessert.

1 egg white
1 cup light brown sugar
  Few grains salt
1 tablespoon flour
1 cup chopped pecans

Beat egg white until stiff and gradually beat in brown sugar. Continue beating until meringue holds shape. Fold in salt, flour, nuts. Drop on buttered cooky sheets leaving plenty of room for expanding. Bake at 250° F. for about 15 minutes. Cool for several minutes, then remove from pan with a spatula.

PLAIN KISSES AND VARIATIONS   *Four* DOZEN

Even a plain kiss is nice!

4 egg whites
1⅓ cups sugar
¼ teaspoon salt
1 teaspoon vanilla

Add salt to egg whites and beat to a stiff foam. Add sugar about a tablespoon at a time and beat until stiff and glossy. Fold in vanilla, after adding about half the sugar. Drop the mixture onto heavy ungreased paper on cooky sheets, allowing room for spreading. Bake at 300° F. until lightly browned, about 25 minutes. Cool and remove from paper with a spatula.

KISS VARIATIONS

1. Fold in 1½ cups chopped pecans, walnuts, black walnuts, or other nuts just before dropping cookies, or fold in 2 cups coconut, corn flakes, or wheat flakes.

2. Fold in 1½ cups semi-sweet chocolate pieces.

3. Fold in mixture of nuts, corn flakes, coconut, and raisins, about 2 cups in all, just before dropping.

4. Kisses may be flavored with maple or almond instead of vanilla.

◘

PUDDING MIX COOKIES WITH VARIATIONS

Four DOZEN

This recipe originated in the test kitchens of the Chicago Public Schools. The kids love them!

1 cup (2 sticks) butter	2 cups flour
2 packages (4 ozs. each) pudding mix	1 teaspoon soda
	1 teaspoon cream of tartar
¼ cup sugar	¼ teaspoon salt
2 eggs	

Cream butter, mix in pudding mix and sugar. Add eggs; beat until fluffy. Sift flour, soda, cream of tartar, and salt together. Add to creamed mixture. Blend thoroughly. Drop by teaspoonfuls or roll into small balls and flatten with fork on greased cooky sheet. Bake at 350° F. for 15 to 20 minutes.

VARIATIONS

If butterscotch or vanilla pudding mix is used, add 2 cups crushed corn or wheat flakes or 1 cup chopped nuts. One cup raisins or dates or the same amount of coconut might be added. Put a cherry or half nut on each cooky, if you wish.

If chocolate pudding mix is used, add 1 cup chopped nuts and 1 teaspoon vanilla.

Anise or caraway seeds may be sprinkled on plain vanilla cookies before baking.

PRALINE COOKIES

Three DOZEN

They look and taste rather like the candy they're named for.

1/2 cup (1 stick) butter
1 1/2 cups brown sugar, packed
1 egg
1 1/2 cups flour
1 teaspoon vanilla
1 cup pecans, coarsely broken

Cream butter, add sugar and egg. Add flour, vanilla, and nuts; mix well. Shape in balls the size of a walnut, place on buttered cooky sheet, and flatten out to about 1/8-inch thick. Bake at 375° F. 12 minutes.

△

RUSSIAN FEAST CAKES

Six DOZEN

These flaky pastries are rich and delicious.

5 eggs
1 cup sugar
1 cup sour cream
About 5 cups flour
1 1/2 cups (3 sticks) butter
1/4 cup sugar
1 teaspoon cinnamon
3/4 cup finely chopped almonds

Beat eggs until light, add sugar, then sour cream. Stir in enough flour to make a dough which will just roll. Roll out 1/4-inch thick and spread with softened butter. Fold dough to center, roll, and spread again with butter. Repeat this process four times. Then chill dough overnight. Roll out 3/8-inch thick, sprinkle with mixture of sugar and cinnamon, then chopped almonds. Cut in 10 strips about 4x6 inches, and roll up the narrow way, to make a roll 4 inches long. Cut into slices about 3/8-inch thick, top again with sugar and almonds, and bake at 350° F. for about 15 minutes.

ROCKS

Here's the best recipe I've ever found for these traditional cookies, but the name is very misleading. They are soft, not hard cookies!

1 cup (1 stick) butter	½ teaspoon allspice
1½ cups packed brown sugar	¼ teaspoon nutmeg
3 eggs	1½ teaspoons cinnamon
3 cups flour	2 cups raisins
1 teaspoon soda	1½ cups chopped nuts
¼ teaspoon cloves	

Cream butter and sugar until light and add eggs one at a time, beating well after each. Sift flour with soda and spices and add gradually. Stir in raisins and nuts. Drop from a tablespoon onto lightly greased baking sheets and bake at 375° F. for 8 to 10 minutes.

SALTED PEANUT DROPS

Here's an unusual cooky you can't let alone.

1 pound salted Spanish peanuts
3 eggs, well beaten
1 cup brown sugar, packed
3 tablespoons flour
¼ teaspoon baking powder
1 teaspoon vanilla

Force peanuts, skins and all, through coarse knife of meat grinder. Add sugar to eggs and beat until thick and light. Add flour and baking powder and mix well. Add peanuts and stir until blended. Drop from a teaspoon on lightly greased cooky sheet. Bake at 400° F. for about 8 minutes. Remove from sheet at once.

SCANDINAVIAN COOKIES   *Two* DOZEN

Want to try a small recipe for a very attractive holiday sweet?

½ cup (1 stick) butter
¼ cup brown sugar, packed
1 egg, separated

1 cup flour
½ cup chopped nuts
Apple or currant jelly

Cream butter, add sugar, and beat until light and fluffy. Add beaten egg yolk. Add flour and blend. Form into small balls about 1 inch in diameter. Dip balls in slightly beaten white of egg, and then in chopped nuts. Place on baking sheet about 3 inches apart. Bake at 350° F. about 10 minutes. Take pan out of oven, and with the tip of a teaspoon make a slight depression on top of each cooky, return to oven and bake about 5 minutes longer. When cookies are slightly cooled, place a small amount of jelly in the depression. Jelly will not melt, but will form a thin crust if placed when cookies are almost cool. Cookies are more attractive if the nuts are shaved instead of chopped as they curl a little while baking.

x

SHERRIED BUTTERNUT DROPS   *Seventy-five* COOKIES

This is the crisp, buttery nut cooky everyone loves at holiday time.

1½ cups (3 sticks) softened butter
1¾ cups sifted confectioners' sugar
¼ teaspoon salt
3⅓ cups flour
½ cup sherry
1 cup finely chopped walnuts or pecans

Cream butter and sugar thoroughly; add salt. Add flour alternately with wine, mixing well after each addition. Drop by teaspoonfuls onto lightly greased baking sheets and bake 18 to 20 minutes at 350° F. Roll while hot in confectioners' sugar.

SWEDISH SPICE COOKIES *Twelve* DOZEN

You can roll these paper thin—easily!

5½ to 6 cups flour
1 teaspoon baking powder
½ teaspoon soda
¼ teaspoon salt
1 cup sugar
1 teaspoon cinnamon

1 teaspoon ground cardamom
¼ teaspoon cloves
1 cup melted shortening
1 cup light or dark corn sirup
1 cup cold strong coffee, brewed
  or instant

Sift 5½ cups flour with other dry ingredients, add mixture of shortening, sirup, and coffee and mix well. If necessary, add a little more flour to make a soft dough. Chill, roll out paper thin, and cut into desired shapes. Bake on lightly greased cooky sheets at 350° F. about 10 minutes.

△

FROSTED SHERRY COOKIES *Five* DOZEN

A double dose of sherry and a sprinkling of nutmeg give character to these little sweet-treats.

2 cups flour
2 teaspoons baking powder
¼ teaspoon salt
½ cup (1 stick) butter
1 cup sugar

1 egg, well beaten
3 tablespoons sherry
Nutmeg
Sherry Frosting (see below)

Mix and sift flour, baking powder, and salt. Cream butter and sugar together until light and fluffy; beat in egg. Add flour mixture alternately with sherry, beating well after each addition. Shape into balls about the size of a large marble and place on a greased baking sheet. Flatten each ball slightly with a spatula. Bake at 350° F. for 25 minutes. Cool and spread with Sherry Frosting, then sprinkle with nutmeg.

SHERRY FROSTING: Heat 2 tablespoons sherry and 2 tablespoons butter in a small saucepan, add 1 cup confectioners' sugar and stir well, then beat to blend. If mixture stiffens before all cookies are frosted, add a few drops of sherry.

SHORTBREAD

Six DOZEN

These Scottish treats take but three ingredients in their traditional form, which is perhaps the best, but there are enticing variations.

1 pound butter
1 cup sugar
4 cups flour

Cream the butter until light; blend in sugar gradually. Knead in the flour. Roll out to a rectangle ½-inch thick or press into a jelly-roll pan, about 10x15 inches. If you like, press a design on top, or prick with a fork. Bake at 350° F. 20 to 25 minutes. Cut into small bars or squares and cool. Keeping qualities are good if the cookies are stored in a canister.

If you like, coat the baking pan with sugar and roll sugar into the surface of the shortbread.

VARIATIONS

Almond Shortbread. Add 2 teaspoons almond extract and 1½ cups finely chopped almonds to the dough.

Christmas Shortbread. Use brown sugar instead of white and mix in 1 cup slivered blanched almonds and 1 cup chopped candied red and green cherries. Cut in diamond shapes.

△

THREE-LAYER COOKIES

Four DOZEN

Luscious, a confection, and bound to be the most popular cooky on the plate!

BOTTOM LAYER

½ cup (1 stick) butter
¼ cup sugar
⅓ cup cocoa
1 teaspoon vanilla

1 egg, slightly beaten
1 can (1 cup) flake coconut
2 cups crushed vanilla wafers

TOP—*Double-deck Brownies, page 286; Borrachitos, page 288 Cream Cheese Cookies, page 290; Date Swirls, page 2?* BOTTOM—*Crumbly Topped Apple Pie, page 342; Sour Cream Apple Pie, page 343; Apple Slices, page 343*

MIDDLE LAYER

3 tablespoons milk
2 tablespoons vanilla pudding
mix

½ cup butter
2 cups confectioners' sugar

GLAZE: 1½ bars (6 ozs.) sweet chocolate, 1½ tablespoons butter.

Cook over hot water until blended the butter, sugar, cocoa, and vanilla.
Add egg and cook 5 minutes more. Add coconut and vanilla wafer
crumbs and press into a 9x12-inch pan. Let stand 15 minutes. Meanwhile mix milk and pudding mixture. Cream butter, add pudding mix,
and confectioners' sugar. Beat until smooth. Spread over first layer and
let stand 15 minutes or until firm. Melt chocolate with butter, cool, and
spread on second layer. Cut into squares which can be very tiny, if you
wish.

SPRITZ

Eight DOZEN (SMALL)

*We always make these Scandinavian cookies for our Tribune
Christmas egg-nog party.*

1 pound butter
1¼ cups sugar
2 eggs
1 teaspoon baking powder
5 cups flour (about)
1 teaspoon vanilla
¾ teaspoon almond extract

Cream butter and sugar until fluffy. Add unbeaten eggs and blend well.
Mix flour and baking powder and work into mixture. Finally, add flavorings. Force through a spritz tube or cooky press into S shapes and small
circles onto greased baking pans. Bake at 350° F. for 10 to 12 minutes.

*Pumpkin Chiffon Tarts (rear), page 346; Macaroon
Refrigerator Cake, page 333; Orange Apricot Fluff,
page 352; Fresh Fruit in Pineapple Shell*

TREASURE BALLS   *Four* DOZEN

You'll treasure the recipe, for these cookies are mighty good!

½ cup (1 stick) butter
3 tablespoons brown sugar
1 teaspoon vanilla
½ cup semi-sweet chocolate pieces, chopped fine (use
    blender, if you have one, or nut grinder)
1 cup minus 2 tablespoons sifted flour
    Confectioners' sugar

Cream butter and brown sugar well, then add vanilla, chocolate, and flour. Mix well and shape into 1-inch balls. Bake at 350° F. on ungreased cooky sheet, for 15 to 20 minutes. Cool and shake in a paper bag with confectioners' sugar.

◎◆◎◆◎◆◎

DESSERTS

THE rich, luscious dessert is out of tune with the times.
There are too many dieters, and a plush finale to a meal
often throws a menu out of balance. Few modern busy homemakers have the time to spend hours preparing something
elaborate for a party. Luckily, the prepared and semiprepared
dessert is readily at hand in the supermarket, delicatessen, or
bakery, so that even entertaining does not present much of a
problem.

Often the best dessert is fresh fruit. I know a charming
hostess, an excellent cook, who makes a practice of serving
fresh fruit with an array of toppings. In a punch bowl she
combines peaches, pears, orange sections, melon balls, seeded
grapes, scattering fresh bright berries over the combination.
One helps oneself, placing the bright fruit and its juice in a
glass dessert dish, then spooning toppings from a collection
of small bowls nearby. Such glamorizers are offered as honey,
flake coconut, yogurt, chopped nuts, diced dates, perhaps
baby marshmallows. The activity inspires comment, and may
even offer a choice of fruit. I have seen a guest pluck only
watermelon balls from such a bowlful, with the comment, "I
go for watermelon!"

Fresh raspberries or strawberries may be served alone

with a topping of sour cream and brown sugar, or softened vanilla ice cream. One fruit, several, or many may be lightly bathed in the serving dish or sherbet glass with Kirsch, Grand Marnier, Cointreau, Framboise, Crème de Menthe or Sauterne, the brandy, liqueur, or wine adding an ineffable fragrance and flavor. A tablespoon per portion of fruit is about right.

THE POSSIBILITIES IN ICE CREAM

A computer or a bright child could possibly tell you how many different combinations will make a sundae for a Sunday dinner if there are a dozen ice creams and sherbets, and a dozen toppings available for mix-matching. There are many more possibilities than a dozen. You'll know when you shop for ice creams and toppings.

Take peppermint ice cream as the first of the dozen. Top it with chocolate sauce or marshmallow cream or crème de menthe for mint-on-mint. Or chopped nuts, crushed toffee, fresh raspberries, or coconut. You've barely begun to explore the possibilities.

For company it pays to buy top-quality ice cream, and you'll find a wide variety: fudge, coffee, mint, butter pecan, toffee. Peach, lemon, cherry, strawberry. Even pumpkin at holiday time. Concentrate on serving it prettily in stemmed sherbets or parfait glasses or champagne saucers.

For very "gourmet" occasions serve something simple and elegant such as lemon sherbet with crème de cassis over it; rich chocolate or coffee ice cream with coffee liqueur; vanilla ice cream topped with cherry pie filling which has been flavored with cherry liqueur; rum ice cream topped with toasted chopped pecans. At holiday time, eggnog or pumpkin or vanilla ice cream with hot mincemeat topping.

Many another kind of dessert that takes little time and pleases a husband, a family, or guests is to be found in this collection of easy-do recipes. Included are some gourmet specialties for the nicest dinner parties. I hope you will find bright ideas for your entertaining among them.

DEVILISH ANGEL DESSERT   *Sixteen* SERVINGS

Better buy the cake, since you're going to tear it apart.

1 small angel food cake
2 packages (6 ozs. each) chocolate pieces
2 tablespoons sugar
3 eggs, separated
2 cups heavy cream, whipped

Melt chocolate in top of double boiler. Add sugar and well-beaten egg yolks, mixing thoroughly. Remove from heat and fold in stiffly beaten egg whites. Cool. Fold in whipped cream. Tear angel food cake into bite-size pieces. Sprinkle a layer of cake in a buttered pan about 9x13 inches, using about half of the cake. Cover with a layer of chocolate mixture. Then add remaining cake and chocolate mixture. Chill overnight. Cut in squares.

CHERRY ANGEL PUDDING   *Sixteen* SERVINGS

This dessert is easy to serve for a party, and so pretty and good!

1 angel food cake, 10 inches, cut in 1-inch cubes
1 can (1 lb. 4 ozs.) cherry pie filling
1 package instant vanilla pudding
2½ cups milk
1 cup sour cream

Turn half the cake cubes into a 9x13-inch pan and spoon the cherry filling over them. Prepare pudding according to package directions, using 2½ cups milk. Add sour cream to pudding and blend with a wire whisk. Spoon mixture over cake and cherries. Chill 6 hours or overnight. Cut into squares to serve.

LIME ANGEL DESSERT   *Twelve* SERVINGS

Buy a small angel food to make this delicious chilled pudding.

 1 package lime gelatin
 1 cup sugar
1¼ cups boiling water
 ⅓ cup lime juice
 1 can (1 cup) flaked coconut
 1 cup heavy cream, whipped
 1 small angel food, torn into small pieces

Dissolve gelatin and sugar in boiling water. Add juice and chill until partly thickened. Fold in coconut and whipped cream. Place a layer of cake pieces in a 9x13-inch pan and spread half the lime mixture over them. Repeat. Chill for several hours or overnight and cut into squares.

APPLE CRUMBLE   *Twelve* SERVINGS

Ridiculously simple, this party dessert is economical also.

 1 package honey spice cake mix
 2 cans (1 lb. 6 ozs. each) apple pie filling
 1 tablespoon lemon juice
 1 cup water

Sprinkle half the dry cake mix into a pan 9x13 inches. Spoon apple filling on top and cover with remaining cake mix. Pour lemon juice and water mixture over all. Bake at 350° F. for 1 hour and 10 minutes.

SICILIAN CASSATA   *Twelve* SERVINGS

An unusual dessert with a sponge cake base, this is a delectable choice for a holiday meal.

 1 10-inch sponge or chiffon cake, split in 3 layers
 1 tablespoon plain gelatin
 ¼ cup cold water

1 pound creamed cottage cheese, sieved
1 cup sugar
2 teaspoons crème de cacao
¼ cup semi-sweet chocolate pieces, chopped
½ cup candied fruits, chopped

Soften gelatin in cold water. Dissolve over hot water. Mix cheese with sugar, flavoring, chocolate, and fruits. Blend gelatin into cheese mixture. Chill until thick enough to spread. Fill cake. Chill for several hours or overnight. Sprinkle confectioners' sugar on top before serving.

x

BUTTERFLY CUP CAKES   *One* DOZEN

So pretty! Yet they're easy to fix.

⅓ cup butter or margarine
¾ cup sugar
2 eggs
1 teaspoon vanilla
1½ cups sifted cake flour
2 teaspoons baking powder
⅓ teaspoon salt

½ cup milk
1 package vanilla or custard pudding, prepared by package directions
Packaged or prepared chocolate butter frosting

Cream butter and sugar until light; beat in eggs, one at a time. Add vanilla. Add sifted dry ingredients alternately with milk, beating until smooth after each addition. Fill greased muffin pans ⅔ full and bake at 375° F. for 20 minutes. When cakes are cool, remove a thin slice from the top of each and cut in half. Scoop out the center of each cake, leaving a half-inch shell. Fill with cooled custard. Carefully frost the top slices with chocolate butter frosting and insert them at an angle in the custard to resemble the wings of a butterfly, pushing up part of the filling to form the body.

Orange Cup Cakes. Use this recipe, making butterflies or not, substituting 2 teaspoons grated orange rind for vanilla and replacing half the milk with orange juice.

COCONUT-PINEAPPLE CUP CAKES
Twenty CUPCAKES

These are very good plain; the topping is just lily-gilt.

1 cup shredded or flaked coco-
    nut
¼ cup water
½ cup shortening
1 cup sugar
2 eggs
2½ cups sifted cake flour

3 teaspoons baking powder
½ teaspoon salt
1 cup crushed pineapple (do not
    drain)
1 teaspoon vanilla
    Butter cream frosting, extra
    coconut (optional)

Combine coconut and water and let stand while mixing cake. Cream shortening and sugar until light; add eggs, one at a time, beating well after each. Add coconut and water. Add sifted dry ingredients alternately with pineapple, mixing well. Add flavoring and fill greased muffin pans lined with fluted paper cups ½ full. Bake at 375° F. for 25 to 30 minutes. Cool cupcakes and frost tops, if you wish, with butter cream frosting. Sprinkle with coconut.

MAPLE-NUT CUP CAKES
Sixteen CUPCAKES

These are fine-textured little cakes with real maple flavor.

2 cups sifted flour
2 teaspoons baking powder
¾ teaspoon salt
⅓ cup shortening
1 egg, well beaten

1 cup maple sirup
⅓ cup milk
⅓ cup chopped nuts
    Maple Butter Frosting (see be-
    low)

Sift dry ingredients and cut in shortening. Combine egg, sirup, and milk and add, beating well. Stir in nuts and bake in greased muffin pans at 350° F. for 20 to 25 minutes. Frost with Maple Butter Frosting.

MAPLE BUTTER FROSTING: Cream 3 tablespoons butter and add alternately ⅓ cup maple sirup and 2 cups confectioners' sugar. Beat well.

CHOCOLATE CHEESE CAKE   *Sixteen* SERVINGS

This was a $100 favorite recipe; the dessert is smooth, be-guiling.

CRUMB MIXTURE

    1 cup fine graham cracker crumbs
    ¼ cup ground walnuts
    ¼ cup sugar
    ¼ cup butter or margarine, melted
    ¼ teaspoon cinnamon

FILLING

    1 pound cream cheese
    3 eggs, separated
    1 teaspoon vanilla
    ½ cup sugar
    3 tablespoons cocoa

TOPPING

    ¼ cup sugar
    2 tablespoons cocoa
    1 teaspoon vanilla
    2 cups sour cream

Mix crumbs, nuts, sugar, butter, and cinnamon. Press into 10-inch spring form pan to make thin bottom layer and side crust. Chill while preparing filling. Beat cheese, egg yolks, and vanilla with rotary beater until smooth. Add sifted sugar and cocoa; beat until blended. Fold in egg whites, beaten stiff. Turn into prepared shell. Bake at 375° F. for 20 minutes. Remove from oven and cool. Stir sugar, cocoa, and vanilla into sour cream. Spoon mixture gently over first part. Increase oven heat to 475° F. and bake cake 10 minutes longer. Chill until serving time.

■

LOU'S BLUEBERRY CHEESE DESSERT

Eight SERVINGS

By changing pie fillings, one could vary this dessert con-siderably.

> Graham Cracker Base (see below)
> 2 eggs
> ¼ cup sugar
> ½ teaspoon vanilla
> 1 package (8 ozs.) cream cheese
> 1 can blueberry pie filling
> 1 cup heavy cream, whipped (optional)

For base, crush 12 double (24) graham crackers and mix with ½ tea-spoon cinnamon, ¼ cup sugar and ¼ cup soft butter. Press into an 8-inch square cake pan.

Mix together well the eggs, sugar, vanilla, and cream cheese and spread over crumbs. Bake at 375° F. for 15 minutes. Cool. Top with blueberry filling. Chill. Serve with layer of whipped cream on top, if you wish, in squares or rectangles.

RUM AND CHOCOLATE POUND CAKE

Six SERVINGS

Variations are endless: Try orange liqueur instead of rum; lemon or coconut pudding mix instead of chocolate.

> 1 bakery pound cake loaf, sliced crosswise in three layers
> ¼ cup rum
> 1 package chocolate pudding mix, prepared
> Whipped cream or dessert topping

Sprinkle the layers of cake with rum and refrigerate for several hours. Prepare pudding mix as directed, adding, if you like, a teaspoon of instant coffee, and using ¼ cup less liquid than the directions ask for. Put cake together with filling, chill again and slice. Serve with whipped cream or dessert topping.

CINNAMON CAKE
Ten SERVINGS

The cake is delicate in texture, and has such good cinnamon flavor!

½ cup shortening
1¼ cups brown sugar, firmly
    packed
2 eggs
1 cup sour milk or buttermilk
2 cups sifted cake flour

1 teaspoon soda
½ teaspoon salt
1 tablespoon cinnamon
Coffee Butter Frosting (see below)

Cream shortening and sugar well, add eggs and beat fluffy. Alternately add milk and sifted dry ingredients, beating after each addition until smooth. Bake in 2 greased or waxed-paper-lined 8-inch layer pans at 350° F., about 25 minutes. Cool, fill and frost with Coffee Butter Frosting.

COFFEE BUTTER FROSTING: Cream ¼ cup butter and work in 2 cups confectioners' sugar, 3 tablespoons strong coffee, 1 teaspoon vanilla. Beat smooth.

COUNTRY MEETING CAKE
Nine SERVINGS

Expect the batter to be thin for this very dark, full-flavored cake.

2 ounces unsweetened chocolate,
    melted
1 cup milk
2 tablespoons butter

1 cup sugar
1 egg yolk
1 cup flour
1 teaspoon soda

Melt chocolate over low heat. Add half the milk and stir until thick. Remove from heat. Add butter and stir until melted. Add sugar and then stir in egg yolk and mix well. Add sifted flour and soda alternately with rest of milk. Beat well. Bake in greased, floured 8x8x2-inch pan at 375° F. for 30 minutes. Frost as you wish.

CRAZY CHOCOLATE CAKE   *Eight* SERVINGS

This method just doesn't make sense, but the cake makes good eating!

Place your flour sifter in an 8-inch square cake pan and turn into it:

1½ cups sifted flour
1 cup sugar
1 teaspoon soda
½ teaspoon salt
3 tablespoons cocoa

Sift the ingredients into the pan and make three indentations in the mixture. In each well, place one of these:

1 teaspoon vanilla
1 tablespoon vinegar
5 tablespoons oil or shortening

Pour in gradually, stirring:

1 cup water

Beat cake in the pan until smooth. Bake 35 minutes at 350° F. Cool on a rack 10 minutes; loosen around the edges, turn upside down and leave until cake falls out of the pan. Frost as you wish.

Yes, there are no eggs!

△

DOUBLE TREAT POUND CAKE   *Six* SERVINGS

Cherry, peach, apricot, and strawberry preserves may be used in such a dessert also.

1 bakery pound cake loaf, cut crosswise into three layers
Red raspberry preserves
1 pint vanilla ice cream

Spread first cake layer with preserves, add second layer, and cover with softened ice cream. Add third layer and more preserves. Freeze firm, then slice.

DEVIL'S FOOD WALNUT CAKE

Ten to Twelve SERVINGS

"Delicious, delicious!" says everybody who eats it.

⅓ cup shortening	1 teaspoon soda
1¼ cups brown sugar	1 teaspoon baking powder
2 eggs, beaten	½ teaspoon salt
2 ounces unsweetened chocolate, melted with ½ cup boiling water	1 teaspoon vanilla
	½ cup sour milk or buttermilk
	¾ cup fine chopped walnuts
1½ cups sifted cake flour	Fluffy white frosting mix

Cream shortening and sugar until fluffy. Add eggs, mixing well. Add cooled chocolate. Alternately add sifted dry ingredients and sour milk and vanilla, beating well after each addition. Fold in nuts. Bake in 2 greased, waxed-paper-lined 8-inch layer pans 25 to 30 minutes at 375° F. Fill and frost with fluffy frosting.

MACAROON REFRIGERATOR CAKE

Twenty SERVINGS

Serve this rich dessert after a light meal or in very small portions after a holiday dinner.

2 cups whipped sweet butter	1 teaspoon grated lemon rind
1 pound confectioners' sugar	2 dozen lady fingers
4 eggs, separated	2 dozen almond macaroons, crumbled
½ cup orange juice	
¼ cup lemon juice	1 cup heavy cream, whipped
1 teaspoon grated orange rind	Strawberries for garnish

Beat confectioners' sugar into butter, add beaten egg yolks and mix well. Add juices and rind; blend thoroughly and fold in stiffly beaten egg whites. Line 10-inch spring form pan with split lady fingers. Spread ⅓ butter mixture in pan, add a layer of macaroon crumbs, another layer of butter mixture, then more crumbs, and a third layer of butter mixture and crumbs. Refrigerate at least 24 hours, wrapped in plastic. Before serving, garnish with whipped cream and berries.

ANNIVERSARY CAKE *Fifty* SERVINGS

By baking ahead and freezing the layers, you can make your own spectacular cake, easily! Cake is baked in several batches.

1 cup butter
2 cups sugar
3 cups sifted cake flour
½ teaspoon salt
1 tablespoon baking powder
1 cup milk
1 teaspoon vanilla

½ teaspoon almond extract
6 egg whites
Lemon Curd Filling (see next page)
Butter Cream Frosting (see next page)

For a 50-serving cake, pictured opposite page 352 make this batter in 3½ separate batches. Cream butter and 1½ cups sugar until very light on mixer. Sift dry ingredients and add alternately with milk to butter and sugar. Add flavorings. Beat egg whites until peaked; add remaining ½ cup sugar gradually and beat until stiff. Fold into batter. Bake as directed in buttered, waxed-paper-lined pans.

You need three pans: a jelly-roll pan, about 15x10x1 inch; a 7x11x1½-inch pan, and a 9x13x2-inch pan.

Fill jelly-roll pan and 7x11-inch pan with first batch of batter. Bake at 375° F. for 25 minutes. Cool in pans 5 minutes, then turn out on racks. Bake a second batch of batter in the same pans.

Bake third batch in the 9x13-inch pan for 50 minutes (you'll have a bonus of 5 cupcakes, which will take 15 minutes to bake!) Bake a half-batch in the 7x11-inch pan again.

ASSEMBLING THE CAKE

Make the Lemon Curd Filling when convenient. It keeps well in the refrigerator when covered. Cut a heavy piece of cardboard slightly smaller than the jelly-roll pan (you can mark around the pan, then cut within the lines) and overwrap with foil to make a firm base. Put the two jelly-roll-size cakes together with filling, on this base. Split the 9x13-inch cake to make the next tier, with more filling between the layers. For the third tier use two of your three 7x11-inch cakes, with filling between. Cut the third and last 7x11-inch cake to make two more layers, your fourth tier. All of the cake may now be placed in the freezer to firm, then overwrapped and frozen until you wish to frost it. Or it may be completed, frozen, then wrapped until wanted. Allow about half a day to thaw the frozen cake.

Lemon Curd Filling (Fills Anniversary Cake)

>   Grated rind and juice of 6 lemons
> 2 cups sugar
> 1 cup butter
> 6 eggs, well beaten

Stir together in top of double boiler over hot, not boiling, water the lemon rind, juice, sugar, and butter. Add a little of the hot mixture to eggs, mix well and turn eggs into mixture, stirring constantly. Cook and stir until thick and smooth. Cool, then refrigerate if not wanted immediately.

Butter Cream Frosting (For Anniversary Cake)

Prepare two batches for the four-tiered cake.

1½ cups sugar
½ teaspoon cream of tartar
⅛ teaspoon salt
½ cup hot water

½ cup egg whites
1 teaspoon vanilla
1½ cups butter (3 sticks)

Combine sugar, cream of tartar, salt, and hot water in heavy saucepan; stir until smooth. Cook without stirring to 240° F. on candy thermometer, washing sides of pan occasionally with pastry brush dipped into hot water to prevent formation of crystals. Start beating egg whites to very stiff stage when sirup reaches about 225° F. When sirup has reached 240° F., remove it at once from heat and pour in thin stream into center of beaten whites, while beating slowly. Continue to beat until lukewarm and light. Add vanilla and blend in well. Beat softened butter to consistency of whipped cream; then add egg-white mixture a little at a time, beating well. You will have a thick, fluffy mixture that holds well. Cover first batch with plastic wrap and keep at room temperature while you make second batch. Tint first, if you want a pastel, using yellow or pink food color.

   This isn't as much work as you might think, and it is a most satisfactory frosting. But, of course, you could use three packages of fluffy frosting mix to cover the cake, following package directions.

x

ORANGE VELVET SPONGE CAKE

Ten SERVINGS

This cake is not a true sponge with the baking powder, but has a velvet texture nevertheless.

5 eggs, separated
1¼ cups sugar
½ cup orange juice
½ cup water
2 cups sifted cake flour
2 teaspoons baking powder

⅛ teaspoon salt
1 tablespoon grated orange rind
Lemon or vanilla pudding mix, prepared according to directions

Beat egg yolks with sugar and orange juice for 10 minutes with electric or rotary beater. Add water and beat 2 minutes longer. Add sifted cake flour, baking powder, and salt. Beat about 1 minute, or until dry ingredients have been blended. Fold in orange rind and egg whites, beaten stiff. Bake in an ungreased 9-inch tube pan at 350° F. for an hour and 10 minutes. Invert pan and let hang until cold. Remove from pan, split into 3 layers, and fill with pudding. Sprinkle confectioners' sugar on top or top with whipped cream before serving.

VARIATIONS

Pudding mix may be flavored with orange rind.
Lemon pie filling may be used.

POPPY SEED CAKE

Twelve SERVINGS

This fine textured, flavor-perfect cake can be glorified with an almond-custard filling.

½ cup poppy seeds
1 cup milk
½ cup butter or margarine
1½ cups sugar
1 teaspoon vanilla

⅛ teaspoon salt
2 cups sifted cake flour
2 teaspoons baking powder
4 egg whites, beaten stiff

Add poppy seeds to milk and let stand 1 hour. Cream butter with 1 cup of sugar. Add poppy seeds in milk, salt, vanilla. Mix well. Add sifted dry ingredients gradually, mixing well. Add ½ cup sugar to beaten egg whites and beat until sugar is dissolved. Fold into batter. Bake in 2 greased 9-inch layer pans 30 to 35 minutes at 350° F. Fill with almond-flavored custard filling, and top with whipped cream, or fill and frost with fluffy white frosting.

△

QUICK APPLE TORTE   *Six* SERVINGS

One-two-three, and it's in the oven!

¾ cup sugar
⅓ cup flour
1 teaspoon baking powder
1 egg, beaten

1 teaspoon vanilla
1½ cups diced apples
½ cup chopped nuts
Sprinkles of cinnamon, nutmeg

Add dry ingredients to egg and vanilla. Add apples and nuts. Turn into an 8-inch pie pan, sprinkle with cinnamon and nutmeg, and bake at 350° F. for 30 minutes. Serve warm topped with cream or ice cream.

✗

GRAHAM CRACKER TORTE   *Eight* SERVINGS

Typical comments: "Very, very good"; "Really wonderful."

¼ cup shortening
¾ cup sugar
1 egg
¾ cup milk

1 teaspoon vanilla
22 graham crackers, crushed
1¼ teaspoons baking powder
½ cup chopped nuts

Cream shortening and sugar; beat in egg. Add milk and vanilla, then mixture of crushed crackers, baking powder, and nuts. Bake in greased 7x11-inch pan at 375° F. about 20 minutes. Serve in squares with whipped cream.

BLACK WALNUT TORTE   *Six* SERVINGS

This light, fluffy nut cake is easy to make and practically failureproof.

> 3 eggs, separated
> 1 cup sugar
> 1 tablespoon flour
> 1/2 teaspoon baking powder
> 1 cup black walnuts, chopped fine
> 1 cup cream, whipped

Beat egg yolks until thick and lemon colored; beat in 1/2 cup sugar gradually. Stir in flour, baking powder, and nuts. Beat 1/2 cup sugar into stiff-beaten egg whites gradually. Fold whites into first mixture. Bake in a buttered 10-inch pie pan at 325° F. for 40 minutes. Serve topped with whipped cream.

WHIPPED CREAM CAKE   *Twelve* SERVINGS

Such good flavor; such delicate texture!

> 1 cup whipping cream, whipped
> 4 egg whites, beaten stiff with 1/4 teaspoon salt
> 1/2 cup water
> 1/2 teaspoon almond flavoring
> 1/2 teaspoon vanilla
> 2 cups sifted cake flour
> 1 1/2 cups sugar
> 3 teaspoons baking powder
> 1/2 teaspoon salt
> 1 can ready-to-spread lemon velvet frosting

Combine the cream and egg whites carefully, and fold in water and flavorings. Fold sifted dry ingredients into whipped-cream mixture, a small amount at a time. Bake in 2 greased, waxed-paper-lined 9-inch layer pans at 375° F. 25 to 30 minutes. Fill and frost cooled layers with prepared frosting.

COOKY OR CAKE PUDDING   *Four* SERVINGS

This good dessert is seldom served at our house. Reason: no cooky or cake crumbs left around!

1 cup heavy cream, whipped
½ cup diced canned or sweetened fresh fruit, drained
2 cups coarse cooky or stale cake crumbs

Fold ingredients together and serve in sherbet glasses.

◥

SHERRIED CHOCOLATE   *Six to Eight* SERVINGS
WALNUT REFRIGERATOR CAKE

It is simply made, luxuriously rich and winey.

½ pound semi-sweet chocolate
¼ cup sherry wine
  Dash of salt
4 eggs, separated
1 cup chopped walnuts
1 dozen lady fingers, split

Place chocolate, sherry, and salt in top of a double boiler and stir over hot water until ingredients are blended. Add slightly beaten egg yolks; cook and stir 1 minute longer. Remove from heat and add walnuts. Let cool, then fold in the stiff-beaten egg whites, blending gently. Line a 9x5-inch loaf pan with waxed paper. Use 2 strips of paper, one going lengthwise and the other crosswise, with ends extending a little above the sides of the pan. Arrange split lady fingers, round side out, around the sides and over the bottom of the pan. Pour in chocolate mixture. Any remaining lady fingers may be arranged over the top of the dessert. Chill 12 hours or more. Unmold on a platter, slice, and serve with whipped cream.

PHILA'S CARAMEL FRUIT CAKE   *One* LOAF

*A fabulous cake concocted by a former airlines stewardess
who loves to cook—you'll agree it deserved that $100 award!*

1 pound dates
¾ cup candied cherries
1 slice green candied pineapple
1 slice red candied pineapple
2 slices white candied pineapple
¼ cup candied orange peel

¼ cup candied lemon peel
¼ cup candied citron
1 cup chopped pecans
1 can moist coconut
1 can sweetened condensed milk
  (1⅓ cups)

Cut dates and cherries into thirds. Cut remaining fruits about the same
size. Mix all ingredients together thoroughly and press in a small greased
loaf pan lined with greased brown paper or an 8-inch tube pan greased
and lined with brown paper. Bake at 300° F. for 2 hours. Turn out on
a cake cooler. Decorate with candied cherries and blanched almonds.
Cover with waxed paper and store in refrigerator. Keeps for several
months.

◾

QUICK FRUIT CAKE   *One* LOAF

Here's an easy recipe for the girl with the kitchenette.

½ package standard size white cake mix or 1 package mix
   for 1 layer
2 eggs
3 tablespoons water
1 teaspoon vanilla
1 teaspoon salt
½ pound light raisins
2 cups coarsely chopped pecans
½ cup chopped candied cherries
2 slices candied pineapple, chopped

Place cake mix in a bowl. Add eggs, water, vanilla, and salt and beat
with electric mixer until smooth. Stir in remaining ingredients. Spread

340

in a greased, small loaf pan lined with waxed paper. Bake in a slow oven (275° F.) for 2 hours. Place a shallow pan of water in bottom of oven while cake is baking.

△

QUICK CHERRY PUDDING   *Eight* SERVINGS

This is one of those miracles—you don't see how it can possibly work. But it does!

>   1 can (1 lb. 6 ozs.) cherry pie filling
>   1 small package (for 1 layer) or ½ standard package white
>   or yellow cake mix
>   ½ cup (1 stick) butter, melted
>   ½ cup chopped pecans

Turn pie filling into an 8x8-inch pan and sprinkle dry cake mix on top. Pour butter over cake mix and cover with nuts. Bake at 350° F. for 45 minutes. Serve warm or cold, plain or topped with whipped cream or ice cream.

LEMON CAKE PUDDING   *Six* SERVINGS

When baked, you have cake on top, sauce beneath.

1 cup sugar	¼ cup lemon juice
¼ cup flour	1 teaspoon grated lemon peel
⅛ teaspoon salt	2 eggs, separated
2 tablespoons melted butter	1 cup milk, scalded

Combine sugar, flour, salt, and butter. Add lemon juice and peel, well-beaten egg yolks, and milk. Mix well. Fold in egg whites, beaten stiff. Pour into a buttered 1½-quart casserole and set the casserole in a pan of hot water. Bake at 325° F. for 50 to 60 minutes.

BLUE PLUM PUDDING *Six servings*

You'll see why this recipe was a $100 award winner—what happens to this kind of plum in the oven is amazing!

1 pound blue or Italian plums, halved, pitted
¼ cup sugar
1 cup flour
1 cup sugar
1½ teaspoons baking powder
1 teaspoon salt
1 egg, well beaten

Arrange plums in greased casserole and sprinkle with the ¼ cup sugar. Blend remaining dry ingredients together, add egg and mix well. Sprinkle over plums. Bake at 350° F. for 30 minutes or until lightly browned. Serve with cream or whipped cream.

CRUMBLY TOPPED APPLE PIE *Ten to Twelve* SERVINGS

Bake an apple pie in a pizza pan for a change!

2 quarts sliced tart apples
⅓ cup butter, melted
1½ cups white or brown sugar
1 teaspoon cinnamon

1½ cups flour for topping
1 cup brown sugar
⅔ cup butter
Pastry mix for 2-crust pie

Stir sliced apples into butter and then mix with sugar and cinnamon. Blend flour, brown sugar, and butter with fingers until crumbly. Line pizza pan with rolled pastry, arrange apples evenly in pan, and cover with the crumbly mixture. Bake at 425° F. about 45 minutes. Serve plain or with ice cream.

SOUR CREAM APPLE PIE   *Six* SERVINGS

Try the same recipe with whipping cream—that's good, too!

 6 cups sliced apples
 1 cup brown sugar
 ½ teaspoon cinnamon
 ⅛ teaspoon nutmeg
 ⅛ teaspoon salt
 ¼ cup flour
 1 cup sour cream
  Pastry for single 9-inch crust, using mix

Mix brown sugar, spices, salt, and flour and spread ¼ of the mixture over bottom of pastry-lined pie pan. Stir the remainder into sour cream and combine with sliced apples. Turn into pie shell. Bake at 450° F. for 10 minutes; reduce heat to 350° F. and continue baking for 40 minutes, or until apples are tender. Cool before serving.

APPLE SLICES   *Twelve* SERVINGS

These delights freeze well, if you can keep any to freeze!

1 package pie crust mix
2 egg yolks
1 teaspoon lemon juice
2 jars or cans apple pie filling

1 tablespoon lemon juice
Sprinkle of nutmeg
Confectioners' sugar icing

Add egg yolks and lemon juice to pie crust mix and use ¼ cup water in mixing. Pat out a little more than half the dough to line a shallow 9x13-inch pan. Spread pie filling in pan and sprinkle with lemon juice and nutmeg. Make lattice strips of remaining dough to decorate tops of slices. Crimp edges and cut a design for escape of steam. Bake at 450° F. for 25 to 30 minutes. Dribble icing over pastry while still warm. (Confectioners' sugar with a little water to make it runny and a few drops vanilla). When cool, cut in squares.

 Other pie fillings—peach, cherry, pineapple—may be used for such slices.

AVOCADO PIE

Six SERVINGS

Cool and summery, this is a lovely pie!

2 large avocados, mashed or sieved
¾ cup lemon juice
1 cup sweetened condensed milk (not evaporated milk)
Prepared 9-inch graham cracker shell

Mix avocado pulp with lemon juice and the sweet canned milk. Fill graham cracker shell and bake at 350° F. for 20 minutes. Cool and chill.

COCONUT PIE

Six or Eight SERVINGS

It reminds you of pecan pie; it is very rich.

2 eggs, beaten
½ cup sugar
1½ cups corn sirup
½ teaspoon salt
2 tablespoons melted butter
   or margarine

1 teaspoon lemon juice
1¼ cups shredded coconut
Unbaked 9-inch pie shell,
   from a pie crust mix

Mix ingredients and pour into the pie shell. Bake at 400° F. for 15 minutes. Reduce heat to 350° F., and bake 30 minutes longer.

LEMON CHIFFON PIE

Six SERVINGS

Who doesn't love lemon pie?

1 tablespoon plain gelatin
¼ cup cold water
4 egg yolks, slightly beaten
⅓ cup lemon juice
1 tablespoon grated lemon rind
½ cup sugar

⅛ teaspoon salt
4 egg whites
¼ cup sugar
9-inch baked pie shell from
   a mix
¾ cup heavy cream, whipped

Soften gelatin in cold water. Beat egg yolks; add lemon juice, rind, ½ cup sugar, and salt. Cook until thick in top of double boiler, stirring constantly. Remove from heat, add gelatin, and stir until dissolved. Cool. Beat egg whites until stiff. Beat in 1/4 cup sugar. Fold this meringue into lemon filling and pour into pie shell. Chill for several hours before serving. Top with whipped cream.

SNOW PIE
Six to Eight SERVINGS

Looks just like new-fallen snow! Gorgeous flavor, too.

1 tablespoon plain gelatin
1/4 cup cold water
1/4 teaspoon salt
3 egg whites, beaten stiff
1/2 cup sugar

1 cup heavy cream, whipped
1 teaspoon vanilla
1 9-inch graham cracker
   crumb crust

Soften gelatin in cold water and dissolve over hot water. Sprinkle salt over egg whites and beat until stiff. Fold sugar into egg whites; mix in dissolved gelatin slowly. Fold in whipped cream and vanilla, pour into chilled crust and chill until firm.

Sprinkle chocolate decorettes over the pie to relieve the whiteness, if snow gives you a chill.

STRAWBERRY PARFAIT PIE
Six SERVINGS

It's quick, easy, delightful!

1 1/4 cups boiling water
1 package lemon-flavored gelatin
1 pint vanilla ice cream
1 1/2 cups sliced fresh strawberries
   Baked 9-inch pie shell (use pie crust mix)

Add hot water to gelatin and stir until dissolved. Add ice cream, cut into pieces, to hot liquid and stir until melted. Chill until mixture is thickened but not set, 15 to 20 minutes. Fold in strawberries. Turn into cooled, baked pie shell. Chill until firm, about half an hour. If desired, top with whipped cream and garnish with whole strawberries which have been gashed to form flower petals.

PUMPKIN CHIFFON TARTS   *Eight* SERVINGS

Use pie crust mix for the tarts and whipped cream from a squirt-can.

1 cup canned pumpkin
3 eggs, separated
1/2 cup white or brown sugar
1 cup milk
1/2 teaspoon salt
1/2 teaspoon ginger
1/4 teaspoon nutmeg
1 teaspoon cinnamon

1 tablespoon plain gelatin
1/4 cup cold water
1/4 cup sugar for egg whites
Salted pecans, whipped cream, or dessert topping (optional)
8 baked tart shells

Heat pumpkin in top of double boiler. Add slightly beaten egg yolks, sugar, milk, salt, spices. Cook and stir until of custard consistency. Remove from heat; add gelatin softened in cold water and stir until dissolved. Chill until partly thickened. Fold in egg whites beaten stiff, into which you've folded the 1/4 cup sugar. Turn into tart shells, chill until firm, and garnish if you wish with whipped cream and pecans.

△

FRESH FRUIT TART   *Twelve to Sixteen* SERVINGS

You could use fewer fruits or different ones, but the dessert might not be quite so pretty!

Oat pastry (see next page), or the regular kind
1 package instant vanilla pudding
1 3/4 cups milk
2 tablespoons orange liqueur
1 quart strawberries
1 banana
1 ripe avocado
1 can (1 lb., 13 ozs.) apricot halves
1 can (13 ozs.) pineapple chunks
Glaze (see next page)

To make the crunchy oat pastry, mix ½ cup rolled oats, grated rind of 1 lemon, 2½ cups flour, ½ cup sugar and ½ teaspoon salt. Cut in 1 cup (2 sticks) butter until mixture is in coarse crumbs. Add gradually ⅓ cup milk and toss with a fork until all dry ingredients are moistened. Form into a ball. Press on bottom and sides of a 12-inch fluted pan or a pizza pan, using your fingers. The mixture is moist. Prick generously with the tines of a fork and bake the crust at 400° F. for 20 minutes or until golden brown. Cool.

Meanwhile prepare pudding mix according to package directions, using 1¾ cups milk. Stir in orange liqueur. Spoon chilled pudding into cooled crust. Top with fruits, arranging them in a pretty pattern. Be sure canned fruits are well drained and dried on a paper towel. Brush fruit gently with glaze and chill.

GLAZE: Melt ½ cup apricot preserves over low heat, press through a sieve and cool. Stir in 2 tablespoons orange liqueur.

FROZEN NEAPOLITAN PUDDING   *Six to Eight* SERVINGS

This dessert is festive looking, easy to serve, and delicious.

- 2 cups crushed vanilla wafers
- ⅓ cup butter or margarine
- ½ cup confectioners' sugar
- 2 eggs
- ½ teaspoon vanilla
- 3 tablespoons each: chopped walnuts, raisins, maraschino cherries
- 1 cup heavy cream, whipped
- 1 teaspoon lemon juice

Cover bottom of large (7x11 inches) freezing tray with one half of wafer crumbs. Cream butter and sugar until fluffy, beat in 1 egg and 1 yolk. Spread over crumbs. Beat the other egg white until stiff, fold in vanilla, walnuts, raisins, and cherries, then whipped cream and lemon. Spread over first 2 layers. Top with remaining wafer crumbs. Freeze.

ANGEL PARFAIT

Eight SERVINGS

You'll be proud to serve this puffy, fluffy stuff. It's truly angelic!

1 cup sugar	Few grains salt
1/4 cup water	1 pint heavy cream
2 egg whites	2 teaspoons vanilla

Boil sugar and water without stirring until sirup spins a thread, about 236° by the candy thermometer. Pour slowly into stiff-beaten egg whites to which salt has been added, beating constantly. Beat until thick. Cool and add vanilla. Fold in whipped cream. Freeze in tray or a melon mold, without stirring, at coldest temperature. Serve with crushed fresh peaches or berries.

VARIATIONS

Brandy Parfait. Flavor with 3 tablespoons cognac, instead of vanilla.

Chocolate. Fold in 2 squares melted, cooled, unsweetened chocolate.

Coffee. Add 1 tablespoon instant coffee to sirup.

Macaroon. Fold in 1 cup crumbled macaroons and use 1 tablespoon brandy, rum, or fruit cordial in place of vanilla.

Peach. Add 1 1/2 cups crushed peaches.

Strawberry. Add 1 1/2 cups crushed berries.

⊠

CINNAMON ICE CREAM

One QUART

It has creamy texture, real spice flavor.

1 1/2 cups milk, scalded
3/4 cup sugar
1/8 teaspoon salt
2 1/2 teaspoons cinnamon
3 egg yolks, beaten
1 pint heavy cream

Combine sugar, salt, and cinnamon and add to milk; stir until sugar is dissolved. Pour mixture gradually over beaten yolks in top of double boiler, stirring constantly. Place over hot water and cook until thickened, stirring constantly. Chill. Stir well and fold in whipped cream. Turn into freezing tray and freeze until firm, stirring well three or four times during freezing.

◘

BUTTERSCOTCH RICE CREAM   *Four* SERVINGS

This quick and easy dessert is long on flavors.

1 cup cooked rice
1 tall can evaporated milk
¾ cup brown sugar, firmly packed
2 tablespoons butter
¼ teaspoon vanilla

Cook rice, evaporated milk, sugar, and butter over moderate heat about 10 minutes, stirring constantly. Add vanilla, cool, and serve with top milk.

△

FRESH COCONUT DELIGHT   *Eight* SERVINGS

A bright berry sauce dresses up this delicate pudding.

2 tablespoons plain gelatin
½ cup cold milk
2 cups milk, scalded
½ cup sugar

½ teaspoon salt
1 fresh coconut, grated (use your electric blender)
2 cups cream, whipped

Soften gelatin in cold milk. Dissolve gelatin, sugar, and salt in scalded milk. Chill until partially thickened. Fold coconut and first mixture into cream. Turn into a quart mold. Chill until firm.

CHERRIES JUBILEE   *Eight* SERVINGS

Everybody loves the drama of a flaming dessert!

1 can (1 lb., 4 ozs.) dark sweet
    cherries, pitted and
    drained

1 tablespoon cornstarch
½ cup cognac or kirsch
1 quart vanilla ice cream

Add a small amount of cherry juice to cornstarch; mix with rest of juice. Cook and stir over moderate heat until thick and smooth. Add cherries and heat thoroughly, then transfer sauce to chafing dish. In a small pan, warm liquor, carefully pour it over sauce, and ignite. Spoon flaming cherries over individual servings of ice cream.

STRAWBERRY CREAM   *Six* SERVINGS

Stir the frozen berries into the hot gelatin to speed preparation.

1 package strawberry gelatin
1 cup boiling water
1 package (10 ozs.) frozen sliced strawberries
1 cup heavy cream, whipped

Dissolve gelatin in boiling water, stir in berries and blend until fruit is thawed, mixture thickened somewhat. Fold in the whipped cream. Turn into dessert dishes and chill until firm.

MAPLE CUP CUSTARDS   *Four* SERVINGS

Some of the best things in life are maple flavored!

1 pint milk, scalded
2 eggs, slightly beaten
⅓ cup maple sirup
⅛ teaspoon salt

Scald milk and combine remaining ingredients. Pour milk gradually into eggs, stirring while adding. Bake in 4 large or 6 small custard cups set in a pan of hot water, at 350° F. until custard has set, about 30 minutes. If desired, a marshmallow or a tablespoon of maple sirup may be placed in bottom of each cup before custard is added.

AMBROSIA MOLD
Six SERVINGS

Here's the perfect holiday dinner dessert—not too rich or filling.

1 can (1 lb.) fruit cocktail
2 tablespoons (envelopes) plain gelatin
1 cup orange sections, membrane removed
1 cup flake coconut
2 cups dairy eggnog

Drain fruit, saving sirup. Soften gelatin in sirup and melt over hot water. Combine all ingredients. Turn into a 6-cup mold and chill until firm.

HELEN'S SNOW-CAPPED GRAPEFRUIT
Four SERVINGS

Very simple, very elegant, this is a refreshing conclusion to a full-course company dinner.

4 grapefruit, cut in half   2 egg whites
4 tablespoons crème de menthe   ¼ cup sugar

Remove grapefruit sections from halved fruit and drain. Discard membrane. Pile sections into 4 of the best-looking half-shells, fluting the edges first, if you wish. Add 1 tablespoon crème de menthe to each portion. Place in shallow baking pan. Beat egg whites (at room temperature) until they form soft peaks, then gradually beat in sugar until meringue stands in stiff, shiny peaks. Cover grapefruit with meringue. Bake at 400° F. for 5 to 7 minutes or until tinged with brown. Serve warm or at room temperature.

BLUEBERRY SPONGE   *Six* SERVINGS

A light, frothy dessert you'll love for warm weather meals.
It could have a whipped cream garnish.

1 tablespoon (envelope) plain gelatin
1/4 cup cold water
1 pint fresh blueberries
1/4 cup sugar
1/4 teaspoon salt
1 tablespoon lemon juice
2 egg whites, beaten stiff

Soften gelatin in cold water. Wash berries thoroughly and crush 1 cup. Bring to boiling point. Add gelatin, sugar, salt, and lemon juice and stir until gelatin is dissolved. Chill until partially thickened. Fold in remaining berries and egg whites; chill in individual molds or dessert dishes until firm.

◘

ORANGE-APRICOT   *Twelve* SERVINGS
FLUFF DESSERT

Light dessert after a heavy meal is a good idea; this mold
could wind up the holiday dinner. It may serve as buffet
"salad" also.

5 tablespoons plain gelatin
2 cans (12 ozs. each) apricot nectar
6 cups orange juice
  Grated rind of 1 orange and 1 lemon

Soften gelatin in 1 cup nectar. Dissolve over boiling water. Add to other ingredients, turn into a 2½-quart mold, and chill until firm. Turn out on serving plate and garnish with canned apricot halves, mandarin orange slices, and maraschino cherries.

If you like, use 1 cup orange liqueur instead of the same amount of orange juice. The flavor is a little exotic.

352

Anniversary Cake, page 33

CHILLED SPICED FRUIT *Six or More* SERVINGS

This simple combination has an amazingly elegant flavor.

1 can Bartlett pears
1 can cling peaches
1 can greengage plums
1 stick cinnamon, broken in pieces

Drain the juices, combine and boil together with cinnamon to concentrate the sirup and add flavor. Heat fruit in sirup and serve hot in dessert dishes, or pour sirup over fruit and chill. Prepare several days early, if you wish.

PEACHES CECILE *Six* SERVINGS

Here's a lovely dessert, and certainly an easy one.

½ dozen macaroons
½ cup sherry
8 marshmallows, quartered
½ cup cream

6 peach halves, canned or fresh
½ cup cream, whipped
6 maraschino cherries

Break up macaroons and soak in sherry 2 hours. Soak marshmallows in ½ cup cream 2 hours. Mix together lightly. To serve, place peach half in dish cut side up. Spoon macaroon mixture into each peach. Garnish with whipped cream and a cherry. Serve very cold.

BLACK MAGIC DESSERT *Four* SERVINGS

One for the Cola addicts, simple but different!

1 package prepared chocolate pudding, instant or other
1 cup bottled cola beverage
½ cup heavy cream, whipped

Use the bottled cola beverage in place of the usual 2 cups of milk. When almost set, fold in whipped cream, and fill individual serving dishes. Chill.

esh Fruit Tart, page 346

CHAMPAGNE ICE   *Eight to Ten* SERVINGS

This is a most refreshing ice; serve it as dessert, or with poultry or meat.

2 cups sugar
2½ cups water
   Peeled rinds (yellow only) of 2 lemons
1 cup lemon juice
1¼ cups champagne or dry white wine
   Sprinkle of salt

Combine sugar, water, and lemon peel in saucepan. Stir over moderate heat until sugar dissolves. Boil 5 minutes. Place lemon juice, wine, and salt in blender container, and at low speed add the sirup in a steady stream, until all is added and lemon peel is fine. Turn into freezer trays and freeze firm, stirring occasionally. Serve plain or with crème de menthe as sauce, or with frozen raspberries whipped to a sauce in the blender.

■

PHYLLIS ANN'S MIXED FRUIT FLIP   *Eight to Ten* SERVINGS

"This is a 10-minute version of the 24-hour salad, good as salad or dessert, and yummy even for breakfast!" says the contributor of this recipe.

1 can (11 ozs.) mandarin orange sections, drained
1 can (1 lb. 14 ozs.) fruit cocktail, drained
1 cup sour cream
   Miniature marshmallows, if you want them

Combine ingredients and chill.

CREAMY COFFEE DESSERT · Eight SERVINGS

This mixture is thick but not firm. Garnish with toasted nuts, if you wish.

1 tablespoon plain gelatin	¼ cup sugar
¼ cup cold water	⅛ teaspoon salt
1¾ cups strong coffee	1 cup cream, whipped

Soften gelatin in cold water and dissolve in hot coffee with the sugar, and salt. Chill until partly thickened. Fold in cream. Chill and serve in dessert dishes.

Coffee liqueur may take the place of the water or ¼ cup of the coffee in the recipe if you are serving the dessert to gourmets.

CRÈME BRULÉE · Eight SERVINGS

This rich custard is one of the most delectable desserts in the world.

1 quart cream (half-and-half will do)
2 tablespoons sugar
2 teaspoons vanilla
8 egg yolks, well beaten
Maple sugar or brown sugar

Scald cream; remove from heat and add sugar and vanilla, mixing well. Pour slowly over beaten egg yolks, beating constantly. Pour into greased shallow baking dish. Bake in a slow oven (300° F.) for 1 hour and 15 minutes, or until just set. Remove from oven, cool, then chill. When cold, cover top of custard with ¼-inch layer of maple or brown sugar. Place custard under hot broiler just long enough to caramelize sugar, being careful that sugar does not burn. Chill before serving in individual dessert dishes.

LEMON CREAM PUDDING   *Six* SERVINGS

Fresh or canned mandarin orange sections or berries might garnish this refreshing combination.

3 cups cold milk
2 packages instant vanilla pudding mix
2 cups sour cream
1 tablespoon grated lemon rind
  Fruit for garnish (optional)

Pour milk into mixing bowl or blender, add mix and beat until blended. Add sour cream and lemon rind. Mix only until smooth. Pour into serving dishes and garnish with fruit, if you wish.

CHARLOTTE RUSSE   *Twelve* SERVINGS

An old-fashioned dessert, this lovely concoction is never out of date.

2 tablespoons plain gelatin
½ cup cold water
4 egg yolks, well beaten
1 cup sugar
1 cup milk

1 teaspoon vanilla
2 cups cream, whipped
2 dozen lady fingers
12 maraschino cherries

Dissolve gelatin in cold water. Combine egg yolks, sugar, and milk in top of double boiler and cook until mixture begins to thicken. Add gelatin and stir until dissolved. Fold in flavoring. Chill, fold whipped cream into custard lightly. Arrange four lady finger halves in each custard cup and fill with whipped cream mixture. Chill thoroughly before serving, then decorate with rosettes made of whipped cream, and top with maraschino cherries.

RASPBERRY MOLD *Eight* SERVINGS

Three flavors, all raspberry, make this a triple treat.

1 tablespoon plain gelatin
1/4 cup cold water
2 packages raspberry gelatin
2 cups hot water
2 packages (10 ozs. each) frozen raspberries, thawed, drained
1 pint raspberry sherbet

Soften gelatin in cold water. Dissolve raspberry gelatin in hot water. Add plain gelatin and stir until dissolved. Add juice from berries and sherbet and mix until sherbet is melted. Chill until partly thickened. Fold in berries and turn into a mold. Chill until firm.

SPANISH CREAM *Four to Five* SERVINGS

Sliced, sweetened berries, cherries, or peaches make a wonderful topping.

1 tablespoon (envelope) plain gelatin
2 cups milk
1/3 cup sugar
    Dash salt
2 eggs, separated
1 teaspoon vanilla

Soften gelatin in 1/4 cup cold milk. Scald remaining milk and dissolve softened gelatin, sugar, and salt in it. Beat egg yolks slightly, add a little of the hot mixture, and stir well, then turn back into pan and cook and stir over very low heat until mixture makes a custard that will just coat a spoon. Remove from heat, add vanilla, and chill until mixture begins to set. Beat until fluffy. Fold in stiff-beaten egg whites. Chill in sherbet glasses until firm.

POTS DE CRÈME   *Six* SERVINGS

Pronounce it "Poh duh Krem." It will make a reputation for you.

½ pound sweet chocolate
¼ cup light cream
2 tablespoons rum

2 egg yolks, slightly beaten
1 cup cream, whipped

Melt chocolate in cream over gentle heat; add rum. Stir until smooth. Pour small amount over egg yolks, mix well; return all to double boiler and cook about 3 minutes, stirring constantly. Cool. Fold in whipped cream. Turn into *pots de crème* cups (demi-tasse cups may be used). Chill for several hours or over night.

RUSSIAN CREAM   *Eight* SERVINGS

Fresh crushed or frozen strawberries make a beautiful dessert of this.

2 cups sweet cream (may be half-and-half)
¼ cup sugar
1 tablespoon plain gelatin
¼ cup cold water
2 cups sour cream
1 teaspoon vanilla

Combine sweet cream and sugar and heat to scalding, but do not boil. Soften gelatin in cold water and dissolve in scalded cream mixture. Cool to lukewarm, then stir in sour cream and vanilla. Chill in a fancy mold or in 8 or 10 individual molds until firm. Serve with fresh fruit.

INDEX

INDEX

363

Printed in U.S.A.